ART OF THE WORLD

NON-EUROPEAN CULTURES

THE HISTORICAL, SOCIOLOGICAL

AND RELIGIOUS BACKGROUNDS

THE ART OF GREECE

Its Origins in the Mediterranean and Near East

by

EKREM AKURGAL

CROWN PUBLISHERS INC., NEW YORK

Translated by Wayne Dynes

Frontispiece: PLATE I – *Assurnasirpal II (883–859 B.C.) hunting lions. Alabaster relief from the Northwest Palace at Kalkhu (Nimrud). British Museum. Height 92 cm. Cf. pp. 30 ff.*

FIRST PUBLISHED IN 1966
© 1966 HOLLE VERLAG GmbH, BADEN-BADEN, GERMANY
FIRST PUBLISHED IN GREAT BRITAIN IN 1968
ENGLISH TRANSLATION © 1968 BY METHUEN & CO. LTD
LIBRARY OF CONGRESS CATALOG CARD NUMBER: 68-9056
PRINTED IN HOLLAND

CONTENTS

PART TWO: GREECE

LIST OF COLOUR PLATES

LIST OF HALF-TONE ILLUSTRATIONS

LIST OF FIGURES

9

ACKNOWLEDGEMENTS

The line-drawings and the map were executed by R. Epikman and M. Erdim in accordance with sketches and directions given by the author. R. Epikman: Figs. 27, 59, 67–69, 71, 99, 129, 135, 136; M. Erdim: Figs. 3–17, 32–39, 44, 45, 48, 49, 53, 54, 66, 70, 72–98, 100–2, 111–19, 125–8, 130–4, 139–49, 152–5, 158–65, 168–70.

SOURCES OF ILLUSTRATIONS

The following museums kindly allowed reproduction of the plates on the following pages:

Adana, Archaeological Museum 92 left, 120, 121
Aleppo, Archaeological Museum   92 right
Ankara, Archaeological Museum   57, 58, 63,
    81 above, 82 below, 216
Athens, Kerameikos Museum   152, 153
Athens, National Museum   172, 206
Baghdad, Iraq Museum   146, 151
Baltimore, The Walters Art Gallery   156
Berlin, Staatliche Museen   33, 35 above, 36,
    70, 76, 91, 145
Istanbul, Archaeological Museum   119, 123,
    203, 213

London, British Museum   3, 18, 23, 24, 29, 34,
    35 below, 154, 158, 175, 178, 179, 182, 184,
    185
Munich, Antikensammlungen   177
New York, Metropolitan Museum   171
Olympia, Museum   64, 186, 189, 191, 194, 195
Oxford, Ashmolean Museum   81 below
Paris, Louvre   20, 26, 128, 168
Rome, Villa Giulia   68
Tübingen, Archäologisches Institut der
    Universität   197
Van, Archaeological Museum   167

Photographs were kindly supplied by: E. Akurgal, Ankara, 119, 142, 164, 167; Deutsches Archäologisches Institut, Athens, 64, 152, 205, 206; E. Berna, 120, 121; M. Chuzeville, Vanves, 20, 26, 128,
168; Photo Derounian, Aleppo, 92 right; M. A. Düğenci, 123, 130, 163, 164, 167, 203, 213, 216, 220;
R. Gnamm, Munich, 177; B. Görgüç, 58 below, 63; A. Güler, 58, 133; Hirmer Foto-Archiv, Munich,
146; N. Kontos, Athens, 153, 172, 186, 191, 194; The Mansell Collection, London, 34; Foto Marburg, 91 above, 92 left; J. Remmer, Munich, 68; J. Skeel, Pluckley, Kent, 158, 175, 182, 184, 185.
The other photographs were provided by the museums mentioned.

FOREWORD

Particular aspects of the problem of the relation between early Greek art and the civilizations of the ancient Near East have engaged the attention of many scholars over a period of several generations. But only two monographs exist that treat the problem as a whole. The first general survey came from the pen of the Danish scholar Frederik Poulsen: *Der Orient und die frühgriechische Kunst*, Berlin, 1912. A second comprehensive study, *The Greeks and Their Eastern Neighbours*, was published in London in 1957 after the early death of its author, the English archaeologist T. J. Dunbabin. While both writers discuss the most important Greek elements of style and iconography that can be traced to Near Eastern sources, they do not attempt a systematic examination of the eastern models themselves.

Emil Kunze and Humfry Payne made progress in this field, although they had only a limited opportunity to deal with eastern art works. Other important contributions came from Paul Jacobsthal, Gerhart Rodenwaldt, Karl Schefold and Pierre Demargne, who also, however, were restricted to questions of detail, since the mass of the material lay outside their field of specialization. In the last few decades our knowledge of this subject has been further enlarged by the work of a number of scholars. Such distinguished archaeologists as Pierre Amandry, R. D. Barnett, G. M. A. Hanfmann, Helene Kantor, Massimo Pallottino, P. J. Riis and Hans Walter deserve mention here. As we have duly noted on several occasions in this book, many Classical archaeologists, working in the context of their special fields of research, have added important observations bearing on the question of the relationship between East and West.

By contrast, this volume gives full coverage to the main art centres of the Near East between 1000 and 500 B.C., presenting and discussing the most important works of art. The identification of a large body of Near Eastern models should put the question of East-West relations in this period on a sound basis.

Every work of art depends on an existing tradition and upon the circumstances in which it was created. To some extent every art work reflects the characteristics of earlier and contemporary artistic trends in its immediate setting and broader environment. In seeking to place an art object chronologically and geographically, we must first identify the component features of its style and iconography. Only through this preparatory tracing of the significant features to their various sources can we fix with some precision the time and place of production as well as the interpretation of the work in question. The validity of the results depends on the scope of the material available for comparison. This method, which I have used over the past twenty years to classify and to date artistic creations of several cultures and areas of the Near East and Anatolia, is employed more intensively in this book, inasmuch as for the first time I have an opportunity to treat the artistic production of the Near East in its totality.

Wilhelm Pinder's maxim, to the effect that 'styles have no sharp chronological boundaries and do not follow one another, but they overlap and interact', suggests that archaeologists in their stylistic investigations should think not simply in terms of dating, but should attempt—along the lines of the method outlined above—a more thorough-going classification according to stylistic developments. Chronological data define themselves. Starting from a detailed examination of the material, the following chapters present a number of art styles and ateliers which are clearly distinguishable geographically and chronologically.

For this series of volumes the publishers have developed a special method of presentation that has allowed the author to direct the work to art connoisseurs and those interested in ancient archaeology, on the one hand, and to specialists in the field, on the other. The notes at the end of the book will permit the reader to check the author's statements and to pursue the subject further. The numerous line drawings should lighten the reader's task, but they also have a special function of their own: to 'describe' as much as possible, and especially to clarify the stylistic features of individual works, for these are not always easy to discern in the photographs. Since Near Eastern artists usually do not model bodily parts and muscles but stylize them, these aspects can be more exactly rendered in the graphic medium. Our drawings, many of which are published here for the first time, should not be regarded as substitutes for photographs but as a 'graphic description and commentary' to the objects under discussion.

The procurement of the colour and black-and-white illustrations was made possible through the courtesy of the directors and keepers of the following museums and institutes: Richard D. Barnett, Keeper, Department of Western Asiatic Antiquities, British Museum; Prof. Dr. Kurt Bittel, President of the Deutsches Archäologisches Institut, Berlin; Dr. Dietrich von Bothmer, Curator, Department of Greek and Roman Antiquities, Metropolitan Museum of Art, New York; Necati Dolunay, Director of the Archaeological Museum, Istanbul; R. W. Hamilton, Keeper, Department of Antiquities, Ashmolean Museum, Oxford; D. Haynes, Keeper, Department of Greek and Roman Antiquities, British Museum; Miss Dorothy K. Hill, Curator of Ancient Art, Walters Art Gallery, Baltimore; Prof. Dr. E. Homann-Wedeking, University of Munich; Prof. Dr. Emil Kunze, Director of the Deutsches Archäologisches Institut, Athens; Prof. Dr. Gerhard Rudolf Meyer, General Director of the Staatliche Museen, Berlin; André Parrot, Membre de l'Institut, Conservateur en Chef, Musée du Louvre; Raci Temizer, Director of the Archaeological Museum, Ankara; Dr. N. Yalouris, Director of the Museum at Olympia; the National Museum, Athens; the Kerameikos Museum; the Iraq Museum, Baghdad; the Museo della Villa Giulia, Rome; Tübingen Museum.

Ankara, July 1966   Ekrem Akurgal

PART ONE

The Orient

Thou canst not, and that dost make thee great,
Thou never dost begin—that is thy fate.
Thy song wheels round as does the starry frame,
End and beginning evermore the same,
And what the middle brings we clearly see
Is what the opening was, the end shall be.

Goethe, West-Eastern Divan, II Book
of Hafiz, 6th poem, 1st stanza[1]

I. NEO-ASSYRIAN ART
(1045–610 B.C.)

SYSTEM OF
NEAR EASTERN
ART

It is generally held that the 'conceptual' and conventional nature of Near Eastern art excluded any real stylistic development during the course of its history, and that consequently the art works of this region are unsuited to style analysis. Yet Neo-Assyrian art, for example, shows at least five successive stylistic phases during its four hundred years of existence. Thus the style did change considerably, although the basic conceptual approach, which ignores the third dimension, persisted relatively unaltered during these four centuries. Later we shall see that in Neo-Assyrian art individual styles developed under almost all the great kings who actively patronized art. In the reign of Shalmaneser III (854–824 B.C.) there were even three different styles that flourished alongside one another. But most of the pictorial formulae of the conceptual attitude held firm until the end of the empire.

Five stylistic phases

The basis for distinguishing a time sequence of five stylistic phases in Neo-Assyrian art lies primarily in iconographic changes and in technical devices and achievements, since these provide the surest criteria for dating works of art. But I have often given special emphasis to stylistic peculiarities in order to show that in ancient Near Eastern art personal or local inflections of idiom did exist, if infrequently. In the course of our account it will become clear that Assyrian art underwent an artistic evolution in some ways comparable to those that took place, for example, in the Greek Archaic period and in fifteenth-century Italy. This cumulative or progressive development in Assyrian art, which brought artists almost to the point of discovering perspective, will be stressed in the discussion that is to follow. Here by way of introduction we shall only mention briefly certain general factors underlying the dominant artistic attitude of the Near East.

Fundamentals of 'conceptual' approach

Linear perspective is an artistic achievement that we owe to the Greek civilization of the first half of the fifth century B.C. All art works of the ancient world, including those of the Greeks, that date before this discovery were executed according to the principles of conceptual art. The essential aims of conceptual art[1] are clarity and distinctness of form and content, together with idealization of the figures and objects represented.[2] These basic principles govern the artistic forms and stylistic rules of the conceptual approach. Frontality is perhaps the most obvious consequence of this programme, for works shaped or drawn frontally offer the clearest, simplest and most ideal representation of external reality. Oblique views and foreshortening are therefore avoided.

As has been indicated, Neo-Assyrian sculptors and painters worked within the limits of the stylistic norms prescribed by conceptual art. Therefore they drew not so much what their eyes saw, but what their minds selected as important or characteristic. Thus an Assyrian statue in the round—just as in Egyptian or any other conceptual art—was created by synthesizing four planes standing at right angles to one another; the sculptor would cut in from straight sides front and back, left and right.[3] The term *Richtungsgeradheit*, i.e. frontality, which has been coined by H. Schäfer,[4] is a useful way of describing this aspect of the conceptual rendering.

On the plane surface conceptual art presents the human body according to the following system[5]: the head appears in its clearest aspect, in profile, but the eye is seen frontally—the clearest view of this part. The shoulders and the chest are presented frontally, while the legs and feet appear in profile (Pl. 3). This is not to be regarded as an unsuccessful attempt at representation; for the Assyrians it amounted to an *ideal* rendering of the human body. Adherence to the conceptual representations is not a matter of the presence or lack of skill; rather it reflects the affirmation of certain preferences to the exclusion of others. The artists choose to show the chest and shoulders frontally because this aspect displays these parts of the body most clearly and most 'beautifully'. If necessary, the Assyrian artist can dispense with the principle of conceptual representation. While slaves, prisoners and unimportant persons[6] required by the subject matter may appear in profile, contrary to the dictates of conceptual art, the king—even when he is shown in action—retains the noble form of the full breadth of the bust[7] (Pls. 1–4).

The idealized art of the Assyrians naturally called for a proud and dignified bearing in the human figure. The king, who personified the might of the state, had to be noble and absolutely superior. The attitude and gestures of the ruler and the important personalities of the court were consequently always calm, measured and aristocratic (Pls. 1–8). They symbolized the political supremacy of the Assyrians and served to overawe neighbours and enemies.

Attitudes and gestures

Neo-Assyrian artists departed from their principle of ideal attitudes and aristocratic gestures only when they had to depict foreign peoples, enemies or slaves. Here they could adopt a more realistic rendering. With their wild and vehement gestures the Arab figures of the time of King Assurbanipal are a striking instance of this realistic representation of the language of gesture.[8]

The demand for idealism in the representation of the human figure was the reason why the Assyrians had no art of portraiture. Nowhere in their art do we find a real portrayal of individual human features.[9] The depiction of the human face, whether of a king or a simple soldier, always took a conventional form. The ruler stood out by virtue of his larger scale and the noble expressiveness of his gestures, not to mention his splendid coiffure and elaborate clothes. By contrast, foreigners in Assyrian art are immediately recognizable by their deviant hair style and dress.

Ideal representation

The cruel conduct of warfare and the grisly scenes depicted in relief on the orthostats (upright slabs forming the base of walls) reflect a thoroughly absolutist concept of government in which all power was concentrated in the state as represented by the figure of the king. Barbaric atrocities—mutilations, massacres, impalements and flayings—were prominent instruments of Assyrian policy, which was exclusively directed towards domination. In their annals the Assyrian kings openly boasted of these acts. Assurnasirpal II had this written about himself:

Atrocities

17

'I conquered the towns of the country of Luhuti. I made a great slaughter among them, destroying, rending asunder and burning with fire. I captured living warriors and impaled them on stakes before their towns.'[10] Scenes of this type were often shown in orthostat reliefs to impress the spectator with the immense power of the king and the gruesome fate of his enemies.

Perpendicular positioning When Assyrian artists want to show things in rising country, they depict them at right angles to the slope of the ground-line, so that trees and buildings stand vertically in relation to the incline rather than in relation to the horizon.[11] This accords with the conceptual rendering of the design. The Assyrian artist knows that all objects tend to stand vertically, but he always places them (as Unger rightly notes)[12] in immediate relation to the little piece of ground where they are situated. This conception, which neglects the totality of the picture in order to treat parts of it separately, fitting them together as relatively autonomous units,[13] reflects preference and not incapacity as one might at first assume. It is interesting to note that in the orthostat reliefs of Nineveh an artist of the Assurbanipal period shows a row of figures descending a 45-degree-angle slope[14] not vertical to the

PLATE 2 – Tiglath-Pileser III (745–727 B.C.) on his war chariot. Alabaster relief from the South-west Palace at Kalkhu (Nimrud). *British Museum. Length 1.95 m. Cf. pp. 32 f.*

slope on which they stand but vertical to the horizon—just as we would expect in western art. The artist seems to have recognized that his figures would look like falling men if they were placed at right angles to the ground according to the principle of conceptual representation. But even in this period trees and buildings on sloping ground continue to appear in the old way: perpendicular to the ground-line.[15] In the mind of the Assyrian artist the trees and buildings were so firmly anchored to the ground that he felt little temptation to betray the basic principle of conceptual representation.

The artists of the Sennacherib period found a clever device for retaining this conceptual principle on which they set such great store. Some slaves toiling up a hill with baskets filled with stones are perpendicular to the ground-line and to the horizon, for the artist has introduced 'steps' into the slope which were not present in reality but which served as ground-lines for the figures.[16]

An unmistakable 'escape' from the conceptual principle occurs, however, in a relief of King Assurbanipal in which the figures, who are climbing a hill, appear at right angles to the horizon.[17] Yet in the rendering of the trees on this relief the artist has remained true to the conceptual rule. In such instances one sees artists trying out new devices, but without ever freeing themselves completely from the bonds of the conceptual attitude.

'Escape' from conceptual principle

Adherence to the demands of clarity and distinctness of form and content made the conceptual artist renounce overlappings within the picture plane. Consequently, figures are lined up in rows, which could be stacked parallel in tiers. Serial arrangement is especially dominant in the Archaic and Classical styles. 'Stacking' of the tiers is known in the first three Neo-Assyrian styles, but it occurs seldom and is restricted to two or three tiers. Yet the narrative history scenes of the Assyrians, which tended to report events in as much detail as possible, impelled artists to multiply the superimposed strips of figures and scenes so as to extend their illustrations vertically up the surface of the orthostats. This procedure formed the basis for the richly illustrated reliefs of the reigns of Sennacherib and Assurbanipal, which are among the outstanding achievements of ancient Near Eastern art.

Perhaps the most remarkable creation of this period is the relief showing the transport of a colossal bull statue across a river, which comes from the South-west Palace of King Sennacherib in Nineveh and is now in the British Museum (Fig. 1).[18] This carving displays two important accomplishments of Neo-Assyrian art: the rendering of the third dimension and the principle of a unified compositional design. Using the rudimentary perspective device of the lines of men snaking diagonally up the relief to the left and right, the artist succeeded in creating the effect of depth, an effect enhanced at the bottom by the river, which is understood as foreground, as well as by the friezes of the row of soldiers and of the mountain landscape at the top, which is understood as background. Moreover, the artist enlivened the scene with formal ingenuity and vivid incidents; he placed the main element of the action, the colossal statue, at the focal point and the chariot of the king, who directed the enterprise, on the upper left. In

Third dimension and composition

PLATE 3 – Sargon II (721–705 B.C.). Alabaster relief from Dur-Sharrukin (Khorsabad). *Louvre, Paris. Height 2.68 m. Cf. p. 40.*

this way a complex but unified composition emerges that is unique in the history of ancient Near Eastern art. Furthermore, it is noteworthy that in the mountain landscape the artist shows some of the trees in front of the mountains and others behind them, so as to endow also this part of the scene with a certain effect of space.

There is no mistaking the effort to provide a kind of 'horizontal' perspective. Yet despite this great advance the artist still puts many of the trees at right angles to the slope of the ground-line.[19] Although this Assyrian sculptor had a well-developed sense of the third dimension, he seems to have been unaware of any comprehensive system that would have enabled him to conquer it definitively.

Horizontal perspective

A different type of spatial rendering appears on another relief of Sennacherib's time, which shows the king and his retinue crossing a river that runs through a mountain valley (Fig. 2).[20] Here the artist has inverted the trees and hills on the section below the river. Some scholars have interpreted this method of representation as a kind of 'mirror perspective'.[21] However, the Assyrian artist did not consider his reliefs from the standpoint of the viewer, but in terms of the column advancing to the right. If one examines the scene from the viewpoint of the king and his retinue, one will see that the trees right and left of the river are represented in the same lying or standing position. The trees on the tributary are also shown in the same fashion on both sides of the stream.

FIG. I – *Transport of a colossal bull statue across a river. Relief of Sennacherib (704–681 B.C.). From Nineveh. British Museum. Cf. note 18 and p. 19.*

FIG. 2 – *The king crossing a river. Relief of Sennacherib (704–681 B.C.). From Nineveh. Cf. note 20 and p. 21.*

Progressive development

The foregoing considerations suggest that the art of the ancient Near East underwent a gradual development that involved an advance from linear drawing to plastic modelling (p. 44), from schematism to naturalism (p. 45), and from simple parallelism to complicated design and composition with effects of depth.

Threshold of discovery of perspective

It is probably right to assume that the artists who created the great compositions of the time of Sennacherib and Assurbanipal were on the verge of discovering the principles of perspective. Consequently, it seems unjustified to regard the slow and ultimately incomplete evolution of art in the Near East as simply indicating stagnation. The quick tempo of life in our modern age, and the love of innovation that has affected mankind since the beginning of Greek civilization, have raised the level of our expectations so that we are tempted to measure earlier conditions by our own standards.

The shift from conceptual to perspective vision was achieved by the Greeks in the course of a cumulative development.[22] In a period of two and a half centuries, from about 750 to 500 B.C., the Greeks worked in a conceptual manner essentially like that of the Near Eastern peoples and their own Minoan and Mycenaean forerunners.[23] Following H. Schäfer, we may say that for all peoples of the world conceptual art represents a first stage in the rendering of the physical environment. So it would not be correct to assert that the Greeks had an innate or *a priori* capacity for artistic expression that differed from that of Near Eastern peoples.[24] The Greeks themselves created their almost photographically objective method

PLATE 4 – Assurbanipal (668–630 B.C.) on horseback hunting an onager. Alabaster relief from the North Palace at Nineveh. *British Museum. Height of detail 53 cm. Cf. p. 42.*

PLATE 5 – Fleeing and wounded onager. Alabaster relief from the North Palace at Nineveh (cf. Pl. 4). *British Museum. Height of detail 53 cm. Cf. pp. 42, 43.*

of design only after a long period of development that required much experimentation.

How then can we explain the remarkable phenomenon that the principle of perspective representation was never revealed to the peoples of the East, despite millennia of activity in sculpture and painting? Art historians have suggested a number of different reasons for this failure. Here we need mention only the most important: 'racial and ethnic characteristics'; 'incapacity', 'inability' or 'unwillingness';[25] 'attachment to old traditions';[26] the highly developed 'sense of artistic idealism';[27] and (the most general explanation of all) the 'world view' of the peoples concerned.[28]

Causes of failure

Anyone intensively concerned with the art and culture of the Near East will admit that there is some truth in all these proposed factors. It seems to me, however, that an entirely different cause, which acted strongly to maintain the 'rigidity' of art forms in the Near East, has not been taken into consideration. The chief reason for the retention of the conceptual approach must lie, I believe, in the political and social structure of the states of the ancient Near East.

The strongly centralized control exercised over Near Eastern art and its almost complete dependence on the royal courts must be one of the main factors retarding the organic evolution of artistic creativity. Pictorial art was the most effective means of propaganda available to Near Eastern rulers and, like writing, was a privilege reserved to the royal family and the priestly caste.

Political and social structure

Art in service of state

Greek art owes its rich and creative development to the democratic structure of the city-state system. The best works of the Greek Archaic period were made for private citizens as well as on commission from members of the ruling circles. Consequently the monumental art of the Greeks, which ranks as one of the great achievements of craft enterprise, is directly dependent on economic conditions. The intense commercial and artistic competition of the city-states and their citizens set a challenging series of tasks for artists and workshops, promoting an organic development of artistic activity as a whole. This economic and cultural competition meant that artists—who were still working mainly within the framework of conceptual procedures during the Archaic period—were under constant pressure to seek out new and better methods; this laid the foundations for the unfolding of western culture and art. In the Near East too there were art objects that were produced commercially to be sold on the market, but these were confined mainly to works of the minor arts (Pls. 36–43) and pottery. As long as the monumental art of the Near East remained a state monopoly,[26] it could not develop in the conditions of freedom offered by the democratic states of Greece.

State monopoly

In the course of our discussion we shall see that in the Near East also, wherever art was fostered by a broad segment of the population and especially by the wealthy strata of the middle classes, artists anticipated Greek sculptors and painters in that they were stimulated by commercial and artistic competition to explore new paths and try out new methods. But since the East enjoyed opportunities of this kind infrequently and only for short periods (cf. Pls. 26–28, 36–43), its craftsmen had no chance to overcome the conceptual point of view.

The Neo-Assyrian empire, which was founded at the end of the second millennium, dominated the Near East from 883 to 626 B.C. During this period the Near Eastern peoples were directly or indirectly subject to Assyrian hegemony. Paralleling this political domination, Assyrian art, which ranks as one of the finest achievements of the ancient Mesopotamian world, exercised an important influence upon the art of other countries. The imposing sculptures that adorned Assyrian palaces became the Classical style of the ancient Near East and were taken as models by all neighbouring peoples.

Assyrian art as Classical model

Among Near Eastern artistic centres of the first half of the first millennium there were hardly any that managed to remain free of Assyrian influence. The late

PLATE 6 – Assurbanipal on his war chariot. Alabaster relief from Nineveh. *Louvre, Paris. Height of detail 90 cm. Cf. p. 41.*

Hittites, the Urartians and the Syro-Phoenician peoples, as well as the great cultural complexes of the Iranians and Scythians, were deeply affected by Assyrian art. For a time Babylonia too submitted to the domination of Assyrian art. This remarkable pre-eminence of Assyrian art permits us to use Assyrian style elements as a criterion for chronological comparison of the various dependent traditions and by this means to work out a fairly satisfactory picture of the overall evolution of art during the first half of the first millennium B.C.

As has been noted above, the Assyrians maintained an official imperial art which was closely supervised by the bureaucracy. Propaganda was a prime aim of this art, together with the glorification of the king and his deeds. The greatest artistic achievement of the Assyrians lay in the realm of orthostat reliefs, which decorated the imposing palaces of Kalkhu (modern Nimrud), Dur-Sharrukin (modern Khorsabad) and Ninua (Biblical Nineveh; modern Kuyunjik). These splendid pictorial narratives, which have been called 'picture prose' by A. Moortgat[30] and 'pictorial epic' by H. Frankfort,[31] display a continuous montage comprising various scenes of a particular event, especially victorious campaigns of the Assyrian kings. The picture cycles were usually accompanied by explanatory inscriptions on the surface of the reliefs (Pls. 9–11).

Sculptors of Neo-Assyrian times were the creators of this new art of narration.[32] *Art of narration* Although the Egyptians also had a kind of narrative art,[33] their wall reliefs show only separate scenes of an event without linking them in an integrated sequence of successive phases of a single action. Nor is the famous Sumerian victory stele of Eannatum,[34] which does present several actions but not a precise sequence covering the whole event, a continuous narrative of the type found in Neo-Assyrian wall reliefs. The well-known Akkadian victory stele of Naramsin[35] depicts a particular moment,[36] but does not provide a continuous description.

A typical example may help to clarify the character of the art of narration in the Neo-Assyrian period.[37] A relief from the time of Assurbanipal, which shows a hunting and sports exercise of the ruler in the royal game park,[38] presents the same lion in different positions three times in succession (Pl. 12b). On the right a keeper releases the lion from a cage by raising the gate. In the centre we see the same lion springing to the attack, although it has already been hit in the back with an arrow. In a third phase, on the left, the same wounded lion leaps towards the king and his bodyguards, who fend him off with bows and arrows.

This continuous narration of a connected series of actions is an Assyrian dis- *Continuous narration* covery, found as early as the Middle Assyrian period. The symbolic base of the light god Nusku, dating from the years 1241–1205 B.C. and now in the Berlin Museum, shows a male figure, probably King Tukulti-Ninurta I, in two successive moments of adoration before the altar.[39] Neo-Assyrian artists developed this procedure further, and in the wall reliefs of Nineveh that illustrate war campaigns created magnificent examples of the genre (Pls. 9–11).

Pictorial narration according to the continuous principle ceases with the end of Assyrian art. Later the device emerges again in the Hellenistic Telephos frieze at Pergamon[40] and perhaps earlier in the north frieze of the north porch of the

Erechtheion on the Athenian Acropolis.[41] Strictly speaking, the depiction of a set of historical events as seen in Assyrian monuments recurs only in Roman art in the Column of Trajan in Rome.[42] As L. Schnitzler has convincingly shown,[43] the architect Apollodoros of Damascus had the idea of illustrating the commemorative column of his imperial patron after the fashion of ancient Near Eastern obelisks.

ARCHAIC STYLE Neo-Assyrian pictorial art first appears in the reliefs of an obelisk erected in the second or third year of the reign of Assurnasirpal II (883–859). This monument, which E. Unger ascribed to Assurnasirpal I,[44] has been shown by B. Landsberger *Obelisk of* to belong to the age of Assurnasirpal II.[45] Despite its mediocre quality, this work *Assurnasirpal II* reveals the basic Neo-Assyrian elements of form and content, pure and uncontaminated by foreign admixture. This is the first monument in world history to depict several scenes of a particular event in a continuous sequence. It is important to note that the reliefs of the obelisk correspond to the text incised on the monument, which they illustrate. This text could have been read only by a select few—scribes, high priests and some princes. For the average viewer the pictures played the leading role, and consequently they receive more space than the text.[46] The obelisk was erected to glorify the achievements of Assurnasirpal II, who appears on the monument no less than twenty times. Similar picture cycles commemorating the *res gestae*, the deeds of the ruler, will concern us in splendid examples from later periods in Neo-Assyrian art history. This obelisk marks the beginning of the new art of sculptural narration, which ranks as one of the greatest creations of Neo-Assyrian art.

The obelisk documents the main 'pictorial laws' of Assyrian art, which were to remain in force until the fall of the empire two hundred and fifty years later. The guide-lines of the conceptual approach have already been discussed above. Here we shall emphasize a few iconographic features that distinguish the reliefs of this obelisk from the works of the following periods. Certain technical details have been pointed out by E. Unger.[47] The chariots do not terminate at the rear in shields as they do in the succeeding Classical style. The outline running from the upper border of the forward part of the chariot box to the end of the shaft is low and there is never a richly decorated band, as in the works of the Classical style. The royal chariots lack the third man who regularly appears in scenes from the following style periods. The head-dress of the horses includes three feathers, which are inserted in a rosette rather than in the horseshoe-shaped clamp found in reliefs of later times. The head-dress also lacks the two long pennants which are usual in the horses of royal chariots of the Classical style.

The reliefs of the obelisk may be distinguished from the carvings of the succeeding style by the entirely different handling of the hair at the nape of the neck of the figures. Coiffure played an important role in Assyrian art. The long, diagonally placed hair knot that is characteristic of the Classical style does not appear on the obelisk. Rather the sculptor uses for his figures short, often spirally rolled neck hair or else a long queue that falls far down the back. This hair style indicates the persistence of the fashions of Middle Assyrian art.

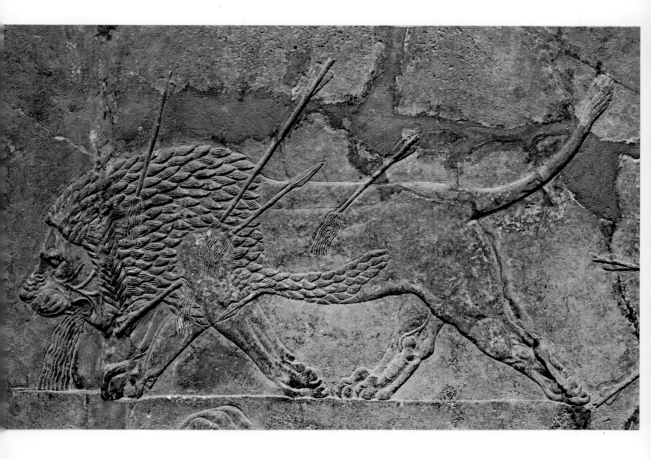

PLATE 7 – Wounded lion. From the great lion-hunting relief of Assurbanipal in the North Palace at Nineveh. *British Museum. Height of detail about 40 cm. Cf. p. 42.*

As has already been suggested, the major difference between this first Neo-Assyrian style, which arose under Assurnasirpal II, and the period to follow lies in the quality of execution. The clumsiness of the artist, who was without doubt the best master to be found at the royal court, shows that at the time Neo-Assyrian art was still in its formative stage. Consequently, we can describe this style as the 'Archaic' phase of Neo-Assyrian art, of which the obelisk may be the last important document. In any event it gives us a vivid idea of pre-Classical work. In view of the great difference between this obelisk and the splendid orthostat reliefs that are almost contemporary, one is entitled to wonder whether E. Unger may not have been right after all in attributing the obelisk to the time of Assurnasirpal I.

The Classical style was created in the time of the great king Assurnasirpal II (883–859), that is during the first efflorescence of the Neo-Assyrian empire. Its iconographic features as well as the conceptual pictorial laws were largely anticipated in the Archaic obelisk we have been discussing and even earlier in the Middle Assyrian art[48] of the second half of the second millennium. Neo-Assyrian classicism raised the traditional art forms to true monumentality. The high quality

Harmony

of execution, the stately calm, and the ripe harmony give these carvings an imposing dignity and grandeur. The works of this period, like the Classical works of other civilizations, were eagerly imitated in later times. The middle phase of Neo-Hittite art took a great many stylistic and iconographic details from the Assyrian Classical style, and Urartian art came into being under the strong influence of the Assyrian Classical style.

Flat relief,
powerful contours

The general character of the Classical style is defined by the flat upper surface of the reliefs with its powerful, but linear contours. Most of the body parts are set off by inner drawing lines and stylizations. Even the highly schematized arm and leg muscles show modelling that is flat in execution. The finest carvings in this art style (Pls. 1, 8), which are now preserved in the British Museum,[49] come from the North-west Palace of King Assurnasirpal II at Kalkhu. Among these are the lions[50] of the portal of the Ninurta Temple at Kalkhu and a half-life-size statuette of the king from the same temple.[51]

Although they lack homogeneity of style and differ somewhat from the sculpture of Assurnasirpal II in iconographic details, the carvings of Shalmaneser III (854–824) still belong to the Classical phase of Neo-Assyrian art. Noteworthy objects from the reign of this king are his Black Obelisk from the citadel of Kalkhu,[52] dated about 829 B.C. and now in the British Museum, and his statue from Assur, now in the Museum of the Ancient Orient in Istanbul.[53] During excavations at Imgur Enlil (Balawat) in 1878 and 1956 bronze revetment reliefs were found that came from two gates of Assurnasirpal II and one gate of Shalmaneser III.[54] Best preserved are the reliefs of Shalmaneser III's gate, which now belong to the British Museum.[55] The reliefs, which are somewhat summarily executed, tell of the military campaigns of the king in various border districts and neighbouring states adjoining the Assyrian empire. Short captions explain the scenes. The scene of the dedication of the royal stele erected in 853 B.C. is interesting. Here we find for the first time the indication of a particular landscape setting, an original rendering of the grotto sources of the river Tigris.[56]

Stylistic and
iconographic features

The iconographic and stylistic aspects of the Classical style are of great importance, for they provide firm criteria for the chronological ordering of the artistic traditions of the Near East. The club-like stylization of the lower-arm muscles is one of the most significant stylistic features of human figure representation in this period (Fig. 3a). Not until the reign of Tiglath-Pileser III was it replaced by a fan-shaped form (Fig. 3b). Moreover, the big diagonally placed shock of hair of the human figures (Pls. 1, 8)[57] as well as the felt cap recalling a fez with a conical attachment,[58] and the royal tiara (Pls. 1, 2, 6) are characteristic features of the Classical style, providing useful indicators for dating.

Dependable criteria for dating are also provided by some details of the chariot *Chariots* representations, such as the small chariot box with quivers arranged criss-cross fashion and the shield, placed at the back to close the box, which is decorated with notching and sometimes with a lion's head as well (Pl. 8). An important feature is the band with transverse decorations that connects the shaft-end with the upper rim of the chariot box. The head-dress of the horses consists of three plumes or a single wide plume in the form of a flat purse,[59] inserted in a horseshoe clamp, from which two long pendents hang fluttering in the wind (Fig. 4).

In this connection the lions must not be neglected.[60] Typical features of the lion *Lions* figures of this period are the gaping mouth with the tongue just slightly projecting, the triangular, half-open ear and the two furrowed rolls of flesh beneath the eyes (Pl. 8a). It is also characteristic that these folds press closely against the lower edge of the eyes and that the upper fold has a gland-like shape and is thicker and larger than the lower one.

Of great importance is the W-shaped stylization of the thigh muscles, which *W stylization* appears not only in the lion figures, but in all the animals depicted in this period.[61] In many cases this stylization is purely W-shaped (Fig. 5a);[62] in other instances, especially in the British Museum bronze reliefs from a gate at Balawat, it takes the guise of a four-tined fork (Figs. 5b, c).[63] As we shall see, this stylization underwent formal transformation within Assyrian art and was imitated in many artistic styles of the Near East. Thus it is a useful pointer for the dating of art works of the first half of the first millennium B.C.

Unlike the relatively homogeneous forms of the sculptures of Assurnasirpal II, *Three different styles* the carvings of Shalmaneser III show three different styles. While the statue of Shalmaneser II in Istanbul is entirely in the Classical manner,[64] the relief scenes on the Black Obelisk[65] (note especially the lion figures) are rather different in style and iconography. A third style, which belongs in a category of its own, is represented by the bronze reliefs from Balawat, in which the elongated figures are executed somewhat summarily although still in a plastic fashion.[66] This last style also shows some peculiarities in details of the iconography. The quivers of the chariot box, for example, are not crossed, as in the reliefs of Assurbanipal II, but are arranged in a different way: while one of the quivers keeps the diagonal position, the other is set upright on the front of the chariot box.

Our identification of three contemporaneous but distinct styles in the Shalmaneser *Style as vehicle for* period shows that the Near East was not unfamiliar with local and personal *local and personal* variations in art, although the dominant centralizing tendency restricted their scope. *inflections*

FIGS. 3a, b – *Left, Fig. 3a: Assyrian arm-muscle stylization. 9th century B.C. After A. Parrot, Assur, Pl. 41. Cf. p. 30. – Right, Fig. 3b: Assyrian arm-muscle stylization in use from reign of Tiglath-Pileser III (745–727 B.C.) onward. Cf. pp. 30, 37.*

FIG. 4 – *Assyrian horse's head-dress. 9th century* B.C. *Cf. note 59 and p. 31.*

No change in Assyrian art from 823 to 746

In the obscure period of Assyrian history that lasts from 823 to 746 B.C. art seems to have undergone no real change. The stele of Shamshi-Adad V (823–810) in the British Museum,[67] together with the stelae of Adadnirari III (809–782) and of the vizier of King Shalmaneser IV (781–772), both in the Istanbul Museum,[68] show male figures, whose head-dress, hair and beard style, arm-muscle stylization and dress are just the same as those we have encountered in works of the Classical style.

TRANSITIONAL STYLE

After the death of Shalmaneser III Assyria underwent a period of decline, and the first half of the eighth century represents a real pause in its development. But during the reign of Tiglath-Pileser III (745–727) Assyria clearly recovered, for in this period the empire became the greatest power ever seen in the ancient Near East. Not only did Tiglath-Pileser III restore Assyrian hegemony in Asia Minor, but he evolved a new social and cultural policy. He declared himself king of Babylonia and thus found a solution for the tangled problem of Assyro-Babylonian relations by providing for a seemingly equal association of the two states in a personal union. As A. Moortgat has rightly said, he was more interested in forging a unified culture in the Near East than in affirming Assyrian hegemony for its own sake.[69] This same comprehensive vision permitted him to reorganize the administrative structure of the empire and to rehabilitate the neglected provinces.

The reign of Tiglath-Pileser III, which saw a complete overhaul in the social and cultural spheres, also witnessed a change in the approach to art, which found new paths for the Classical trend of the ninth century. Some modest efforts represent the first hesitant steps in this artistic reformation. Consequently, one may appropriately term this phase of Neo-Assyrian art the 'transitional style'.

New compositions

The transitional style is less elegant than its Classical predecessors. The relief is even lower, and the bodily forms are lightly modelled. The main accomplishment of this style lies in the artists' striving to forge a type of composition suited to broad, high wall surfaces. The reliefs from the time of King Tiglath-Pileser from the Central Palace at Kalkhu clearly show that the artists of this period were

PLATE 8 – Assurnasirpal II (883–859 B.C.) hunting lions. Alabaster relief from Kalkhu (Nimrud). *Staatliche Museen, Berlin. Height 97 cm. Cf. p. 31.*
PLATES 9–11 – Battle scene: King Assurbanipal's victory at the river Ulai over Te'umman, king of Elam. Alabaster relief from the South-west Palace of Sennacherib (704–681 B.C.) at Nineveh. *British Museum. Height 1.32 m. Cf. pp. 42, 45.*

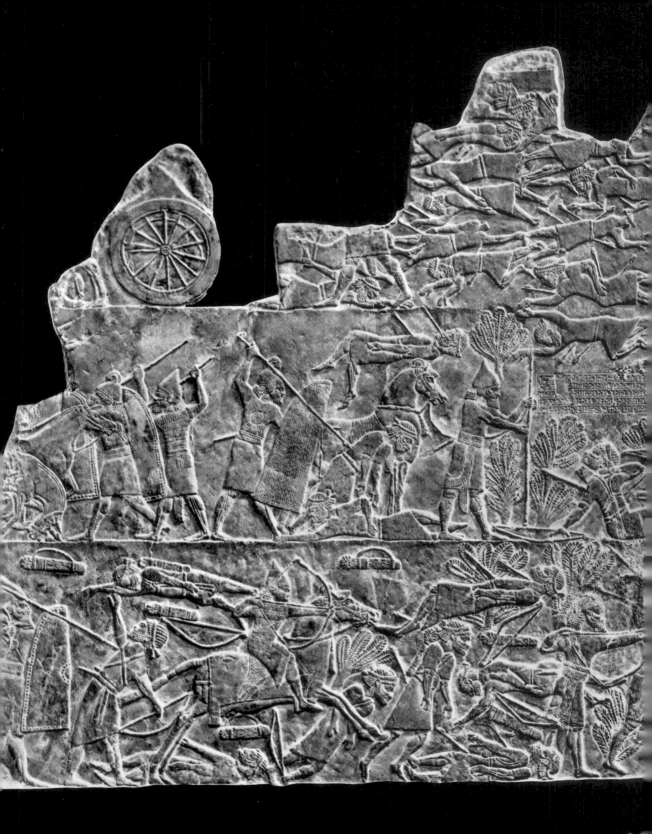

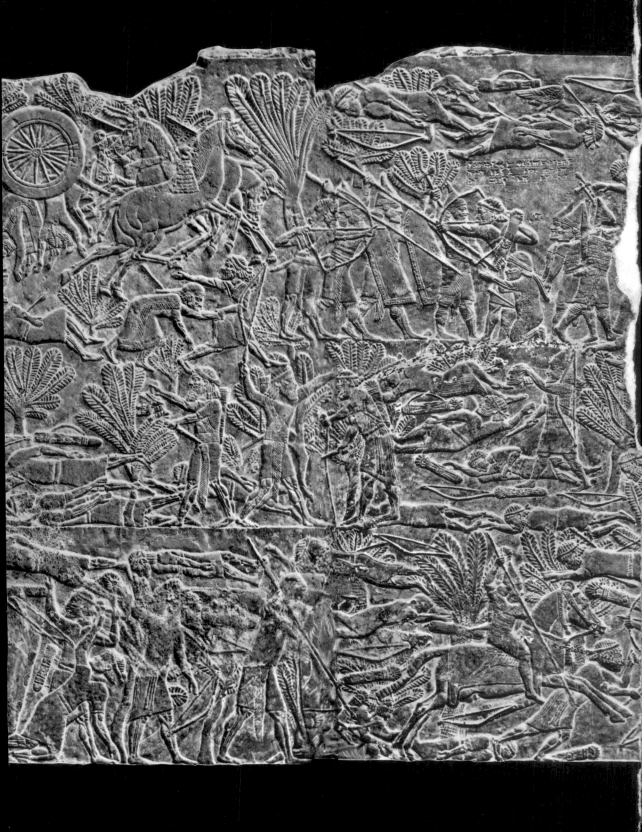

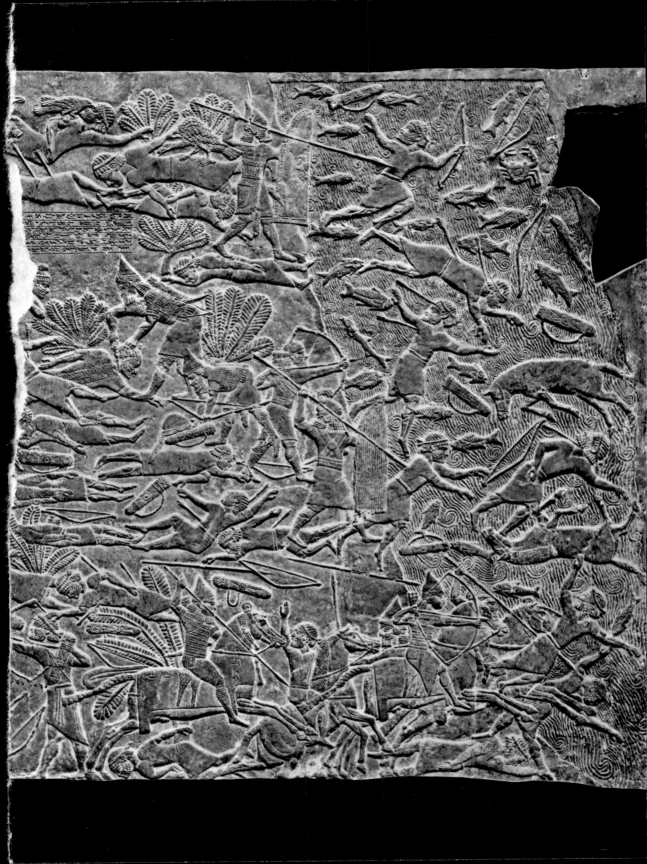

prepared to grapple with the problem of rendering spatial relations on the pictorial surface. This phase of experimentation yielded a number of interesting results. A relief illustrating the transportation of booty and people taken from a conquered city[70] shows a surface composition on the left side of the picture that may be regarded as an effort to work out a perspectival solution. The diagonal line formed by the hooves of the five uppermost animal figures does in fact give the impression of a line receding towards a vanishing point. In the Classical style standing or lying figures were carefully stacked in rows one above the other.

Another sculptor of the time of Tiglath-Pileser III depicted the figures of three enemies, who are to be thought of as lying next to one another, in the stacked arrangement.[71] If the artist of the above-mentioned series of five animals represented them not one atop the other, but in overlapping fashion, this procedure cannot be an accident. Moreover it is important to note that the upper rows of animals and the scribe figures have no ground-line. It seems clear that the sculptor has left the earliest known attempt at a perspectival rendering of spatial relations. The two palm-trees that appear in his composition are space dividers, which are meant to suggest the third dimension. We shall see below that these efforts were carried further in the realistic style of the seventh century.

A number of stylistic and iconographic features of the Classical style underwent *Transformations* a transformation in the transitional phase. The head-dress of the kings became somewhat taller; in addition to the diagonal band at the base found in examples of the Classical style, some horizontal bands appeared as well.[72] A novelty is the fact that these bands are decorated with rosettes.

The conical extension of the head-dress has become larger (Pl. 2). Conversely the hair knot has become a bit smaller than in the Classical style, and it is not placed so markedly diagonally as in the works of the ninth century, but in many instances approaches a vertical position.[73]

The club-like stylization of the lower-arm muscles persists, but at the same time a *Fan-like muscles on* new fan-like stylization is employed (Fig. 3b).[74] It is not unusual for the two *lower arm* interpretations of the muscles to appear side by side on the same slab.

The lion figure also undergoes considerable change. In the time of Tiglath-Pileser III *New features of lion* the flesh folds stylized in the form of two palmette leaves beneath the eyes are modelled more clearly and plastically (Fig. 6).[75] In the ninth-century examples the upper of these two palmette-like stylizations takes the form of a protruding gland[76] and the second form below is noticeably smaller. But in the time of Tiglath-Pileser III the two bulges are equal in size and form. It is also characteristic that these forms found immediately below the eyes in the ninth century become

PLATE 12a – King Barrakab and his secretary. Corner orthostat from Zincirli (Sam'al). Basalt. Aramaean style. About 730 B.C. *Staatliche Museen, Berlin. Height 1.12 m. Cf. pp. 55 f.*
PLATE 12b – Continuous narration of an event. Orthostat relief from Assurbanipal's Palace at Nineveh. *British Museum. Cf. p. 27.*
PLATE 13 – Princess at a funerary meal. Stele from Zincirli (Sam'al). Basalt. Aramaean style. About 730 B.C. *Staatliche Museen, Berlin. Height 1.12 m. Cf. p. 56.*

even larger in the time of Tiglath-Pileser III, so that they fill the whole cheek area of the lion's face.[77]

The lion's ear also changes its shape. To be sure, it is still open in this period, but a disk-like form appears on the upper surface,[78] which is to persist as an identifying characteristic of the Assyrian figure.

The W-shaped stylization of the thigh invented during the Classical style hardly changed: it is now more nearly a W, but the part next to the belly of the animal is somewhat altered.[79] The original form of the stylization can be easily recognized (Fig. 5d, e).

Changes in chariot details
In the representation of chariots many features take on new standard forms, though these flourish side by side with those of the Classical style (Pl. 2). The richly decorated band that links the shaft-end with the upper rim of the chariot box persists in the reign of Tiglath-Pileser III,[80] but it disappears completely in the following period. In many chariots depicted by artists of the transitional style it gives way to a simple rope,[81] and this is usual in chariots of the succeeding styles.[82] The rope is found as early as the chariots of the obelisk of Assurnasirpal II. There, however, it hangs slack so that it is hidden behind the horse; but henceforth it is pulled up high and is always visible under the reins. The crossed quivers of the chariot box, which were fashionable in the Classical style, have disappeared. From the time of Tiglath-Pileser III one sees only a vertical quiver on the front of the chariot; the second quiver has apparently been banished to the other side of the chariot in the background.

In the transitional style both the wheel and the chariot box are larger. The number of wheel spokes is now fixed at eight, and the wheel no longer has only one rim (as in the Classical style) but three, two thin ones and a heavy one, held together

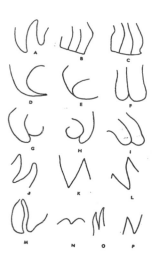

FIGS. 5a–p – *Thigh stylizations from Near Eastern animal figures (9th–7th century B.C.). – a: Assyrian art. 9th century B.C. Cf. Pls. 1, 8, p. 33. – b, c: Assyrian art. 9th century B.C. Cf. Barnett, Assyrian Palace Reliefs, Pl. 155. Cf. p. 31. – d, e: Assyrian art. Second half of 8th century B.C. Cf. Strommenger, Mesopotamien, Pl. 218. Cf. above. – f: Assyrian art. Reign of Sargon. After Strommenger, Mesopotamien, Pl. 220. Cf. p. 41. – g–i: Assyrian art. Reigns of Sennacherib and Assurbanipal. Cf. Strommenger, Mesopotamien, Pls. 234, 238, 249. Cf. p. 41. – j, k: Aramaean-Hittite art. 730–700 B.C. Cf. Figs. 12, 15, p. 60. – l, m: Aramaean-Hittite sphere. Early 7th century B.C. (Cf. Capena Bowl, Brown, Etruscan Lion, Pl. 5a; Cauldron base from Praeneste, Akurgal, Kunst Anatoliens, p. 58, Pl. 26.) Cf. p. 60. – n–p: Urartian art. 7th century B.C. Cf. Akurgal, Kunst Anatoliens, p. 36, Pl. 13; Erzen, AA, 1962, p. 410, Pl. 18; Akurgal, Kunst Anatoliens, p. 37, Pl. 15. Cf. Fig. 127, p. 197.*

with clamps at four places.[83] The enlarged size of chariot box (and wheel) is probably due to the fact that it now usually accommodates three persons, instead of two as in the ninth century.[84] The surfaces of the chariot box now display ostentatious ornament. In the chariot the king is often shaded by a richly decorated canopy (Pl. 2).

A characteristic feature of the reliefs of Tiglath-Pileser III are soldiers with helmets ending in a point, long lances and a short round shield.[85] The three-staged, cylindrical horse's head-dress for the attachment of streamers[86] as well as the royal attributes in the form of a flower or a fan, which the king carries in one hand, and the Aramaean scribe, accompanied by an Assyrian scribe[87]—all these are motifs and themes that first appear in the time of Tiglath-Pileser III.

New warrior types

Equine head-dress

One of the most important changes in the artistic situation under Tiglath-Pileser III was the reaction against the highly centralized Classical style of the preceding period, which encouraged a lively art production in the provincial cities. The orthostat reliefs of Arslan-Taş[88] and the wall frescoes of Til Barsib[89] come from two palaces in the province of Syria. Since the figural scenes from these two sites belong fully to the transitional style, they have been correctly dated to the time of Tiglath-Pileser III.[90] Both the Til Barsib frescoes and the Arslan-Taş reliefs show all the peculiarities of the transitional style we have been discussing. The Arslan-Taş works do not have the high quality of the contemporary carvings of the South-west Palace in Kalkhu. On the other hand, the wall frescoes from Til Barsib rank as the finest pieces of Assyrian painting that have survived. (A portion of these wall-paintings comes from a later restoration in the time of Assurbanipal.)[91]

Activity in provinces

Sargon II (721–705) was a worthy successor of Tiglath-Pileser III. He was successful in preserving everything that his great forebear had constructed and established. In the field of art patronage he even surpassed him.

PLASTIC STYLE

After Sargon ascended the throne, he began to look for a new site for his capital, which he fixed in the neighbourhood of Nineveh. This royal city, which was called Dur-Sharrukin or 'fort of Sargon' (the modern Khorsabad), was an imposing metropolis, with great monuments proclaiming the Assyrian ruler's might. The entrance to the palace, which led to the king's throne-room, was decorated with orthostat reliefs over four metres high as well as with *Lamassu* demons in high relief, which must have made a powerful impression on the visitor.

The kings of friendly neighbouring states and the vassals and envoys, who came to seek an audience with the great king, had to pass along sculptured walls depicting the heroic deeds of the ruler until they reached the throne, which was supported by a base with a cautionary scene. This showed Sargon borne in his war chariot across the bodies of fallen enemies, while his soldiers erected pyramids of human heads.[92]

The monumentality of the orthostat reliefs led to a rounded or 'plastic' style that assured the carvings of the time of Sargon their pre-eminence as the finest and best art works of Assyrian history (Pl. 3). If one examines a splendid winged-bull god, the *Lamassu* figure in the Louvre which comes from Sargon's palace,[93] one

Monumentality and plasticity

FIG. 6 – *Lion's head. Detail of a portal lion from Arslan-Taş. Assyrian art. Reign of Tiglath-Pileser III (745–727 B.C.). Cf. note 78 and p. 37.*

can see that the limitation of the flat treatment of the two preceding styles has been overcome. Here the figural elements are worked well out of the relief ground with all details carefully shaped.

The new plastic rendering of forms is especially apparent in the treatment of the hair. While in the Lamassu figures of the Classical style[94] the flatly worked locks appear in the form of clusters of vertical wavy lines, here we see the hair plastically worked and modelled with corkscrew curls. As a relief of a winged god in the Museum of the Ancient Orient in Istanbul[95] and several other reliefs show, the corkscrew curl was already known in the ninth century,[96] although it was rarely[97] employed.[98]

The new 'plastic' treatment enabled the sculptor to render forms naturalistically. Thus the beard and hair are no longer decorative adjuncts, but living forms presented in their full natural roundness. This plasticity is also felt in the relatively flat orthostat reliefs (Pl. 3), where the body and muscle forms are more salient than in the carvings of earlier styles (Pls. 1, 8).

Most of the iconographic and stylistic elements introduced in the transitional style became fixed rules in the period of the Sargonid style. The fan-shaped stylization of the lower-arm muscle[99] first employed in the time of Tiglath-Pileser is now the only accepted way of showing this part of the body (Fig. 3b), and this convention persisted in the following periods. In the plastic style the stylization of the knee-cap acquired a new form (Fig. 7b). Whereas in the reliefs of the ninth century it had consisted of three rolls of equal thickness[100] (Fig. 7a), in the carvings of the time of Sargon (Pl. 4) a new stylization appeared; the middle roll was reduced in size, acquired a pearl-like form and was enclosed by the upper and lower rolls meeting in the form of an arch (Fig. 7b).[101]

Stylization of knee-cap

The royal tiara keeps the shape usual in earlier times. However, the tendency to enlargement has gained ground, so that the tiara and its conic finial become noticeably higher.[102] Moreover, the head-dress is more ornate.

Coiffure

The coiffure style of the transitional style was developed further. In comparison with previous work, the shock of hair on the nape of the neck is shorter and smaller, lying only at a slight diagonal on the shoulders, not yet quite vertical[103] (Pl. 3) as in the succeeding styles of the time of Sennacherib and Assurbanipal. The fashion for richly decorated chariot boxes that appeared in the transitional style[104] continued (Fig. 8). The rope connecting the top front of the chariot box with the shaft-end is now general. The luxurious band which was normal in the ninth century and common in works of the Tiglath-Pileser style instead of the rope, fell out of fashion. For horses the cylindrical tassel holder, which appeared in the transitional style, is now a fixed rule.

In this style the lion type undergoes a noteworthy shift. The pouches beneath the eyes now usually consist of three stringy folds. They may be clearly recognized in the lions of the big hero figures from the palace of King Sargon II, now in the Louvre (Fig. 9).[105] In the time of Sargon the W-shaped thigh stylization of the animal figures commonly resembles that of the previous transitional style.[106] But often the half of the W next to the animal's belly is remodelled. In some instances the form seems to consist of two joined U shapes (Fig. 5f).[107] Other animals have a disk held in place by a rolling arch on the thigh (Fig. 5g-h).[108] Since artists of this period did not represent the muscles in a linear style, but modelled them plastically, these forms cannot be worked out exactly, even through careful study of the trial pieces in the Louvre. But there is no doubt that they adhere in a general way to the W scheme.

Modification of lion type

The general process of accommodation of Assyrian culture to Babylonian models continued even after Sennacherib (704–681) destroyed Babylon and carried off the Marduk figure to Assur. His son Esarhaddon (680–669) restored the god Marduk to his place and began to reconstruct the destroyed city. Assurbanipal (668–626), who from his youth was devoted to the tasks of peace and to works of scholarship and art, worked towards a synthesis of Babylonian and Assyrian culture.[109]

Assyrian sculpture, however, remained untouched by the influence of Babylon, since it was managed entirely by the court. The reliefs in the British Museum from the time of Sennacherib and Assurbanipal come from the South-west Palace in Nineveh. The art works of the reigns of the two kings show easily recognizable differences, so that two sub-styles may be distinguished; but since most iconographic elements in works of the two periods are almost the same, we may disregard the fine points of this differentiation.

REALISTIC STYLE

In this period the royal tiara with its conical finial is even larger and more ornate than its predecessors in the Sargonid style (Pl. 6). The wheels of the chariots are larger and consequently easy to distinguish from those depicted in older works (Pl. 6). Since the capacity of the chariots also increased, the number of people accommodated is usually four and only rarely three.[110] In the time of Sennacherib the wheel regularly had eight spokes, but in the reliefs of Assurbanipal a sixteen-spoke type is found as well. The royal canopy over the chariot is broader and in many cases has a richer decoration than in the earlier styles. From the time of Sennacherib, however, one finds chariot boxes without any decoration.[111] The chariots shown in the art of Sennacherib's reign may be easily distinguished from

those of the Assurbanipal period. Typical of Assurbanipal era work is that the sides of the chariot box are enclosed and strengthened by several (usually four) metal bands.[112]

The head-dress of horses took on a new form in this period. It is no longer conical, but almost horseshoe-shaped or nearly circular (Pl. 4) and is decked out with fine, closely set feathers.[113]

As in the preceding plastic style the lower-arm muscle is modelled in a fan-like shape (Fig. 3). However, a distinction is observed, for in the Sargonid period the stylization consisted of three dissimilar lines, whereas here there are two lines of almost equal length and one short line.[114]

Change in hair style

One of the main characteristics of this style is the vertical placement of the shock of hair on the nape of the neck. Unlike the royal tiara, from the ninth century until the time of Sennacherib the hair shock decreased steadily in length, so that it reached its shortest form in the seventh century. As a consequence of this shortening the formerly diagonal shock of hair took on a fully vertical position.

From the time of Sennacherib the comparatively short shock of hair lay with its full weight vertically on the shoulders.[115] The generally reduced plasticity in the rendering of the forms is expressed in the treatment of the hair. The hair shock of the Sargonid period (Pl. 3) has a round and open form, in which the individual ringlets are plastically treated. This type of design was cultivated with especial success by an outstanding master, who seems to have created the Lamassu figures as well as the orthostat reliefs with the king accompanied by his priests (Pl. 3) and the Assyrians with drinking vessels.[116]

In carvings of the Sennacherib and Assurbanipal periods the individual ringlets of hair are schematically arranged so as to form horizontal and vertical rows (Pls. 4, 6).[117] It must be added that in comparison with the Sargonid style the realistic style worked less plastically (though still with more modelling than in the two styles preceding the realistic one). Thus, for example, the curls in the carvings of the realistic type are always clearly stylized as coiled spirals, calling for a certain plasticity in their rendering. By contrast, the flatly executed reliefs of the Classical style generally have hair and beard locks that are exclusively characterized by a cluster of vertical wavy lines.

Change in lion type

In the realistic style the lion type undergoes a fundamental change. In place of the palmette stylizations beneath the eyes one now has four thin string-like folds (Pl. 7).[118] The thigh stylization of the animal figures remains unchanged with respect to the plastic style (Fig. 5g–i). We also find the scheme of the two paired U shapes of unequal width[119] as well as the round disk[120] accompanied by a rolling arch (Pls. 5, 7, 9–11). It is easy to see that both types are simply transformed W stylizations. In later times this thigh stylization was borrowed by various art traditions, which further modified and developed it.

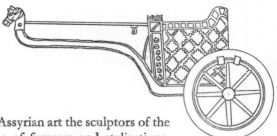

Egyptian lion form

It is especially noteworthy that for the first time in Assyrian art the sculptors of the realistic style created a lion type with a face free of furrows and stylizations. Beside the lion type we have been discussing with four thin skin folds (Pl. 7) there are lions preserved from the North-west Palace at Nineveh with faces carefully modelled without the skin fold.[121] There is no doubt that these lion figures were created under the influence of Egyptian models. As is well known, Egyptian lion figures have a smooth face without furrows or stylizations.[122] It is understandable that Egyptian influence should have been effective in this period, since under Esarhaddon the Nile kingdom was temporarily incorporated into the Assyrian empire. Below we shall see how hints of Egyptian art appear in the design of Assyrian battle scenes.[123]

The animals shown in the art of Assurbanipal mark the climax of Neo-Assyrian art (Pls. 4, 5, 7). These naturalistic figures, which show remarkable qualities of observation and capture the excitement of momentary actions, rank not merely as one of the greatest achievements in the art of the ancient Near East, but are outstanding landmarks in world art as a whole (Pl. 7). The naturalistic rendering of emotional states and of sudden movement is so far advanced that in the case of one lion driven by whips we can sense the animal's rage and fury as he crouches ready to spring while his tail flays the ground.[124] Then how touching is the anxiety of the mare on the relief with the fleeing and wounded onager, which comes from the North Palace of King Assurbanipal at Nineveh.[125] She looks back in terror to see her helpless foal for the last time before she starts her gallop, leaving it to be devoured by the dogs (Pl. 5). The attitude of the head, the position of the ears, the trembling lips and nostrils as well as the tense leg muscles convey perfectly the fleeing animal's distress.

Climax of Assyrian sculpture

The orthostat reliefs from the North-west Palace of King Assurbanipal abound in magnificent figures of animals in various attitudes and emotions. Especially convincing and expressive are the springing and attacking lions, and the wounded and dying ones (Pls. 4, 5, 12b). Comparing these scenes with the reliefs of the Siphnian Treasury at Delphi, the Alexander Sarcophagus in Istanbul and the Pergamon Altar in Berlin, all later Greek works showing lion combats, it is striking how far the realistic creations of the Assyrian artists surpass them.

H. Frankfort has pertinently observed that Assyrian artists often depict real events.[126] Apart from religious imagery, there is nothing in Assyrian art that could not exist in reality. Frankfort has also pointed out that in fact the body-to-body combats of man and lion continued to take place in much the same fashion in the district of the upper Euphrates until fairly recent times. The lion fighter wrapped

Lions in combat

his left arm in a great mass of black goat's hair or in coarse cloth to protect himself against the beast's teeth and claws. When the lion sprang to the attack the man extended his protected left arm,[127] leaving his right arm free to wield the sword against the lion's body.[128] Assyrian kings claimed to have accomplished such heroic deeds single-handed. Assurbanipal, who has left us the finest hunting scenes of antiquity, boasts of having seized a lion by the ear and run it through with a spear.[129] On an orthostat relief of the North Palace at Nineveh, where he is shown holding a lion by the tail, he declares: 'I am Assurbanipal, king of the world, king of Assyria. For my princely enjoyment I laid hold of a lion by the tail, and at the bidding of Ninurta and Nergal, the gods who are my lords, I split his skull with the axe in my hands.'[130]

The preceding considerations show clearly that in the course of two centuries Assyrian art underwent a gradual development leading from schematism to a splendid naturalism. This advance is also recognizable in other matters of style. We have seen, for example, how the figures in the orthostat reliefs of the ninth century seem like enlarged drawings. In the time of Sargon, however, the figures are worked in relatively high relief and the forms of the body are modelled with sculptural fullness. Then in the carvings of the Sennacherib period the plastic tendency diminished to some extent.

In reliefs of the Assurbanipal period human and animal figures give evidence of careful observation of nature.

The W-shaped stylization of the thighs of lions and other animals, which appeared outlined in a linear fashion or simply incised in the ninth century (Pls. 1, 8),[131] was plastically modelled in naturalistic forms in the seventh century. Moreover, the leg-muscle stylization in the guise of a pendent tulip, which was rendered as an incised drawing in the animal figures of the ninth century,[132] acquired plasticity in the orthostat reliefs of the seventh century (Pls. 4–7, 9–11). The flat and linear hair treatment of the ninth century (Pls. 1, 8) moved in the eighth and *Plastic fullness* seventh centuries towards a naturalistic rendering, which captured the plastic fullness of the organic forms in a convincing way (Pls. 3, 4). The stiff 'posed' figures of the lions in ninth-century works (Pls. 1, 8) become living images of roaring, raging and threatening beasts (Pls. 4, 5, 7). The artists were splendidly successful in endowing the animals' countenances with the emotions of pain and wrath, anxiety and menace.

In order to understand the advance that Neo-Assyrian art made in the time of Assurbanipal over the stage reached in the Classical style of the ninth century, one need only compare any horse figure of the Classical style with the mare on the relief of King Assurbanipal (Pl. 5), which we have already discussed. The Assyrian animal figures of the seventh century rank among the finest achievements that exist in the visual arts.

Climax of realism While the realistic treatment of animals in hunting reliefs of Assurbanipal reached astonishing perfection, human figures are still imbued with the time-honoured idealism defined by the standards of the conceptual approach. A comparable tendency was dominant in Greek art throughout its whole course. In the fifth and

FIG. 9 – *Assyrian lion type. Reign of Sargon (721–705 B.C.). Cf. note 105 and p. 41.*

fourth centuries B.C. especially, human figures normally appear with highly idealized features. Greek art similarly avoided the rendering of details and forms of expression that were neither 'beautiful' nor 'ideal'. Here too Neo-Assyrian art could be very severe (see above, p. 17). No disturbing features mar the dignified, serious and proud faces of the men (Pls. 1–4, 6),[133] and no unworthy or low gesture is allowed to disrupt the harmony of the whole. At the same time this artistic concept of working with ideal principles allowed the creation of naturalistic works both in the Near East and in Greece, except that while Near Eastern art follows the 'conceptual approach', the Greek predilection for 'visual reality' permits a corresponding naturalism.

Above we have considered at some length the great advance Neo-Assyrian artists made in the treatment of spatial depth and in the creation of a homogeneous composition (p. 19). In conclusion we must note that the orthostat reliefs of the time of Assurbanipal stand at the summit of Assyrian art. The scenes showing Arabs fleeing, falling, fighting with one another or sleeping in their tents give evidence of the Assyrian artists' superb powers of observation. Especially naturalistic and attractive is a scene in which one Arab falls down from a camel and another tries to bring the prone animal to its feet by beating its legs with a stick, while two others desperately fight one another.[134] The interrelationship of the human figures, with their lively gestures and attitudes, and the camel forms a remarkable design, which compares favourably with the Amazon and Centaur battles in Greek art. The artist points a surprising contrast between the mask-like impassivity of the Arabs' countenances and the expressive movement of the faces of the camel and the horse.

Spatial depth and composition

An outstanding achievement of Neo-Assyrian art is the scene of Assurbanipal's victory over Te'umman, king of Elam, on the river Ulai.[135] The composition is both grandiose and dramatic, depicting the scenes as a vital and well-organized whole (Pls. 9–11). The action moves in stormy vehemence from left to right, ending in the river where the enemy is slaughtered to the last man.

Great battle scene

The brief but expressive words of the inscription on the slab heighten the drama of the relentless struggle. The scene depicted on a separate ground-line on the upper left shows Te'umman kneeling after being struck by an arrow (Pl. 11).[136] An inscription explains what is happening: 'In desperation Te'umman tells his son: Shoot me with your bow.'[137] Nearby on the right is a longer caption that describes the sad end of the king and his son: 'Te'umman, king of Elam, who was wounded in a fierce battle, and Tamritu, his eldest son, who took him by the hand, fled in order to save their lives and hid in a thicket. With the help of Assur and Ishtar I slew and beheaded them.'[138] In the scene below this inscription we see an Assyrian soldier killing the son of Te'umman with a club, while another severs the king's head.[139]

Another tragic episode of the battle is narrated in words and images on an adjoining slab (Pl. 9). An Elamite prince sinks down, struck by an arrow.[140] Above him appears the following inscription: 'Urtaku, the foster son of Te'umman, though wounded by an arrow, had not yet ended his life. He called an Assyrian to behead him with the words: Come, cut off my head, then take it to the king, your lord, and let him show mercy.'[141] But the king showed no mercy. The battle continued in all its horror and ruthless vehemence until no more enemies were left (Pl. 11).

Design and composition Anyone who is acquainted with Egyptian battle scenes will recognize influences from the Nile kingdom in this Assyrian orthostat relief. Paradoxically, the continual fighting with Egypt seems to have strengthened the bonds with this ancient civilization. The Assyrian artist must have known battle scenes such as those still visible in the temples at Thebes on the upper Nile, and have been strongly influenced by them.

But in the naturalism and lively expressiveness of his own figures the Assyrian artist went far beyond his Egyptian predecessors. Especially impressive is the scope of the composition as a whole. The vertical sweep of the river up the slab is a felicitous inspiration that gives the picture spatial depth (Pl. 11). Through this device the figures floating one above the other give the impression of lying or standing on the ground at different distances from the observer. In distributing the isolated trees from bottom to top among the figures and scenes he seems to have wanted to show that the figures do not float in the air but stand or lie on the ground like the trees. This was the last attempt by Near Eastern art, at the end of its glorious history, to advance toward a solution of the problem of space. As in the relief of the transportation of the colossal bull statue (Fig. 1) from the time of Sennacherib, this effort led the artist to the threshold of the discovery of perspective.

ASSYRIAN ARCHITECTURE The kings of the Neo-Assyrian period were great builders who erected imposing palaces and temples. It seems, however, that Assyrian architecture—unlike Assyrian sculpture—did not exercise a significant influence over the cultures of *Hittite building elements* neighbouring countries. On the contrary, from northern Syrian and Hittite centres the Assyrians borrowed such building types and decorative features as the *bit hilani*, columns, ornamental capitals, sculptured bases and orthostats adorned with reliefs. Sargon II states this expressly: 'I erected a *bit appati* in the fashion of a Hittite palace, which is called *bit hilani* in the Amurru language; . . . eight paired lions [that is, portal lions] weighing 4610 talents, in shining bronze; . . . four high columns of cedar wood taken from the Amanus I had placed on lion colossi.'[142] The important question of the borrowing of Hittite building elements, which were also imitated to some extent by the Greeks, will be taken up in a later chapter.

Four centres

The kings of the Neo-Assyrian period (883–606) built not only in Assur, but in the three more northerly capitals of Kalkhu (Nimrud), Dur-Sharrukin or 'Fort of Sargon' (Khorsabad) and Nineveh or Ninua (Kuyunjik).

In the great walled city of Kalkhu, which measures about 2100 by 1670 metres, the outstanding English archaeologist M. E. L. Mallowan has recently uncovered remains of important buildings containing princely finds.[143] Here lay the palaces of Assurnasirpal II (North-west Palace), who had selected this place as his capital, and two buildings of Shalmaneser II, the Central Palace and the so-called 'Fort', together with other notable structures of the succeeding Assyrian periods.[144]

The Central Palace and the South-west Palace of Nimrud were also used as royal residences in the time of Tiglath-Pileser III. The provincial palaces of Til Barsib (Tell Ahmar)[145] and Khadatu (Arslan-Taş),[146] both in Syria, belong to the time of this king.

'Fort of Sargon'

Sargon II built his capital, which has an enclosure wall measuring about 1.8 by 1.7 kilometres, in a very short space of time, six years. He lived there until his death two years later.[147] The palaces and the temple stood at the north-west corner of the citadel. The palace where Sargon lived had three gates, decorated with reliefs showing demons and genii, leading into a courtyard measuring about 100 by 100 metres. Behind this courtyard was a second rectangular one, from which a passage on the left side led to the throne room, with its entrance guarded by Lamassu and Gilgamesh figures over 4 metres high.[148] The palace precinct, which included a temple, where the six great gods were all worshipped, and a ziggurat, was surrounded by an enclosure wall. However, the higher north-western part of the residential palace straddled the city wall, so that from the outside this area gave the impression of a projecting bulwark.[149]

As E. Strommenger has recently noted, Assyrian palace complexes were assembled as courtyard systems, often having a wide throne room between an outer and inner court.[150] The temples, which were also building complexes with courtyard systems, had cult rooms with a broad vestibule and a longitudinal cella.[151] The private dwelling areas were suites of rooms usually consisting of a courtyard, a large and small chamber and a bathroom.[152] The walls were constructed of mud brick. In the more stately buildings the lower parts of the walls were adorned with sculptured or plain orthostats or else with glazed bricks depicting animals.[153]

Nineveh

Sennacherib (704–681) rebuilt Nineveh as a capital.[154] He erected the South-west Palace, where Assurbanipal was later to reside for a time until his new North Palace could be completed. In the Neo-Assyrian period Nineveh extended for 4.2 kilometres in length and 2.1 kilometres in breadth. Most of this area has not yet been explored by archaeologists. From the inscription of a stele of Sennacherib in the Archaeological Museum in Istanbul we learn that Nineveh had a processional avenue called the 'royal street'.[155] This was paved with stone slabs and its width fixed by ordinance at 26 metres. All the citizens had to observe this ruling, for as the inscription states: 'Whosoever among the inhabitants of Nineveh shall build his house on to the street beyond the prescribed limits shall be impaled upon the roof-tree of his own house.'[156]

II. BABYLONIAN ART

Babylonia was one of the oldest civilized countries of the ancient Near East. In the age of Hammurabi, in the eighteenth century B.C., the Mesopotamian world reached a culminating stage of development. Later, when Babylonia became politically dependent on Assyria, its cultural level remained very high, and the victorious Assyrians recognized this superiority. In a sense the Babylonians were the Greeks and the Assyrians the Romans of the ancient Near East. In the fields of religion and literature especially the Assyrians were strongly influenced by this older civilization.

In the seventh century B.C., not long before the Ionic philosophers appeared, Babylon was still the spiritual capital of the world. All the wisdom and knowledge of the ancient East, the legacy of thousands of years of practical experience, were known to the priests of this city.

What then were the intellectual accomplishments of the Near Eastern peoples in the course of two and a half millennia since the discovery of writing about 3000 B.C.? The study of surviving documents suggests that in the middle of the seventh century men had not yet reached the stage of scientific thought that was to be realized two generations later in the Ionian Greek cities of the west coast of Anatolia.[157] Assurbanipal, who had received a careful scholarly and priestly education in his youth and who accumulated a large personal library, has left an interesting account that throws light on the spiritual life of the ancient Near East. 'Marduk, the wise one among the gods, gave me a broad ear, a perceptive mind. Nabu, the scribe of the universe, Ninurta and Nergal gave my figure manliness and incomparable strength. I understood the revelation of the wise Adapa; I have seen the hidden treasure of the whole art of the scribes in the houses of heaven and earth . . . I can solve the most complicated tasks of division and multiplication. I read the artful writing table of Suman and the dark Akkadian, which is hard to ascertain. I understand the text of stones that come from the time before the flood . . .'

Achievements of ancient Near Eastern peoples

The status of the exact sciences among the Near Eastern peoples seems to be clearly expressed in these succinct words of Assurbanipal. The solution of very complicated tasks of division and multiplication must have been the highest achievement that men at that time had devised for practical purposes from their daily experience. Other surviving written sources confirm that the intellectual activity of the ancient Near East in the mathematical and astronomical fields had not reached the stage of scientific research.[158] The strength of the Near Eastern peoples lay in the realms of literature, art and especially religion. Their greatest contribution to world culture was the discovery of cuneiform writing and above all the Phoenician alphabet, which with some modification serves most of mankind today as a common resource.

Literature, art and religion

Babylonia, which had played a leading role in the artistic field in the second quarter of the second millennium, during the Hammurabi period, once more became an important art centre after the end of the thirteenth century. The Babylonian boundary stones of the late second and early first millennium are carvings of outstanding artistic expression with a unique character.[159] The representations of men, animals and fables have a fully Babylonian stamp in both iconography and style. These art works had a great influence upon Luristan bronzes, and many reflections are evident in the products of the late Hittite workshops.[160] Outstanding in the latter group is the Neo-Babylonian feather crown[161] of the genius figures from Malatya and Tell Halaf.[162] Moreover, the unusual coiffure of Queen Gula on the boundary stone of King Nebuchadnezzar I, now in the British Museum,[163] is the same as that worn by King Sulumeli at Malatya.

Only a few sculptures have survived as evidence of Babylonian art from the period of the Neo-Assyrian empire. The political hegemony of the Assyrians seems to have considerably restricted the possibilities of development for Baby-

Boundary stone

lonian art. A boundary stone of King Mardukapaliddina II (721–710), which comes from the year 714,[164] continues the long-established custom of the Babylonian boundary stone in a modified style (Pl. 19). The text records King Mardukapaliddina's gift to the magnate Bêl-âkhe-irba of a tract of land. In his right hand the king holds an object of unknown meaning, possibly symbolizing the gift. The recipient raises his right hand in grateful acknowledgement. Above the two figures we find (from left to right) symbols of Nabu, the mother goddess, Ea and

Vertical pleats

Marduk. Both figures wear a belted tunic that has a cluster of vertical pleats running from the belt to the feet.

This cluster of pleats, which also appears in the figures shown on other Babylonian boundary stones[165] and on a Babylonian seal,[166] is part of a Babylonian fashion in dress that spread over the entire Near East in the last quarter of the eighth century and in the seventh century.[167] We find it at Zincirli,[168] Sakçegözü[169] (Pls. 12a, 13; Figs. 98, 99), Carchemish (Fig. 93) and in Luristan. It recurs on Syrian ivory reliefs (Pl. 41; Fig. 106), and even appears on Assyrian reliefs of the time of Esarhaddon[170] and Assurbanipal.[171]

After the fall of the Neo-Assyrian empire Babylonia regained its independence to enjoy renewed prosperity in the sixth century, the time of its greatest brilliance. Nabupolassar (625–605) and especially his son Nebuchadnezzar II (604–562) built great fortresses, palaces and temples that became a byword for magnificent luxury among later generations. The city walls of Babylon ranked as one of the seven wonders of the world, and sometimes the Hanging Gardens of Semiramis in Babylon were included as well. And as F. Krischen has rightly noted,[172] the Tower of Babel would have been named as a third Babylonian wonder of the world, if this tower had still stood in its original form, or at least as a ruin, when the list was drawn up in Hellenistic times.

Hanging gardens

The 'Hanging Gardens' of Babylon were not in fact built by Semiramis but by Nebuchadnezzar. As E. Unger has suggested,[173] they may have been laid out following an earlier version by Semiramis, if there is any truth in the tradition. An inscription on a stele in Assur[174] states that Sammuramat, that is Semiramis, was the consort of Shamshı-Adad V (823–810), mother of Adadnirari III (809–782) and daughter-in-law of Shalmaneser III (854–824); and the inscription on a relief stele in Istanbul[175] indicates that Semiramis held the regency on behalf of her young son for five years. Since Shamshi-Adad V extended Assyrian rule to Babylon in 812–811 it is not impossible that Semiramis also reigned in Babylon and laid out the first hanging gardens there. A square vaulted structure measuring about 40 metres on each side, to the north-east of the southern citadel of Babylon, which lies west of the Ishtar Gate, has been regarded as the base of the Hanging Gardens.[176] It seems that the building originally consisted of a series of steps forming terraces and reaching a height of 30 metres.[177] The building type was bold and new, and the general layout, with fresh green trees standing out against a mass of imposing constructions in reddish-brown brick, must have been highly impressive.

Babylon was the largest and best fortified city of the ancient Near East. Excavations show that its walls stretched for 20 kilometres. They were built of unbaked mud brick. In projecting and exposed spots, especially those in contact with water, the walls were strengthened with baked brick masonry, using asphalt as mortar.[178] The system consisted of a main wall 6.5 metres thick and a 4 metre-thick advance wall. The general layout closely recalls the Byzantine city walls of Istanbul.[179] *City walls*

The rectangular city lay athwart the river Euphrates, which divided the area into a small western and a larger eastern part, the whole having an almost square shape.[180] In the centre of the city stood the tower of Babel, that is the Etemenanki ziggurat of Marduk with its 'high temple' and south of it the 'deep temple' of Esagila. The main avenue, the so-called processional street,[181] ran from the northern part of the eastern quarter, paralleling the course of the Euphrates, then made a right turn towards the west, and led across a bridge to the western quarter. This processional street linked the main temple of Esagila with a festival building lying outside the city.[182] Parts of the street and one of its great entrances, the Ishtar Gate, have been excavated and then partially reconstructed in the Berlin Museum on a somewhat reduced scale (Pl. 20). The side walls of the street were decorated with striding lions[183] in glazed relief bricks, and the gate had dragons in the same technique. These dragon figures[184] repeat the pictorial type of the dragon we know from the Babylonian boundary stones (Pl. 19), while the lion figures are clearly based on Assyrian models. As the two thick palmette-shaped skin folds beneath the eyes show, the lions go back to Assyrian prototypes from the time of Sargon. Similarly, the softly modelled thigh muscle in the shape of a W derives from the lion figures of Sargon.[185] *Ziggurat*

Ishtar Gate

The Palace of Nebuchadnezzar II betrays close connections with the architecture of the time of Sargon, for it straddles the city wall and consists of numerous court complexes.[186] These links are significant, since they show that the Babylonians, while influencing the Assyrians in many fields, also took important features of their art from the conqueror.

The great architecture of the late Babylonian period could not play the leading historical role it merited, for it entered too late upon the stage of world history.

Ionian architecture, which had already developed in the second quarter of the sixth century, can hardly be considered to have been influenced by Babylonian building. The Persians, who conquered Babylon at that time (538), were the only people of the Near East who had the resources to erect buildings of comparable splendour. The Persian empire took over the entire heritage of ancient Mesopotamia. Cyrus created history's first universal state. 'When I entered Babylon peacefully and took up residence in the palace of the princes amidst joyful celebration, the great lord Marduk inclined the white heart of the Babylonians towards me, because I thought to honour him daily . . . All the kings of all quarters of the world who dwell in throne-rooms, from the upper sea to the lower sea, . . . they all brought their heavy tribute and kissed my feet in Babylon . . .'

Although the intellectual leadership of the world passed from the Near East into the hands of the Greeks in the beginning of the sixth century, Babylon remained a cultural centre of the first rank even into Hellenistic times, so that Alexander planned to establish the new capital of his world empire in this ancient metropolis of the East.

III. ARAMAEAN ART

During the second half of the second millennium, bands of Semitic nomads, who are usually lumped together under the name of Aramaeans, began to stream from their original home in the Arabian desert towards Babylonia, northern Syria and the eastern Tigris district.[187] As early as the first half of the eleventh century the Aramaean Adad-apal-iddina usurped the Babylonian throne.[188] From that time onwards the peaceful Aramaean penetration of Babylonia progressed steadily. In the same way the Aramaeans settled in northern Syria and southern Anatolia, so that in the eighth and seventh centuries B.C. with few exceptions the chief cultural and economic centres were in their hands.

The political history, as well as the language and culture, of the Aramaeans have been discussed in a fundamental monograph by A. Dupont-Sommer.[189] Here I shall confine myself to interpreting[190] the art of this important people.[191]

Below it will be shown, in discussing late Hittite art, that it is primarily to the Aramaeans that architecture owes the creation and development of the *hilani* building type and the elaboration of the tectonic order of columns with bases and capitals (p. 73). At Zincirli (the ancient Sam'al) the Aramaeans also produced fine works of sculpture that may be regarded as their own creation (Pls. 12–17; Figs. 10–16).

The artistic monuments of Zincirli are provided with Aramaean inscriptions and show stylistic characteristics unparalleled in either Assyrian or Hittite art. Among the Zincirli carvings we find a turban-like cap, which recalls the Assyrian tiara in its general make-up, but which can be regarded as an original type of head-dress because of its conical form. It appears in all the Aramaean scenes at Zincirli (Pl. 12a, Fig. 10) and in some Anatolian monuments of the eighth and seventh centuries (Pl. 30).[192] Since Phoenician ivories[193] and metal bowls[194] show a very similar conical cap, it seems that the Aramaeans brought this head-dress with them from the south. *Aramaean head-dress*

A further characteristic of Aramaean art is the spiral hair curl.[195] This actually comes from Assyrian art. The Aramaean artists arranged the spiral curls of the beard in a way that anticipated the Sargonid hair style. The curl by the ear (Pl. 12; Fig. 11) also seems to have been an Aramaean invention. Moreover, the ubiquitous type of fold treatment found on Aramaean carvings seems to derive from an old Aramaean tradition (Pls. 28, 35). Of course, it may be that here the Aramaeans were considerably stimulated by the Hittites and the Babylonians. It is important to note, however, that the particular type of fold treatment, which will be discussed further below, is only found on Aramaean monuments or late Hittite works influenced by them. *Spiral curls, curl by the ear*

One of the most important characteristics of the Aramaeans is, I believe, their generally secular outlook, and this is clearly evident in their art. *Secular outlook*

Funerary stelae   The erection of stelae with funerary scenes of feasting is also a specifically Aramaean practice.

Study of the carvings at Zincirli (Sam'al) reveals that at this site a well-developed Aramaean court art[196] existed alongside the traditional folk art of the small states, at least from the middle of the ninth century onwards. We know that at Zincirli two different ethnic groups lived side by side with one another. For Kilamuwa prided himself on having 'brought to an end feuding between the Mushkabim and Ba'ririm'.[197] In our opinion these two groups can be clearly identified by their works of art.

The Aramaeans were the ruling class; their court art is elegant and graceful (Pls. 12–17). The indigenous Luvians, whose culture had been shaped by the Hittite tradition, were their subjects, but they continued to prefer their own ruggedly old-fashioned art (Figs. 61–66). In order to show the people that indigenous customs were respected, the Semitic princes had the entrances and the orthostats of citadel gates decorated with carvings in the Hittite manner. But in palaces this antiquated art found no place, and monuments in the Aramaean style were preferred (Pl. 12; Fig. 11). The peaceful coexistence of the Mushkabim and Ba'ririm seems to have lasted for a long time, for only in the second half of the eighth century were the Hittite lion figures pulled down (Figs. 71, 72), to be replaced by new lion monuments in the Assyrian manner (Figs. 12, 13). The Aramaeans no longer needed to pay lip service to the Luvian-Hittite tradition. This shows that they had become undisputed lords of the country.[198]

Kilamuwa relief   The oldest Aramaean art work is a ceremonial relief of a king, from Zincirli (Fig. 10).[199] The large tuft of hair gathered at the nape of the neck places the relief in the ninth century, as can be seen from comparison with Assyrian prototypes

(Pls. 1, 8). The head-dress and the spiral curls are Aramaean characteristics. The larger figure in front must represent King Kilamuwa, whose name is indicated on the other pictorial slab.[200] The second figure behind him is dressed in the same way; he holds in his left hand a pouch the size of a fist, and in his right, like Kilamuwa, a chalice-like blossom, evidently an emblem of royal dignity. The second figure is probably the king's son. Both men have faces with hooked noses of Semitic type. The shaven upper lip of the bearded king may derive from Hittite models (p. 96), which the Aramaeans were at first probably glad to imitate.

A colossal statue from Zincirli, now in Berlin,[201] with an Aramaean inscription on the front of the robe of 'King Panamuwa, the son of Karal', represents the god Hadad. The statue, which may be dated by the inscription to about 790, has a stylized beard with Aramaean spiral curls.

An outstanding relief from Zincirli shows the Aramaean King Barrakab with his secretary (Pl. 12a).[202] The short Aramaean inscription on either side of a moon symbol mentions the donor and his god: 'I, Barrakab, the son of Panammu/my God Baal/Harran.' Both figures have the hooked nose of Semitic type. The king wears an Aramaean tiara and has hair and a beard, stylized with Aramaean spiral curls. The elegant curl by the ear is also Aramaean. The shoulder folds of the mantle, an invention of Aramaean artists, appear here for the first time. The king is seated upon an ornate throne. He raises his right hand to emphasize the words addressed to the secretary. In his left hand he holds a palmette-like flower, possibly a sign of royal majesty. The modestly dressed secretary holds under his left arm a hinged book, probably made up of papyrus leaves, and in his left hand a writing case with a place for ink and a brush. With his clenched right hand he salutes the king.[203]

Barrakab relief

Another Aramaean work from Zincirli is the funerary stele of a princess with her lady-in-waiting.[204] The bottom of the slab tapers to a point so that it could be fixed to a pedestal (Pl. 13). The custom of setting a funerary stele over the tomb was unknown in Mesopotamia and is specifically Aramaean.[205] The grave reliefs of the Neo-Hittite principalities that have been found so far are all wholly Aramaean, Aramaeanizing (Pls. 13, 26–30; Figs. 100, 101), or at least influenced by Aramaean carvings. At the top of the funerary stele under discussion we see a winged sun disk decorated with palmettes, the emblem of royal power. This winged sun device derives from Egyptian rather than Hittite sources. The princess sits upon a simple throne with a plaited cushion before a table with a

Aramaean tiara funerary meal. She wears an Aramaean tiara. The brim of this conical cap is decorated with six-leaved rosettes, continuing at the back on to a trailing ribbon. Her skirt has parallel folds recalling the shoulder folds on the mantle of King Barrakab (Pl. 12a). Among her jewels one must note a Phrygian fibula on her breast, a popular fashion accessory in the last third of the eighth century and around 700 B.C. The flower in her left hand must be a princely emblem. The abundant offerings on the table include a bowl with flat loaves and meat patties, which remain favourite dishes in the south-eastern Anatolian provinces even today. Nearby are a smaller bowl with roast fowl and two vessels which probably contained salt and spices. The handmaiden holds a knife in her left hand and in her right a fly-whisk, a princely attribute. The figures belong to the same human type found on the other Aramaean reliefs. The stylistic link of the figures with the relief of King Barrakab dates the funerary stele to the beginning of the last quarter of the eighth century. The Phrygian fibula on the princess's breast confirms this date.

The reliefs from Zincirli we have been discussing, together with other carvings from the same site as well as all the sculptures of Sakçegözü[206] (Pls. 14–16; Figs. 11, 14–16) and finally the statue of a king from Malatya,[207] are all creations of a single sculptural school. We must regard the style of the carvings as Aramaean, since Hittite features, apart from a few details of the animal figures (p. 60), have almost entirely disappeared.

Three characteristic features of this Aramaean style—the cap-like head-dress, the spiral curl and the curl by the ear—have been discussed above. Moreover, the

Hair style hair at the nape of the neck of the Zincirli princess (Pl. 13) seems to be specifically Aramaean, and it recurs even more strikingly in the portal sphinx of Zincirli (Fig. 11), in the sphinxes and genii (Pl. 15a), and in the lion-slayer of the lion-hunting relief (Pl. 22b), all from Sakçegözü. In this hair style several spiral curls fall down to the shoulder in a thick mass. In Assyrian reliefs this coiffure is often used to characterize foreign peoples. Assyrian artists used to render the Babylonians of the seventh century with a similar hair style. Since a strong influx of Aramaean elements makes itself felt from the late second millennium onwards, it follows

PLATE 14 – Royal figure. Orthostat relief from Sakçegözü. Andesite. Aramaean style. About 730 B.C. *Archaeological Museum, Ankara. Height 86.3 cm. Cf. above.*

15

that this hair style must be linked to the Aramaean immigrant population. The sirens of the tridacna shells have similar hair curls falling to the shoulder (Pl. 36c), and these were apparently usual among Semitic peoples. The Syrian reliefs also show a very similar hair style at the nape of the neck (Pl. 43; Fig. 111). It is interesting that a limestone statuette from Amman in Jordan[208] shows the same kind of hair style. Thus the Aramaeans seem to have brought it from their original homeland.

The statuette from Amman, which stands 45 centimetres high, wears a mantle of the type already seen in the Aramaean reliefs of Zincirli[209] (Pl. 12a) and Sakçegözü (Pl. 14). The mantle is arranged in diagonal folds, with one of the ends held in one hand at chest height. This form of mantle recurs in the Malatya royal statue.[210] It is quite possible that Malatya also had come into the hands of the Aramaeans at the end of the eighth century, for the royal statue is a true repetition of the royal relief from Sakçegözü (Pl. 14). We note that apart from the dress the two figures have the same hair and beard style and that in their right hands they bear the same royal symbol. The more ordinary Amman statuette is a somewhat less successful example of the fashion. But there is no doubt that it too follows the same mantle type. It may be that the Aramaeans brought this mantle with them from their homeland, subsequently modifying and refining it. The Aramaean mantle with its thick shoulder folds (Pls. 12a, 14) recurs on the human-headed attachments of an Urartian cauldron found at Vetulonia in Etruria (Fig. 126).[211]

The rendering of the folds themselves is a long-established custom in the Near East, but the mantle falling over the shoulders is a new fashion created by the Aramaeans. Although it derives from Babylonian models (Pl. 19), the long tunic, emphasized at the back with a cluster of vertical pleats, became the normal fashion in the Aramaean world during the second half of the eighth century. It appears in most of the male figures of Zincirli and Sakçegözü (Pls. 12a, 14; Figs. 98, 99). The same garment with vertical pleats behind is, however, also found in contemporary Syrian ivories (Pl. 41; Fig. 106) and on the Araras relief (Fig. 93).

Fold rendering

The costume of the two genii of Sakçegözü fertilizing a palmette-tree (Pl. 15a) follows Assyrian models of the transitional and Sargonid styles (Pl. 3). The figure wears a mantle, which leaves the advanced foot free, with a fringe that forms a buoyant curve over the thigh and then falls straight down to the ankles. The lion-slayer of the lion-hunting relief from Sakçegözü represents a distorted version of the same costume (Pl. 23b). The handsome sandals of the male figures of Zincirli and Sakçegözü (Pl. 14; Figs. 98, 99) also have a special form and decoration, evidently Aramaean inventions. Almost identical sandals appear in the Carchemish Araras relief (Fig. 93).

PLATE 15a – Genii. Orthostat relief from Sakçegözü. Andesite. Aramaean style. About 730 B.C. *Archaeological Museum, Ankara. Height 86.3 cm. Cf. p. 56.*
PLATE 15b – Male sphinx. Orthostat relief from Sakçegözü. Andesite. Aramaean style. About 730 B.C. *Archaeological Museum, Ankara. Height 86.3 cm. Cf. p. 56.*

FIG. 12 – *Portal lion from Hilani III at Zincirli. After AiS, Pl. 57, below. Aramaeanizing Hittite style. About 730 B.C. Archaeological Museum, Istanbul. Cf. pp. 53 and below.*

Modification of Hittite animal figures

Building on the Hittite tradition, the Aramaean artists of Zincirli and Sakçegözü created entirely new types of animal figures. A number of animal carvings from Zincirli belong to this category: the portal lion from Hilani III (Fig. 12), the portal lion from the southern hall P, two portal lions from the inner citadel gate (Fig. 13), the two sphinxes on columns, the portal sphinx from Hilani II (Fig. 11), and finally the animal figures from Sakçegözü (Pl. 16; Figs. 14, 15).

The animal figures mentioned from these two sites have the following common style elements: the ∩-shaped reserve area on the shoulder, which often has an x-sign; the stylization of the front legs, which consists of one (Figs. 12, 13) or two (Pls. 15b, 16; Figs. 14, 15) wedge shapes; the W- or N-shaped stylization of the thighs (Figs. 11–15); and the ∴-shaped stylization of the ankle (Figs. 11, 12, 15). These details—especially the double-wedge schematization of the front legs and ∴-shaped stylization of the ankle—are so unusual and original that they must be hallmarks of a single workshop. Thus the same artists worked contemporaneously for Zincirli and Sakçegözü.

The lion of the lion-hunting relief from Sakçegözü has the same thigh and leg stylization and seems to show the same ankle schematization as well (Pl. 23b). The W- or N-shaped stylization of the thighs in Aramaean art, which develops as a modification of the W-shaped Assyrian scheme (Pl. 16; Figs. 15, 5j–k), was later borrowed by other northern Syrian workshops and by Urartian ones (Fig. 5l–p). Two bronze works of northern Syrian origin found in Etruria, the bowl from Capena[212] and the cauldron base from the Barberini Tomb in Praeneste (Fig. 5m),[213] show animal bodies with W- or N-shaped thighs. L. Brown thought that the thighs of the lion figures on these works show a flame-like stylization,[214] but it is clear that it is really an N-shaped scheme, as comparison of these two examples with the thigh stylization of a lion from Zincirli shows (Fig. 12). Moreover, we have been able to link the sphinx figures of the cauldron base from the Barberini Tomb to Neo-Hittite and Aramaean works on account of other stylistic features.[215]

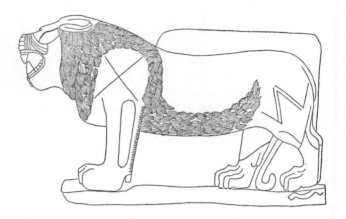

FIG. 13 – *Portal lion from the inner citadel gate at Zincirli. After AiS, p. 342, Fig. 253, Pl. 47, below. Aramaeanizing Hittite style. Reign of Sargon (721–705 B.C.). Archaeological Museum, Istanbul. Cf. pp. 53, 62.*

Among Aramaean sculptures the lion heads (Figs. 14, 15) show predominantly Assyrian traits. The three-flap ear, the rich furrowing of the nose and the two palmette-shaped stylizations beneath the eyes point to particular Assyrian models. Yet despite the added Assyrian style elements these Aramaean lions have kept their overall Hittite character. Like the body, the head has not entirely lost its cubic form. The cheek bones are clearly formed, as was usual among Hittite lion figures (Pl. 21). For this reason the two palmette-like stylizations on the face did not point upwards, as was the case with the Assyrian lion figures (Pl. 8a), but downwards. The excessively large and thick canine teeth are a further trait of middle Neo-Hittite lion figures, which lingers in the lions of Zincirli and Sakçegözü. Aramaean artists created a type of griffin head that was eagerly imitated by later artists (Pl. 15a, Fig. 16). This represents an Aramaean transformation of the

Aramaean-Hittite lion figures

Aramaean-Hittite griffin

FIGS. 14, 15 – *Portal lion from Sakçegözü. Cf. Plate 16 and p. 60.*

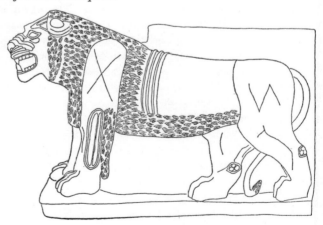

Hittite figure type (Fig. 79), in which traits of the eagle are combined with those of the lion and the horse. The chin area of the bird-men from Sakçegözü is no longer consistently shaped as part of the beak, as in Hittite and Assyrian examples, but clearly takes the form of a lion muzzle (Fig. 16). The wide-open beak with the outstretched tongue and the mane suffice to show that the Aramaean artists of Sakçegözü combined the eagle head with that of the lion to make a single unit. An important modification is the change of the spiral curl at the crown of the head into a knobby thickening (Fig. 16). It is significant that at Sakçegözü the other bird head still shows the spiral ending at the top of the head. This change of the spiral ending into a conical thickening was probably first carried out in figures in the round made by goldsmiths, and reliefs of Sakçegözü seem to have originated as imitations of such metal prototypes.

In summary, the griffin-head type created by Aramaean artists has the following characteristics: horse's ear, horse's mane, wide-open beak, lolling tongue, chin area in the form of a lion's muzzle, mane roll and lock, which at the top and bottom forms a spiral or else a knobby finial at the top. This type of griffin head, which we first defined fifteen years ago,[216] is an Aramaean invention. At Zincirli and Sakçegözü it was given not only to bird-men but also to griffin figures with leonine bodies, as at Carchemish.[217] The griffin relief from an orthostat in Ankara (Fig. 17) is the only example[218] in which the head of a griffin-man of the Sakçegözü type (Pl. 15a) is combined with a leonine body. The head of the Ankara griffin is very much damaged at the top, so that one can no longer determine whether the big lock ended above in a spiral or in a round thickening. Otherwise this head has all the features found in the griffin-man of Sakçegözü.

Flowering of Aramaean art — By association with the relief of King Barrakab (Pl. 12a),[219] which is datable by its inscription, the Zincirli animal figures may be placed about 730. Since the Sakçegözü animal figures come from the same workshop (p. 61), they must belong to the same period. The activity of this remarkable school of sculptors must be placed mainly in the last third of the eighth century. The previously mentioned portal lions from the inner citadel gate of Zincirli (Fig. 13) appear to have been created in the time of Sargon (Fig. 9) on account of the three palmette-shaped stylizations beneath the cheek bones. Although they are the latest examples of such lion figures, they still have the lolling tongues of Hittite lions. It may be that the sculptor intentionally retained this old-fashioned trait, so that his figures, which were erected near lions in the middle Neo-Hittite style (Figs. 71, 72), should not appear too startling. In any case, as the remains of lion claws on the right side of the lower border show, he created his figures by reworking lions of the middle Neo-Hittite style.

Chariot relief from Sakçegözü — The old-fashioned-looking relief of the lion hunt with a chariot in Sakçegözü (Pl. 23b) originated in the last third of the eighth century, like the other carvings from this site. Because of the dress of the lion-slayer and the shoulder and leg

PLATES 16a, b – Portal lion from Sakçegözü. Basalt. Aramaean style with Assyrian-Hittite elements. About 730 B.C. *Archaeological Museum, Ankara. Height 84 cm. Cf. Figs. 14, 15 and p. 60.*

16a

16b

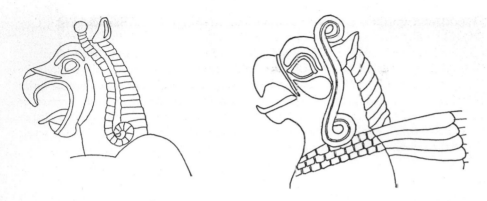

FIGS. 16, 17 – Left, Fig. 16: Griffin head from an orthostat relief from Sakçegözü. Cf. Plate 15a and pp. 61, 185. – Right, Fig. 17: Griffin head from an orthostat relief from Ankara. Basalt. Aramaeanizing Hittite style. About 700 B.C. Archaeological Museum, Ankara. Cf. note 218 and p. 62.

stylizations of the lion—characteristic features which have already been mentioned—it may be linked to the other Sakçegözü orthostats.

As my examination of the original suggests, despite its entirely Hittite face, the lion has a lightly indicated palmette form beneath the cheek bone. The open mouth also lacks the characteristically Hittite feature of the outstretched tongue. Following Hittite practice the nose is furrowed only at the tip. The winged sun disk is more in the Hittite vein than that found in the carving of the genii with the palmette-tree (Pl. 15a). The stylization of the wings is almost the same on both slabs. The richly decorated band connecting the chariot box with the shaft-end appears in Assyrian art no later than the time of Tiglath-Pileser (745–727). Thus there is no objection to a dating about 730. The lion head at the rear of the chariot box, which must be regarded as the decoration of a shield placed there, certainly belongs to the Classical style, though it may be claimed here as a conscious archaism. As O. Nuoffer recognized many years ago,[220] the curving rail of the chariot box is a sign of technical advance. The richly decorated horse blanket also appears on chariots depicted on Syrian ivories,[221] which probably originated in the last third of the eighth century. These works in ivory also have the same small, low box and the same bar behind as in the Sakçegözü relief.

Zincirli, Sakçegözü, Maraş, Karatepe and several other sites have yielded a large number of carvings with strong Aramaeanizing traits. But since in many im-

Other Aramaean-Hittite carvings

PLATE 17 – Lion protome from Olympia. Ornament for the rim of a cauldron. Late Neo-Hittite style with Assyrian-Aramaean and Neo-Hittite elements. Late 8th century B.C. *Olympia Museum. Height about 25 cm. Cf. p. 181.*

portant ways these sculptures rest on indigenous Hittite-Luvian traditions, they will be discussed in the section on the Neo-Hittite style.

Role of Aramaeans in architecture

One last word must be said on the activity of the Aramaeans in the architectural field. In the section on Neo-Hittite architecture (p. 69) it will be shown that the development of the *hilani* building type and the elaboration of the columnar order with capitals and base actually took place in such Aramaean arts centres as Zincirli, Sakçegözü and Tell Halaf. The new approach to building found in Hittite culture, which was on the point of dying out, may only be explained as the result of the life-giving new spirit brought by the immigrant Semitic Aramaeans.

IV. NEO-HITTITE ART

In the first half of the first millennium B.C. the small Neo-Hittite states of southern Anatolia and northern Syria produced outstanding works of architecture and sculpture that strongly influenced other cultures—first the Near Eastern lands and later Greece and Etruria.

Neo-Hittite culture depends on antecedents of the Syro-Hittite-Luvian civilization of the second millennium B.C., which incorporated important Hurrian and Minoan-Mycenaean elements. In the course of the first quarter of the first millennium Assyrian, Phoenician and Aramaean contributions were added, producing, in the ninth and eighth centuries, a great efflorescence of culture in the Hittite centres, from which impressive art works survive. Especially important was the Aramaean part in the formation of the new culture in southern Anatolia and northern Syria, for the Aramaeans began to invade the area at the beginning of the first millennium. *Antecedents of Syro-Hittite-Luvian complex*

The first of their conquests, according to Landsberger,[222] was the seizure of the kingdom of Til Barsib by the tribal chieftain Adin about 950. He was followed by Gabar Sam'al at Zincirli about 920. The Aramaean takeover of the area continued by stages into the seventh century. Art monuments show that Tell Halaf became Aramaean during the eighth century and Karatepe towards the end of this century. By 700 the Aramaeans had infiltrated the area of Maraş and Gaziantep and possibly had reached far as Ivriz, south of Konya. Similarly, Malatya may also have become Aramaean in the second half of the eighth century. Only Hattena and Carchemish stayed Luvian-Hittite until the Assyrian conquest.[223] *Spread of Aramaeans*

The term 'Neo-Hittite art' is best suited to the architecture and figural art of this hybrid culture. In earlier publications I have given a detailed analysis of Mitannian and Syro-Hittite elements together with Assyrian and Aramaean ones in Neo-Hittite figural art, but I have also insisted that the art as a whole is a continuation of the Anatolian Hittite tradition,[224] since the basic features of these monuments bear an authentic Hittite stamp. *'Neo-Hittite art'*

In architecture also, while the Mycenaean-tinged northern Syrian traits of the second millennium come into prominence, such Anatolian Hittite features as gates, orthostats with reliefs, animals flanking the entrance, and animal protomae addossed to piers persist.

Since southern Anatolian and northern Syrian states are also linked to the Hattusa by religious rites and symbols, and by the name of their kings (for example, Lubarna-Labarna, Qatazilu-Hattusili, Muttali-Muwatalli), we must admit that the term 'Neo-Hittite' is justified.[225] Paolo Matthiae has contributed an outstanding study that deals exhaustively with the monuments of Syrian art during the second millennium.[226] In iconography and style the objects assembled in his book are not nearly so close to Neo-Hittite sculpture as the Anatolian and Hittite works of the imperial period were.

PLATE 18 – Griffin protome from Praeneste, Etruria. Bronze. Late Neo-Hittite style with Hittite-Aramaean and Assyrian elements. Late 8th century B.C. *Villa Giulia, Rome. Overall height 27 cm. Cf. p. 185.*

The hieroglyphic script is another important cultural element that links the 'Neo-Hittites' to the Hittites of the imperial period. As B. Landsberger has recently shown,[227] the hieroglyphic script was created in the Luvian-speaking area for that language. But this script seems to have reached its full development only during the period of the Hittite empire and in the Hittite capital. During the fourteenth and thirteenth centuries it was in use also in Kizwatna (that is, in the land of the Luvians) as the official script of the Hittite empire. The use of the hieroglyphic script on public monuments of the Neo-Hittites is therefore a tradition that derives from the Hittite empire.

The most important achievements of the Neo-Hittite cultural centres lie in the field of architecture. The building type known as the *bit hilani* or *hilani*, of which the earliest known instance is King Niqmepa's Palace of the fifteenth-fourteenth century B.C. at Tell Atchana on Syrian soil (Fig. 18), became a standard architectural form in the Neo-Hittite cities of the ninth and eighth centuries. It must be regarded as one of the most remarkable architectural inventions of the ancient Near East. As R. Naumann has justly said,[228] we are dealing with a building that has a vestibule with one to three supports on the front side, behind which lies a large main room with a hearth. Around the main room are grouped smaller rooms.[229] A staircase leading to un upper storey often appears on one side of the vestibule. The door splayings generally feature animal sculptures and the lower parts of the façades have orthostats bearing reliefs.

The earliest example (Fig. 18), Niqmepa's Palace at Tell Atchana, has all the features of the later *hilani* buildings of northern Syria.[230] It is possible, however, as H. Frankfort has suggested,[231] that the eighteenth-century Yarimlim Palace at Tell Atchana represents a first step towards this form. The reception hall of this palace (5, 5a) is divided into two rooms by two short spur walls with four wooden supports between them.[232] Behind the reception hall is a large room with a centre support (2) and two small side chambers. This spatial grouping around a hall, where the main part is reached by an entrance with four supports, recalls the similar arrangement of the official rooms of the Niqmepa Palace (Fig. 18).

R. Naumann has pointed out a number of building elements in Yarimlim Palace that derive from Minoan Crete.[233] Among these are the large windows of the first storey, divided into three lights by two wooden columns on basalt bases, which recall representations on Cretan faience plaques, frescoes in Cretan style showing a bull procession, and the partition of the reception hall, which gives it the appearance of a Cretan state room.

The use of columns in the reception hall of Yarimlim's Palace and in the vestibule of Niqmepa's Palace (Fig. 18) is undoubtedly a case of Minoan-Mycenaean influence, for columned halls are unknown in Mesopotamia. The isolation of the palaces as free-standing buildings is entirely alien to the Near Eastern tradition. Comparable arrangements of rooms are found only in Hattusa, Troy and in the Mycenaean cities.[234]

During the period from the fifteenth to the thirteenth century all fields of artistic activity in Syria experienced strong Minoan-Mycenaean influence. In this con-

Hieroglyphic script

ARCHITECTURE
Bit Hilani

Niqmepa's palace

PLATE 19 – Neo-Babylonian boundary stone from the time of Mardukapaliddina II
(721–710 B.C.). Black marble. *Staatliche Museen, Berlin. Height 46 cm. Cf. pp. 50, 51.*

nection one may point to the chamber tombs of the Isopata type in Ras Shamra (Ugarit) and to the Mycenaean elements in the Mitannian seals of Syria. C. Schaeffer[235] has convincingly shown that a Syro-Mycenaean style flourished in the fifteenth century and that a Mycenaean colony developed there in the thirteenth century. It is therefore possible that the device of supports in the two palaces at Tell Atchana was borrowed from Minoan-Mycenaean buildings.

Building J[236] at Zincirli is the oldest *hilani* of the Neo-Hittite period (Fig. 19). It is dated about 830 by an inscription of Kilamuwa found on the site. The palace (Fig. 20) divides into an official section (J 1–3) and a residential section (J 4–14). The official part includes two big rooms about 25 metres by 6 and 8 metres respectively. In the 8-metre-wide entrance opening we must restore one or two supports, although no trace of them has been found. A hearth was installed in the main room. *Minoan-Mycenaean features*

Later, Building J was enlarged by adding a public reception house, Building K, consisting of official rooms (Fig. 20).[237] At the top of a flight of eight steps stood a vestibule with three columns on decorated basalt bases (Fig. 33). Behind the vestibule was the reception hall with a fixed hearth.[238] On the short side of the reception hall before the hearth was a limestone base, near which many fragments of ivory figures were found, which evidently came from furniture placed in this room. *Building J*

The decorated bases suggest that Building K was erected in about the last third of the eighth century (p. 83). The building inscription of Barrakab[239] found *Building K*

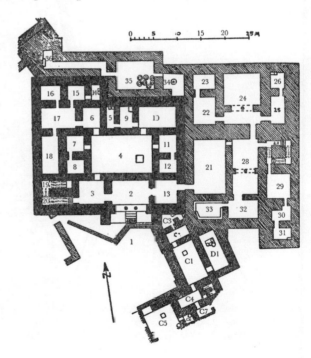

FIG. 18 – *Niqmepa's Palace at Tell At-chana. The earliest hilani building. 15th–14th century B.C. Cf. note 230 and p. 69.*

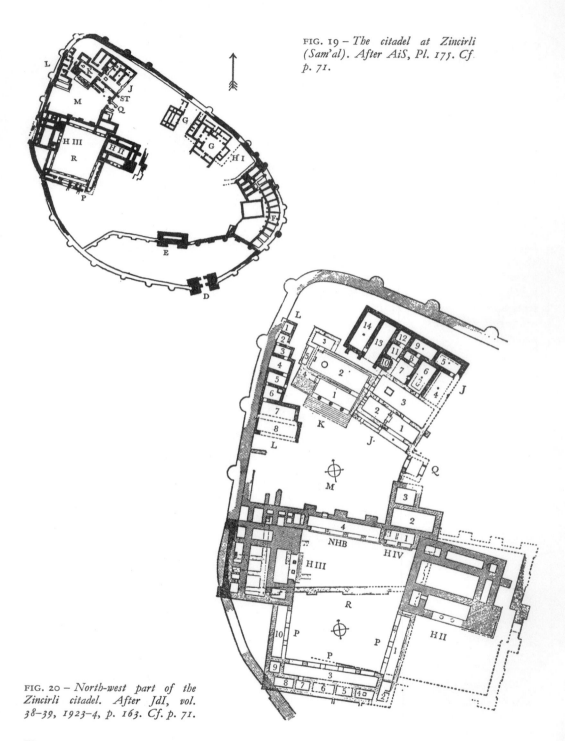

FIG. 19 – *The citadel at Zincirli (Sam'al). After AiS, Pl. 175. Cf. p. 71.*

FIG. 20 – *North-west part of the Zincirli citadel. After JdI, vol. 38–39, 1923–4, p. 163. Cf. p. 71.*

in the débris south of the Barrakab façade may originally have been on the west side of the entrance of the vestibule, as F. von Luschan has maintained.[240] This assumption, which is of course unproved, accords with our dating. B. Landsberger[241] interprets the inscription as follows: 'I, Barrakab, son of Panammu, King of Sam'al, servant of Tiglath-Pileser, lord of the [four] parts of the earth, because of the good conduct of my father and my own good conduct, was placed on the throne of my father by my lord Rakkab-El and my lord Tiglath-Pileser; and my father's house was more miserable than any; and I hunted beside my lord, the king of Assyria, in the company of great kings, lords of silver and lords of gold; and I succeeded to my father's house and made it finer than the house of [any of] the great kings; and my brothers the kings envied every fine thing of my house; and my fathers, the kings of Sam'al, had no fine house. They had the house of Kilamuwa, but this was [both] winter and summer house for them; and I built this house.'

As Wachtsmuth has suggested,[242] the 'house' mentioned in the inscription is probably Building J.

Four other *hilani* buildings have been excavated in Zincirli that are closely linked in date. The oldest of them is Hilani IV, which is not a self-contained building,[243] but part of a hall, which opens on its long side towards the south on to Court R (Fig. 20). The building divides into two parts: a longer western hall (4) with adjoining rooms to the west, and a short eastern hall (1), behind which lie a main room and a subordinate one (2, 3). Rooms 1–3 form a unit that reproduces the *hilani* scheme. The reduced vestibule of Hilani IV had only one column, resting upon a sphinx that has come down to us in a much-damaged state.[244] The fine orthostat relief of King Barrakab[245] with his secretary (Fig. 12a) stood on the west side of the eastern projecting wall of this vestibule.

Hilani buildings

Orthostat reliefs with musicians and other renderings decorated the east, south and west sides of the massive pier[246] that formed the end of the wall between the two parts of the open hall. The eastern part of the long hall thus formed a noteworthy ceremonial façade leading to the reception hall of King Barrakab. The longer section to the west functioned somewhat like a Greek stoa. In fact this long portico hall heralds the early halls of Samos from the age of the Orientalizing style. It seems likely that the Greek stoa derives directly from such prototypes as the Zincirli building. Hilani IV and its western columned extension were built about 730, as is shown by the inscribed orthostat relief with the enthroned Barrakab (Pl. 12a).[247]

Not long after the erection of the northern hall with Hilani IV there followed Hilani III (Figs. 20, 21) and Hilani II (Fig. 20).[248] The orthostat reliefs[249] of Hilani III (Fig. 12) come from the same workshop that created the Barrakab carvings (p. 56). The orthostat relief with a sphinx,[250] which belongs to Hilani II (Fig. 11), also comes from this workshop (p. 56). These links suggest that Hilanis III and II belong to the last quarter of the eighth century. Somewhat later, although evidently still from the same building project, are the three large halls of the southern Building P, which encloses Court R on three sides (Fig. 20).[251] A portal

Hilanis II and III

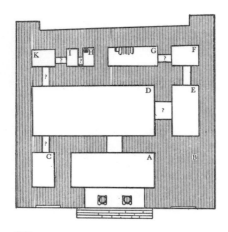

FIG. 21

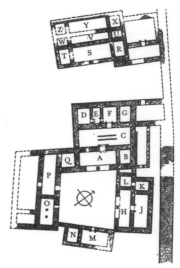

FIG. 22

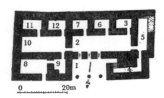

FIG. 23

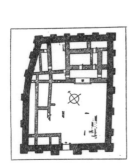

FIG. 24

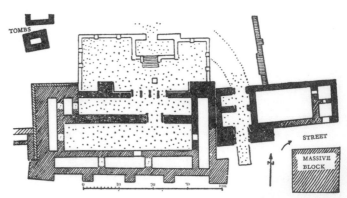

FIG. 25

FIGS. 21–25 – *Fig. 21: Hilani III at Zincirli. 725–700 B.C. Cf. note 248 and p. 73. – Fig. 22: Upper Palace at Zincirli. About 660 B.C. Cf. note 225 and p. 75. – Fig. 23: Hilani at Tell Tainat. About 730 B.C. Cf. note 256 and p. 75. – Fig. 24: Hilani at Sakçegözü. About 730 B.C. Cf. note 257 and p. 75. – Fig. 25: Hilani at Tell Halaf. 730–700 B.C. Cf. note 258 and pp. 75, 77.*

lion, which probably comes from this latter building, shows the same formal type as the lion figures of Hilanis III and II.

Hilani I

The largest building of the town is Hilani I, which measures 52 by 34 metres (Figs. 19, 20).[252] Unfortunately we have no satisfactory point of reference whereby to date it. But R. Naumann[253] has plausibly suggested that it may be the latest of the *hilani* buildings, belonging to the early seventh century. Since Zincirli was not occupied by the Assyrians until Esarhaddon's conquest about 670,[254] the building activity of the Aramaean princes may have reached its height in the first quarter of the seventh century. In the Upper Palace of Zincirli,[255] which the Assyrians under Esarhaddon erected on the ruins of Hilani I (Fig. 22), we find

Upper Palace

two *hilani* structures (A–G and H–L). As is customary in Assyrian architecture, however, they are only parts of a larger palace complex. The overall effect is different, for in the new *hilanis* the staircases flanking the vestibule have been given up, showing that there was no second storey. However, the latest building (R–Z) of Zincirli (Fig. 22) shows that the building norm established in Syria from the second millennium onwards, which provided for palaces as free-standing units (p. 71), still persisted tenaciously in the Assyrian period.

The real flowering of the *hilani* type falls in the second half of the eighth century. The *hilanis* of Tell Tainat (Fig. 23),[256] Sakçegözü (Fig. 24)[257] and Tell Halaf (Fig. 25)[258] belong to this period. The vestibule of the Tell Tainat *hilani* (Fig. 23) has three columns at the front, as does the vestibule of Building K at Zincirli (Fig. 20). The bases of the two buildings come from the same workshop (Figs. 33, 34) and are virtually interchangeable (p. 83). R. Naumann[259] has drawn attention to the close parallels in the plans of the two buildings. The walls seem to have been executed in the same technique,[260] and the two palaces were probably designed by a single master. The period of the erection of the Tell Tainat palace can be determined by the lion base (Fig. 26)[261] of the megaron which is situated close to it. The excavators believe that the megaron structure existed before the rest of the palace was built. But both were in use at the same time. The paired lions of the base in question show two small palmette stylizations of the skin folds beneath the eyes, a characteristic of the reign of Tiglath-Pileser III (745–727; Fig. 6). Allowing for an interval of a decade between its erection and that of the megaron, it would date (at the earliest) from about 730.

Flowering of hilani tradition

The Sakçegözü *hilani* (Fig. 24) also shows close links with the Zincirli monuments. The arrangement of the vestibule of the Sakçegözü *hilani* with only one column on a sphinx base[262] appears earlier in Hilani IV at Zincirli (Fig. 20). Also noteworthy is the close similarity between the orthostat reliefs of Sakçegözü (Pls. 14–16)[263] and the figures of the ceremonial façade of Hilani IV at Zincirli (Pl. 12a). Moreover, the sphinxes[264] of the two buildings seem to come from the same workshop. Consequently the palace of Sakçegözü should be dated about 730, along with Hilani IV.

Sakçegözü hilani

The Tell Halaf *hilani* (730–700 B.C.), which is generally dated in the second half of the ninth century,[265] should rather be attributed to the last third of the eighth century, the height of fashion for the *hilani* form. This temple-palace (Fig. 25)

Tell Halaf hilani

PLATE 20 – Ishtar Gate from Babylon with coloured enamel tiles. Latter part of reign of Nebuchadnezzar II (604–562 B.C.). *Staatliche Museen, Berlin. Height 14.30 m. Cf. p. 51.*

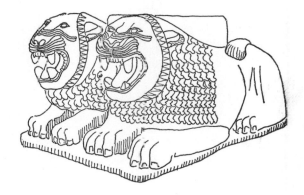

FIG. 26 – *Column-base lions from Tell Tainat. Second half of the 8th century B.C. Cf. note 261 and p. 75.*

has the same simple plan—by this time normal—that appeared in the examples at Zincirli of the last third of the eighth century. Hilanis II and III at Zincirli have the same spatial disposition (Fig. 20). The Tell Halaf *hilani* consists of a vestibule, a central hall and several ancillary rooms laid out in a row behind. Building K (Fig. 20) has a comparable scheme. Only the ancillary rooms could not be introduced in this last building because no space was available. The temple-palace of Tell Halaf also shares the three-support scheme in the vestibule with Building K at Zincirli and the *hilani* at Tell Tainat (Fig. 23). The stairway of the terrace (Fig. 25) also bears a great resemblance to the flight of steps of Building K at Zincirli.

Especially noteworthy is the fact that the temple-palace of Tell Halaf has no dwelling quarters such as are found in the older *hilani* type (cf. Building J, Fig. 20), but served only as an audience building. Thus it belongs to the developed and perfected *hilani* type. These comparisons should suffice to show that, like Hilanis I–IV of Zincirli and the Tell Tainat *hilani*, the imposing temple-palace of Tell Halaf belongs to the last third of the eighth century. It was erected during the height of Aramaean-Hittite civilization—the second half of the eighth century. Aramaean-Hittite sculpture is also a creation of the second half of the eighth century (p. 55). It does not seem likely at all that the earliest *hilani* type should have been invented in the relatively provincial area of southern Anatolia and northern Syria. Other reasons, to be discussed later (p. 111), also indicate that the temple-palace of Tell Halaf is a creation of the late eighth century. The Tell Halaf structure is a mature building in a style that has reached its classic stage of development. Great times create great buildings. The Tell Halaf architect, who was certainly one of the most successful designers of this period, is even known by name: Abdi-ilimu.[266] This sensitive architect must have created other buildings in the Near East, some of them possibly still awaiting the excavator's spade.

Architect Abdi-ilimu

We have seen that another master was active at the same period at Zincirli and Tell Tainat. But Abdi-ilimu was the leading personality. Not only did he create in the temple-palace of Tell Halaf an imposing and formally perfected *hilani*, but with his monumental figures of gods on animal bases he invented a new form

of support (pp. 87, 119) that ranks as an outstanding artistic achievement. The vestibule has an entrance 10 metres wide and 6 metres high with the splayings flanked by two winged sphinxes. The entrance lintel is supported by three powerful gods (Pl. 23a) standing on animal colossi.[267] On the right the 'Great Mother' rose over a lioness, in the middle the storm god stood on a bull and on the left the divine son appeared on a lion. Thus we have a triad[268] in the Hurrian-Hittite sense, such as was found at Yazilikaya in the thirteenth century (Fig. 27). At the entrance to the temple-palace the visitor encountered five animals and three · deities in frontal position. All the figures had inlaid eyes in coloured stone that produced a menacing effect. They served to make the visitor aware of the power of the gods and of the prince as well. Taken as a whole, this was an artistic achievement of unique effectiveness and impressive beauty (Pl. 23a).

Spread of hilani In the second half of the eighth century the *hilani* spread outside the southern Anatolian—northern Syrian area. Tiglath-Pileser III (745–727), who was the first Assyrian king to build a *hilani*, announced: 'In the centre of Kalkhu I built for my amusement a palace in cedar wood and a *bit hilani* after the manner of a palace in the land of the Hittites.'[269] Above we have cited the inscription of Sargon II, where he speaks of a building in the manner of the Hittite *hilani* buildings (p. 46). In fact at Khorsabad a detached building has been found of the type of the *hilani* of Zincirli.[270] Sennacherib and Assurbanipal also boast of palaces built in the Hittite fashion. Assurbanipal speaks as follows: 'I had timbers from first-class cedar trees in Sirara and Lebanon placed over the palace. Doors of sweet-smelling wood I had covered with copper and fixed to the portals. Fine columns I covered with gleaming bronze and I erected the *chittu* of the portal of the *hilani*.'[271] *Hilani* buildings of the two kings have been found in Kuyunjuk as well.[272]

Neo-Hittite building elements The previously noted inscription of Sargon II shows that the Assyrians took from Neo-Hittite architecture not only the *hilani* type but also such building elements

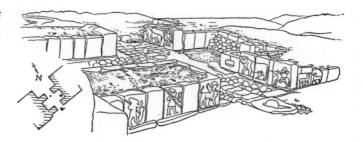

as 'paired lions or columns from tall cedar trunks placed on lions'. Orthostats with reliefs, and such features as bases for supports, columns and capitals were borrowed by the Assyrians from their neighbours in northern Syria and southern Anatolia.

We will first discuss the prototypes in the Neo-Hittite states and then their Assyrian derivatives.

The first orthostats, the big stone slabs used to revet the lower sections of walls to protect them from moisture, have been found as early as in the Yarimlim Palace at Tell Atchana.[273] Like the later examples these orthostats are of basalt, but they have no reliefs. The next examples, also without relief decoration, come from Niqmepa's Palace (Fig. 18) at Tell Atchana.[274] The earliest orthostats with reliefs have been found at Alaca near Hattusa. In the time of the empire they decorated the lower part of the city wall at the Sphinx Gate.[275] The first orthostats with reliefs from Neo-Hittite times come from Malatya and Zincirli,[276] where they also served to embellish the lower part of a gate complex (Fig. 28).[277] Like the orthostats of Alaca they consist of stone blocks running through the thickness of the wall. By contrast, the orthostats created for Assyrian buildings in the following period are slabs that function not as supporting members but as a protective and decorative revetment. The Assyrians took this type of relief orthostat from Hittite monuments. However, they developed these revetment slabs into an essential part of the façade of Assyrian monumental architecture, so that the finest orthostats of Assyrian palaces markedly surpass their Hittite prototypes in form and quality. Possibly on account of contact with Assyrian work, the later buildings of southern Anatolia and northern Syria no longer have the earlier type of orthostats in the form of solid blocks running through the thickness of the wall, but are invariably slabs. Thus, in Zincirli, where orthostat blocks were usual in the ninth century, slabs appear in the eighth. Places that flourished later, such as Sakçegözü and Karatepe, have only orthostat slabs. Not surprisingly, Tell Halaf also employs the slab type exclusively—another reason for dating this building to the last quarter of the eighth century.

History of orthostat

The first standard architectural elements of the ancient Near East, such as bases for supports, columns and capitals, seem to have been under Phoenician influence in the cities of southern Anatolia and northern Syria in the ninth and eighth centuries. Since Mesopotamian architects had no stone for building and even

Other architectural elements

79

FIG. 29 – *Entrance to Niqmepa's Palace. Tell Atchana. (Cf. Fig. 18.) After Naumann, Architektur Kleinasiens, p. 130, Fig. 121. Cf. below.*

had to import wood from the Lebanon, the form of the column with a base and capital could not develop in that country. In second-millennium Anatolia, where the imposing architecture of the Hittites arose, architects would surely have developed fixed types of columns with bases and capitals if relations with Crete and Mycenae had been somewhat closer, and if the Hittite empire had not been cut short at its height.

The Phoenician cities of the early first millennium, which were in close contact with Egypt and whose art continued the Mycenaean tradition of the thirteenth and twelfth centuries (p. 71), invented the type of capital with overhanging crown of leaves (Fig. 58).

Neo-Hittite architecture developed primarily in those cities of southern Anatolia and northern Syria whose population had been Aramaeanized. The Phoenician element and the fresh wave of Neo-Hittite art is thus explained by the invasion of the Aramaeans, who spread north and west from their original home in the Arabian desert.[278] On the other hand, during the ninth and eighth centuries the cities of southern Anatolia and northern Syria seem to have continued the strong Mycenaean tradition with which they had been familiar since the sixteenth century. Through the interaction of various elements in the encounter of Phoenician-Aramaean culture with the Luvian-Hittite tradition, new base and capital forms were created in the small states of southern Anatolia and northern Syria.

Base   The first appearance of a tectonically designed and artistically shaped base to support a column as an independent building element occurred in the cities of southern Anatolia and northern Syria in the eighth century. The column-bases of Egyptian and Minoan-Mycenaean art consist of simple disks, usually rather low. The bases in Tell Atchana[279] belong to this category (Fig. 29). In this connection

PLATE 21a – Lion base from Carchemish. Basalt. Early to middle Neo-Hittite style. Reign of Katuwas, i.e. Pisiris (second half of 8th century B.C.). *Archaeological Museum, Ankara. Height 82 cm. Cf. Fig. 69 and p. 103.*

PLATE 21b – Detail of Plate 21a.

PLATES 21c, d – Lion statuette from Al Mina. Ivory. Middle Neo-Hittite phase. Second half of 8th century B.C. *Ashmolean Museum, Oxford. Length 7.1 cm. Cf. Fig. 77 and p. 181.*

21 a

21 c

21 d

b

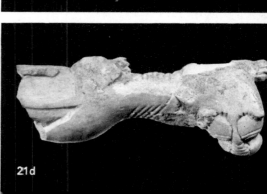

22

it is of some interest to note that the simple base is called a 'plinth' in the Greek language. Originally meaning 'brick', the word appears to come from the Minoan language. It may be that in Minoan-Mycenaean times builders began to place a brick tile under the wooden column, calling this type of base a plinth—a term that persisted into Greek times. The simple plinth served to enlarge the contact surface, to protect the wooden column from damp and to stop it from sinking into the ground. The column-bases of the Neo-Hittite period are essentially distinct from these simple plinths of brick and stone that were in use in Egyptian and Minoan-Mycenaean art, for they formed specially emphasized, tectonically shaped building elements. At Zincirli, Carchemish, Tell Tainat and other Neo-Hittite sites column-bases have been found that are almost Ionian Greek in their tectonic quality (Figs. 30–43). Bases that like the later Ionian ones comprise two parts—a rectangular plinth and a torus in the shape of a cushion or drum—have come to light at Carchemish and especially at Zincirli (Figs. 30, 31)[280]. A base of this kind has also been found at Arslan-Taş.[281] But the best examples are from Khorsabad,[282] Sargon's capital. They were probably imported from one of the Neo-Hittite cities. There are two large basalt bases, of which the torus diameter measures 1.45 metres at the top (Fig. 32). With this large diameter the columns resting on the torus must have consisted of a bundle of wooden shafts held together with bronze rings.

The column-bases of the Neo-Hittite period that have no plinths are just as tectonic in their effect as those with plinths, for they are richly decorated and strongly articulated so that they have an impressive structural character. The finest examples are the bases of Building K at Zincirli[283] (Fig. 33) and from the *hilani* of Tell Tainat (Fig. 34).[284] Almost identical, they come from the same workshop and belong to the same period. They comprise an ornate drum with two rolls of leaf ornament and a middle 'belt'. The leaves of the lower roll are standing and those of the upper one hanging. A closer look at the lower roll (Fig. 33) enables one to make out the individual leaves quite clearly. The leaves taper symmetrically, and each has a stem-like middle rib. Below the individual leaves are in contact and quite thick. Halfway up they begin to taper so that interspaces appear, producing a striking contrast of light and shade. The edges of the individual leaves are marked by a 'seam' that looks like a rib. In the upper roll individual leaves are not distinguishable at first because the ribs of the leaves are twisted like rope and the leaf edges have been obscured, so that the unit is no longer the single leaf but a metope-like spacing from rib to rib.[285] The ornamental composition of the upper roll also shows that the sculptor was not entirely clear in his understanding of the hanging leaves. He has not brought his ornamental form, which consists of two vertical volutes in the shape of a Phoenician capital, into the leaf, but has joined

Bases from Zincirli and Tell Tainat

PLATE 22a – King Sulumeli offering a libation to the storm god. Orthostat block from Malatya. Basalt. Early Neo-Hittite style. 1050–850 B.C. *Height 86 cm. Cf. p. 95.*

PLATE 22b – Priestesses. Orthostat block from Carchemish. Basalt. Middle Neo-Hittite style. Reign of Katuwas, i.e. Pisiris (second half of 8th century). *Archaeological Museum, Ankara. Height 1 m. Cf. p. 99.*

it to two adjacent leaves, so that the shape of the individual leaf is largely obscured by this symmetrical composition of palm volutes. The individual leaves of the upper roll may be understood only by comparing them with those of the lower. As F. von Luschan has rightly perceived,[286] the drop-like form that hangs from the curls of the long upright volutes on either side is a female inflorescence which we find in all Phoenician palm-tree renderings;[287] it recurs on the palm-tree of the Sakçegözü relief (Pl. 15a).[288] Under this female inflorescence there hangs on either side a palm leaf which seems about to drop, which is intended as a space-filler. Above the large upright palm volutes a young palm frond is symmetrically arranged on either side. The narrow middle roll, which has an interlace band, compresses the torus in the centre like a heavy rope and gives the tectonic structure of the base an organic vitality.

The way in which the eyelets of the interlace band on the Zincirli bases are decorated with rosettes is a further indication of Phoenician influence, which has been pointed out above. Interlace bands with rosette decoration appear in the building ornamentation of Hama.[289]

As has been mentioned, the bases from Tell Tainat (Fig. 34) are almost identical reproductions of the Zincirli examples. The only differences are that the back lines of the two great upright palm volutes are not (as at Zincirli) placed parallel and in contact, but diverge in the lower part. Also the interlace band of the middle roll takes a somewhat different form. These differences between the bases of Tell Tainat and the Zincirli pieces are probably attributable to the preferences of two different masters, who were active or who trained in the same workshop.

Other bases from
Zincirli Another base in basalt (Fig. 35), which has been recovered from Zincirli,[290] where its original position could not be determined, has the same tectonic structure. The ornament, however, is simpler, with the same leaf crown in the upper and lower roll, except that it is inverted; moreover, it dispenses with the interlace band in the middle roll. This base probably comes from the same period as the four bases discussed above, which may be dated about 730 by reference to the lion base of the Tell Tainat temple-palace (Fig. 26, p. 75).

Another column-base that should be mentioned was found detached from its original context in the débris of Court R at Zincirli (Fig. 36).[291] The plinth and torus are worked from a single block. The decoration of the torus is a simplified

FIGS. 30–32 (from left to right) – *Fig. 30: Column-base from Carchemish. After Naumann, Architektur Kleinasiens, p. 131, Fig. 130. 8th century B.C. Cf. note 292 and p. 85. – Fig. 31: Column-base from Carchemish. After Naumann, Architektur Kleinasiens, p. 131, Fig. 129. 8th century B.C. Cf. note 293 and p. 85. – Fig. 32: Column-base from Khorsabad. 721–705 B.C. Cf. note 282 and p. 83.*

  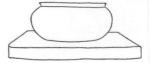

version of the palm motif seen on the two bases of Building K at Zincirli (Fig. 33). There are four palm leaves—each with a female inflorescence—which are conceived as paired double volutes. With its simplified decoration this last column-base may be considered a late work produced towards the end of the eighth century. It deserves special attention since it is designed with two clearly differentiated parts, a plinth and a torus. Socles consisting of a plinth and a torus seem to be an invention of the art centres of southern Anatolia and northern Syria. The column-bases mentioned from Zincirli and some further examples from the Neo-Hittite states (to be discussed below) rank as the oldest instances of the socle type with plinth and torus.

The above-mentioned round base[292] from the vicinity of Carchemish (Fig. 30) is another example of the socle with plinth and torus. Like the Zincirli piece, it is worked from a single block. Its crown of standing leaves is arranged on the principle of the row of leaves found on the bases of Building K at Zincirli, and the leaves take the same form, but the style is different. Another basalt base from Carchemish (Fig. 31),[293] the lower part of which is broken off, appears—to judge from what remains—also to have been a socle with plinth and torus that was carved from a single block. Both the form of the leaves and their arrangement are quite different from the examples at Zincirli (Fig. 33) and Tell Tainat (Fig. 34): the leaves are wide and rounded and the middle ribs take the form of palm fronds. These two socles from Carchemish may be regarded as examples of further development of the cushion base, of which simple prototypes are known from Zincirli and Arslan-Taş.[294] All of these, including the last-named examples, consist of a plinth and a torus. This suggests that the plinth-and-torus base was generally diffused in the area of southern Anatolia and northern Syria.

Assyrian artists took up this Carchemish type of base, which they developed eagerly. Three bases from Khorsabad (Fig. 37)[295] and four bases from Nineveh that were found in front of Sennacherib's Palace (Fig. 38)[296] reproduce the round socle type of Carchemish. In the socle model from Nineveh (Fig. 39)[297] the Carchemish type recurs, although without the plinth, for in this case the torus rests on the back of a sphinx. Assyrian reliefs also depict the simple cushion types of Neo-Hittite architecture—with and without leaf decoration[298]—which have no plinths (Figs. 40–42).[299] The pieces of furniture shown on the relief of Assur-

Carchemish type in Assyria

FIGS. 33–35 (from left to right) – *Fig. 33: Column-base from Building K at Zincirli. About 730 B.C. Cf. note 283 and p. 83. – Fig. 34: Column-base from the hilari at Tell Tainat. About 730 B.C. Cf. note 284 and p. 83. – Fig. 35: Column-base from Zincirli. 730–700 B.C. Cf. note 290 and p. 84.*

baniᴣal's victory banquet[300] have bases and capitals that resemble those found in Assyrian reliefs with architectural façades. In Assyria all the main base types of the southern Anatolia-northern Syria area seem to have been enthusiastically emulated. A rectangular base from Nimrud,[301] on which stands a sphinx (Fig. 43), presents a socle type in which the tectonic structure—two deep scotiae (grooves) separating three torus-like profiles—closely recalls the structure of the base of the Ionic order.

Furniture fragments in ivory

Having encountered the bases as architectural members, we should now examine their appearance in the minor arts. Especially interesting are the ivory throne fragments[302] found in a side chamber next to the bathroom L 5 at Zincirli (Figs. 44, 45).[303] Here we find a very similar decoration to, and the same tectonic structure as, the bases of Building K in several versions (cf. Fig. 33). The ivory carvings are considerably superior to the stone work both in the rendering of the individual forms and in the execution of the whole. The cushion type of torus was employed in the architecture of many Neo-Hittite sites (Figs. 33–36). The ivory carvings incorporated into furniture mainly imitate the art forms of architecture without adding anything of note. Furniture fragments in ivory imported from southern Anatolia and northern Syria have also been found at Nimrud. Richard D. Barnett has identified them and brought them into relation with examples from Zincirli.[304] Building L, in which the ivory throne fragments from Zincirli were found,[305] was built in the time of Barrakab at the earliest. This provides a very welcome point of reference for dating the base and capital forms to the second half of the eighth century.

Animal pedestals

The animal pedestals (Pl. 23a; Figs. 46, 47) played a much greater role in Neo-Hittite art than the decorated column-bases with and without plinths. In any case use of the animal base as a column-bearing architectural member seems to be a Neo-Hittite invention. The impetus for this discovery may have come from Hattusa, where lions and sphinxes took on the function of wall-bearing animals, flanking both sides of the portal as a monolithic block running through the thickness of the wall. The portal sphinxes from the Yerkapi[306] in Bogazköy and a lion figure from Alaca[307] represent portal animals with the upper bodies treated as three-dimensional sculpture projecting from the wall; the main part of the body, however—the part that bears the pier or side wall—is shown in relief. In the context of these portal animals of Bogazköy[308] and Alaca,[309] in which the forequarters of the sphinx appear on the front of the pier,[310] while the other parts are invisible, also were intended as load-bearing members, and not simply as a decorative element.

86

FIGS. 37–39 (from left to right) – *Fig. 37: Column-base from Khorsabad. 721–705 B.C. Cf. note 295 and p. 85.* – *Fig. 38: Column-base from Nineveh. Second half of 8th century B.C. Cf. note 296 and p. 85.* – *Fig. 39: Socle model from Nineveh. 721–705 B.C. Cf. note 297 and p. 85.*

The next-oldest portal animals in the form of palace sculptures are found at Tell Atchana in palaces or temples of the thirteenth century.[311] The earliest Neo-Hittite examples come from Malatya.[312] The Assyrian imitations derive from Neo-Hittite prototypes, as the Assyrians themselves admitted (p. 78). Inspired by portal lions of this type, such as those of the lion gate at Malatya, the architects of Neo-Hittite times (who in contrast to the Hittites of the imperial period were acquainted with column-bases) had the bold and arresting idea of using animal pedestals as substitutes for column-bases. *Portal animals*

The lion base from Carchemish (Fig. 48), one of the earliest column pedestals in animal form,[313] in fact shows two lions attached to a round base like two portal animals. The derivation from portal animals is also clearly recognizable in the contemporary statue bases of Neo-Hittite art (Figs. 48, 74; Pl. 21). Only with the second half of the eighth century do we find properly developed animal pedestals. The lions and sphinxes of the animal socles of the *hilani* buildings of Zincirli, Sakçegözü and Tell Tainat, which all originated in the last third of the eighth century, were no longer applied to the sides, but actually bore a base which in turn supported a column. The only example that is fully freed from the Anatolian Hittite concept of the portal animal is the paired lion piece from Tell Tainat (Fig. 26).[314] It is characteristic that the animal bases of Tell Halaf (Fig. 47)[315] also depart from the old-established motif of the portal animals and show a new concept. This is one more indication that this highly interesting building should be dated to the last third of the eighth century (p. 77). *Lion base from Carchemish* *Animal pedestals in developed form*

Like the Assyrians, the Neo-Hittites probably used 'splendid columns of aromatic cedar trunks from the Lebanon', which they 'covered with gleaming bronze' (p. 47). In any case excavations of Neo-Hittite ruins have not yet brought to light any remains of stone columns from a monumental building. But we do have stone columns of considerable size, such as the column in the Staatliche Museen in Berlin, which was carried off to Assur from a site in the southern *Columns*

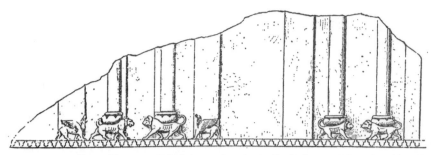

FIGS. 40–42 – *Above, Fig. 40: Relief from Assurbanipal's Palace at Nineveh. After Perrot and Chipiez, Histoire de l'Art, vol. II, p. 143, Fig. 42. Original in British Museum (Barnett, Assyrian Palace Reliefs, Pl. 136). Cf. p. 93. – Below, left, Fig. 41: Relief from Khorsabad. After Perrot and Chipiez, Histoire de l'Art, vol. II, p. 142, Fig. 41. Original in Chicago (Loud, Khorsabad, Figs. 83–89). 721–705 B.C. Cf. note 331 and p. 93. – Below, right, Fig. 42: Relief from Assurbanipal's Palace at Nineveh. After Perrot and Chipiez, Histoire de l'Art, vol. II, p. 143, Fig. 42. Original in British Museum (Barnett, Assyrian Palace Reliefs, Pls. 133–4). Cf. note 332. For Figs. 41, 42 cf. also p. 93.*

Anatolia-northern Syria area (Fig. 49),[316] and a limestone capital with the beginning of a shaft from Khorsabad (Fig. 50),[317] the original purpose of which is not known. Evidently there were columns with shafts that tapered both above and below. The standard column type of this period has a cylindrical shaft (Figs. 50, 52). By contrast the column found at Assur mentioned above, as well as the fragment of a column attached to a capital shown on a relief from Tell Tainat (Fig. 53), are prismatic. One cannot help being reminded here of the Ionian columns of Archaic Greece, in which the flat fluting produces a similar effect.

Necking rings The shaft of the Assur column (Fig. 49) terminates in a torus necking, set off above and below by small but effective rings. The same profile recurs in the necking of a serpentine colonnette[318] from Zincirli (Fig. 52). It is possible, however, that in these instances the torus, as in a Neo-Hittite head-piece of a cauldron stand found at Olympia (Fig. 54)[319] represents a part, not of the column,

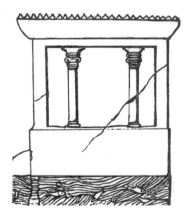

but of the capital. Yet it seems that the column neckings in Neo-Hittite architecture were invariably profiled or at least had shaft rings, for almost all columns in the minor arts (Figs. 44, 45) or depictions on reliefs (Figs. 41, 42) show rings on the necking, which are meant to form a transition between column and capital. The Assur column (Fig. 49) in any case repeats the necking profile of the serpentine colonnette from Zincirli (Fig. 52)—an indication of its origin in the southern Anatolia-northern Syria area. The same conclusion is suggested by the fact that it is of basalt.[320] The lower fragment of the column (which has been restored) has a badly preserved inscription[321] that unfortunately gives no help in dating the column. From the location of the column, which was found in the row of steles at Assur, W. Andrae has argued in favour of the period of Assurnasirpal II.[322] However, the rings on the necking show that it belongs to the standard type of northern Syrian column and could not have been made before the eighth century (p. 90). The lower end is profiled, like the upper end of a Neo-Hittite column, so that a ring stands between the shaft and base, linking the two architectural members organically.

Capital

Like the base, the Neo-Hittite capital had a characteristic form. The surviving examples show clearly that a crown of pendent leaves was the main feature. It was often provided with an abacus-like element (Figs. 44–58) and usually had a lower part consisting of a torus or a circle of standing palmettes. Thus one can distinguish two types of capital according to whether the design is simple or complex. It should be noted, however, that the two are basically variants of a single type.

A smaller capital from Carchemish with an adjoining fragment of shaft[323] has a doubled shaft-ring, pendent leaves and an abacus-like addition (Fig. 55). On a relief from Tell Tainat (Fig. 53) a similar capital is represented; this consists of double shaft-rings on the necking of the column, a circle of pendent leaves and a

Carchemish capital with leaf crown and abacus

89

FIG. 46 – *Niche in façade of hilani at Tell Halaf. After Naumann, Tell Halaf, vol. II, Plan 5. 730–700 B.C. Cf. p. 86.*

high extension on which a Phoenician leaf capital is shown. As R. Naumann has noted,[324] the tree-like ornaments to the right and left of the leaf formation probably depict decorations that in reality would have been attached to the sides of the 'abacus'. The stone capital with part of a shaft from Khorsabad (Fig. 50) is an Assyrian imitation of Neo-Hittite prototypes, as we have come to know them. It also has necking rings, a pendent leaf crown, and a low, round 'abacus'. The column which was carried off to Assur (Fig. 49) likewise consists of a ring and two necking rings, a leaf crown and a low 'abacus'. The figure reproduced here shows a very plausible reconstruction by R. Naumann (Fig. 49).[325] The ten dowel holes above the bowl probably served for the attachment of a large leaf crown in bronze. A column representation from a house model from Tell Halaf (Fig. 51)[326] reproduces the capital type discussed, with a necking ring, pendent leaf crown, upper termination as a high 'abacus' and a saddle beam. The basalt capital from Tell Halaf (Fig. 56), which rested on a basalt column and supported a large bird in the same material,[327] has no 'abacus'—it is just a crown with eight pendent leaves.

It may be that stone capitals with two rows of leaves, one atop the other, were in existence, for examples are known from Nimrud among the ivory works made by Neo-Hittite craftsmen.[328]

Ivory imitations   There are also somewhat more intricate capitals, comprising shaft-rings, torus, standing palmette circle, pendent leaf crown, and often an 'abacus'. A serpentine colonnette from Zincirli (Fig. 52) and Neo-Hittite ivories from Zincirli (Fig. 45) and Nimrud[329] belong to this type. An ivory fragment from Zincirli (Fig. 45) shows the same capital form in two identical, but opposed versions. The previously mentioned head-piece of a bronze cauldron support from Olympia shows the same capital type with torus, crown of standing palmettes and pendent leaves (Fig. 54); consequently it must come from a southern Anatolian-northern Syrian workshop. A small sandstone capital in the British Museum (Fig. 57),[330] which possibly formed part of the balustrade of an Assyrian building, should be added

PLATE 23a – Reconstruction of ceremonial grouping at the entrance to the temple at Tell Halaf. Basalt. Middle Neo-Hittite style with late Neo-Hittite elements. 730–700 B.C. *Tell Halaf Museum, Berlin. Height of divine figures without columnar attachments 2.75 m. Cf. p. 105.*
PLATE 23b – Lion-hunting relief from Sakçegözü. Basalt. Aramaean style. 730–700 B.C. *Staatliche Museen, Berlin. Height 1.18 m. Cf. p. 62.*

23 a

23 b

to this group. The leaf circles were generally either standing on bases or hanging from capitals. There are, however, exceptions.

By contrast the Ionic capital type was not found in the Near East, whether among the Neo-Hittites, the Assyrians or the Phoenicians. A relief from Khorsabad, preserved in the Oriental Institute in Chicago,[331] represents a pavilion in the form of a temple *in antis*, in which the columns appear to carry Ionic capitals (Fig. 41). Unfortunately this detail is shown very sketchily. I believe that photography and the relief itself are deceptive in this regard, and that what is shown must be a capital of Neo-Hittite type (Figs. 51–57). The modern draughtsman who copied another pavilion from an Assyrian relief in the Palace of Assurbanipal at Nineveh[332] has shown the capitals of the left columns in the form of two superimposed Ionic capitals (Fig. 42). But the fine photograph reproduced in R. D. Barnett's *Assyrian Palace Reliefs*[333] shows that this is actually a Phoenician capital of the same type as the other capitals of the pavilion. If one turns the photographs in Barnett's volume upside-down, one sees that the column-base in the form of a crown of standing leaves gives the impression of an Ionic capital, as is the case also with the above-mentioned capitals of the pavilion on the relief from Khorsabad. Indeed, if true Ionic capitals were present in the Near East we should surely have some definite evidence of their existence.

Ionic capital

The Phoenician capital with vertical volutes[334] occurs as an ornament on the abacus of a capital depicted on a relief from Tell Tainat (Fig. 53) and again on the throne of a goddess depicted on a relief from Carchemish.[335] But the Phoenician volute capital (Fig. 58) does not seem to have been employed as an independent feature in Neo-Hittite architecture.

Phoenician capital

Neo-Hittite architecture derives its ornament—especially the decorative motifs of bases and capitals that derive from the palm-tree—from Phoenician prototypes (p. 84). But the tectonic design of such individual elements as the plinth, torus, circles of leaves and palmettes has a pronounced indigenous character. The Neo-Hittite crown of leaves, for example, undoubtedly belongs to the orbit of Phoenician influence, yet the shape is new and original. The same is true of the design of other architectural elements. The tension that appears in the torus of the bases of Building K at Zincirli (Fig. 33), gives the whole base an organic elasticity—a quality elsewhere found only in Greek architecture. From the loosely arranged vegetable forms of Phoenician architecture Neo-Hittite craftsmen created building elements that convey solidity and powerful structural harmony.

Phoenician influence

All three components of the Neo-Hittite column—base, shaft and capital—are independent architectural members made up of various elements. The Neo-Hittite column is an architectonic unity with an organic structure consisting of foot, body and head. As history's first tectonically ordered column type this

PLATE 24a – Deity from Tell Halaf. Basalt. Middle Neo-Hittite style with late Neo-Hittite elements. 730–700 B.C. *Archaeological Museum, Adana. Height 1 m. Cf. p. 115.*
PLATE 24b – Great goddess on lioness; from Tell Halaf. Basalt. Middle Neo-Hittite style with late Neo-Hittite elements. 730–700 B.C. *Archaeological Museum, Aleppo. Height 2.73 m. Cf. p. 116.*

achievement deserves special recognition. A century and a half had to pass before the Ionian architects took up the tectonically articulated column of the Neo-Hittites and developed it further.

NEO-HITTITE
SCULPTURE

In the world of ancient Near Eastern civilization a special place belongs to the sculpture of the Luvian-Hittite principalities, which was carried on vigorously in southern Anatolia and northern Syria after the break-up of the Hittite empire. The work was unexceptional in quality because of its provincial and conservative character. A comparison of these sculptures with the highly accomplished monuments of contemporary Assyrian art makes their modest standing readily apparent. Yet Neo-Hittite sculpture is historically important because of its unique intermediary role in regard to the last Assyrianizing and Aramaeanizing style currents. The geographical position of the Neo-Hittite principalities and favourable historical conditions account for the fact that the art works of these centres stimulated the rise of the Orientalizing style in Greece towards the end of the eighth century.

Three styles

The sculptures produced in the principalities are by no means homogeneous. They vary according to locality, but can be grouped in three main styles: early Neo-Hittite style, the middle Neo-Hittite style and late Neo-Hittite style.

EARLY NEO-HITTITE STYLE
(1100–900/850)

Untouched by Neo-Assyrian influence, this first stylistic phase continues the metropolitan tradition of Hittite art that flourished in Anatolia and northern Syria during the second millennium. In fact it is only known to us from the gate

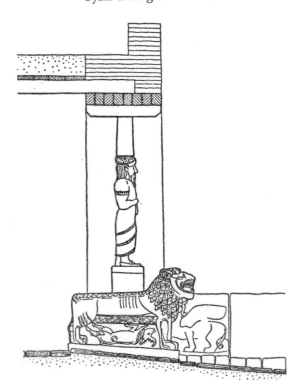

FIG. 47 – *Deity on a lion base. From niche in façade of hilani at Tell Halaf. After Naumann, Tell Halaf, vol. II, Fig. 31. 730–700 B.C. Cf. p. 87.*

sculpture of Malatya (Pl. 22a), which may be regarded as a faithful continuation of the sculpture of Hattusa and Alaca.[336] The iconographic type of the kings with the winged sun disk and the *kalmush* is the same as in the prototypes of imperial times. In reliefs gods wear the same peaked caps as the gods of Yazilikaya (Figs. 27, 59). In both cases the caps are decked out with horns in front and at the rear, while inside they have divine emblems, which appear elsewhere only in Yazilikaya (Figs. 27, 59).[337] The short kilt with the centre pleat and a curved seam above the knees is also found, as well as the belt consisting of a simple leather or metal band, known from scenes at Hattusa. The sword which the gods wear at their side has the same crescent pommel as in the reliefs of the empire;[338] later, in the middle Neo-Hittite stage, it was to be transformed. Other empire elements in the early Neo-Hittite style will be mentioned below in discussing the middle Neo-Hittite phase. Syro-Hittite and Mitannian motifs and stylistic features will also be treated at that point.

Empire tradition

The fine orthostat blocks from Malatya that formerly embellished the façade of the city wall flanking the main gate show the king performing religious rites and are entirely in the manner of the art of the empire (Pl. 22a). On the relief illustrated two successive scenes appear. On the left we see the storm god in his chariot drawn by two bulls. On the right, having descended from the chariot, the god accepts a libation poured by King Sulumeli. The god's right hand holds a boomerang and his left a thunderbolt. Behind him two hieroglyphs placed at head height—the divine ideogram above and below the storm-god emblem—identify him further. The horns and the divine emblem of his peaked cap are very summarily indicated. They are most clearly recognizable on the figures of the relief plaques with the dragon Illuyanka (Fig. 60), who is killed by the storm god in the presence of his son. The round objects in the scene are probably hailstones, which the god hurled down at his adversary.

Malatya orthostat relief

Unfortunately we have no criteria to fix the chronological limits of the early Neo-Hittite style. To go by the date of the destruction of the empire the earliest possible date must be placed about 1180 B.C., but it is hard to say at what point after 1180 the new style actually began. The close stylistic link of the gate sculptures to works at Hattusa and Alaca speaks for a relatively early start. In a special study of the problem I suggested that the upper limits of this style should be set about the middle of the 11th century[339]. The lower boundary may be placed about 900/850 because of the intrusion of Assyrian style elements at that point. But in the absence of reliable clues it seems best to allow a range of two full centuries, from about 1100 to 900/850, for the unfolding of this style.

Dating

Above it was suggested that the early Neo-Hittite style shows no Assyrian features. Yet the Malatya orthostat block with the libation scene (Pl. 22a) has one Assyrian characteristic, for the way the relief shows the storm god first travelling in his chariot and then standing to receive the king's homage corresponds to the principle of continuous narration familiar from Assyrian art (p. 27). Unfortunately this Assyrian trait offers no firm basis for dating: the method of continuous narration is known from the time of King Tukulti-Ninurta (1241–1205) and was

Assyrian elements

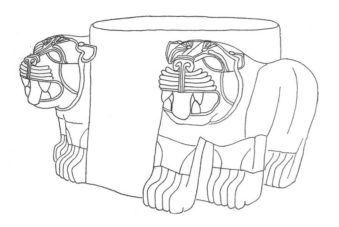

FIG. 48 – *Lion base from Car-chemish. Cf. Plate 68. Early to middle Neo-Hittite style. Second half of 8th century B.C. Archaeological Museum, Ankara. Cf. note 313, p. 87.*

still popular as late as the seventh century.[340]. It must be assumed, however, that the early Neo-Hittite style was practised in Malatya (or some other Neo-Hittite centre) at least as early as the eleventh century; no other conclusion is possible, since the artists had direct knowledge of the art of the Hittite empire.

MIDDLE NEO-HITTITE STYLE (900–750/730 B.C.)

The really important figurative art of the Neo-Hittite principalities was produced in the middle period, which (unlike the early Neo-Hittite style) is not simply a direct continuation of the imperial Hittite tradition of Anatolia. Alongside the persisting strands of imperial origin, new characteristic elements appear. The best and most striking examples[341] were found at Carchemish (Figs. 78–86) and Zincirli (Figs. 61–66). As in the early Neo-Hittite style the male figures depicted on works from these two sites wear the wedge-shaped beard with shaven upper lip (Pl. 22a; Fig. 60), the long hair with a curl at the end sometimes reaching down as far as the elbows, and the short kilt with a centre pleat and a thick seam over the knees. They wear the belt of the imperial period,[342] with a double fold above and below. Such pictorial types as two-headed sphinxes and especially sphinxes with peaked horned caps from Carchemish (Fig. 78) and Zincirli (Fig. 64), hark back to the days of the empire (Fig. 27).[343] As in the Syrian Hittite and many Anatolian Hittite examples, the caps worn by gods are decorated with one or two pairs of horns (Figs. 61, 78, 82). In figures from Carchemish and Zincirli, just as in reliefs from Malatya, Hattusa and Alaca, weapons are generally carried on the shoulder. The type of sword sheath with a curved end found at Carchemish and Zincirli is a lingering relic of Hattusa, although the sword itself has a pommel of modified type. The theme of a divine or human couple developed in Hattusa,[344] with the female figure standing or sitting on the left and the male on the right,

FIGS. 49, 50 – *Above, Fig. 49: Column from Assur. Restoration after Naumann, Architektur Kleinasiens, p. 140, Fig. 154. 8th century B.C. Staatliche Museen, Berlin. Cf. note 316, pp. 88, 90. – Below, Fig. 50: Limestone capital with shaft ring from Khorsabad. After Perrot and Chipiez, Histoire de l'Art, vol. II, p. 216, Fig. 74. 8th century B.C. Cf. note 317, p. 90.*

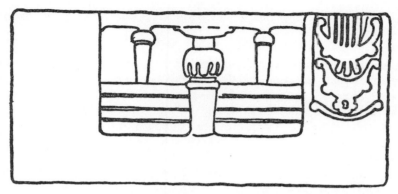

FIG. 51 – *House model serving as a cauldron base. Basalt. Tell Halaf. After Naumann, Tell Halaf, vol. II, Fig. 9. Second half of 8th century B.C. Cf. p. 90.*

persisted in Neo-Hittite art. Noteworthy is the fact that the type of lion characteristic of the empire continues almost unchanged in both the early and middle style stages; this fact will be further discussed below.

The early and middle Neo-Hittite style phases show many iconographic features that are foreign to Anatolian Hittite art. The tassel at the top of the horned cap, the reduced number of horns (Figs. 61, 78, 82), the absence of ear-rings, the upward stretch of one arm are details that stand in marked contrast to the traits of the imperial age.[345] The fact that the other hand of the god always holds some object is non-Hittite, for in the reliefs of the empire the god's hand was always stretched slightly forward but never held anything, as it was clenched. It is also a non-Hittite feature that the storm god should hold a thunderbolt in one hand, even though this attribute appears in his emblem (Pl. 22a). The cluster form of the thunderbolt is likewise non-Hittite. Most of these features that are lacking in empire works are details borrowed from Mitannian and Syro-Hittite prototypes of the second millennium. Similarly—as I have shown in an earlier study following A. Moortgat[346]—the hybrid animals of Neo-Hittite art, the creatures partaking of the qualities of lions and birds, are pictorial types ultimately based on Mitannian and Syro-Hittite models. The mythological scenes from Carchemish and Tell Halaf that show a man killed by two others belong to the repertoire of the Syro-Hittite and Mitannian complex of the second millennium.[347]

Syro-Hittite and Mitannian style elements

After about 850 B.C. this mixture of Anatolian Hittite features and Syro-Hittite and Mitannian components was further enriched by Assyrian, Phoenician, Aramaean and Babylonian contributions, which give an altogether different physiognomy to Neo-Hittite art.

A characteristic aspect of the middle Neo-Hittite style phase is the introduction of isolated Assyrian motifs. The war chariot (Figs. 66, 86) is the main motif that the Neo-Hittite workshops of this phase took over from Assyrian art. The models favoured were chariots of the Assyrian Classical (Pls. 1, 8) and transitional (Pl. 2) styles. Another Assyrian motif is the wounded lion that appears on an orthostat

Assyrian elements

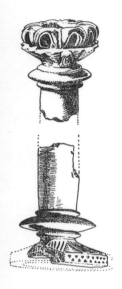

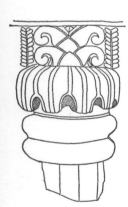

FIG. 52 – *Serpentine colonnette from Zincirli. After AiS, vol. V, Pl. 27. 8th century B.C. Cf. p. 89.*

from Malatya.[348] The replacement of the Hittite sword with its crescent pommel and the sheath curving at the end (Pl. 22a; Fig. 60) by the new long sword, often provided with a long tassel (Fig. 62),[349] is another sign of Assyrian influence. The old-fashioned shoes with their turned-up and pointed toes were no longer popular (Pl. 22a). The traditional hybrid creatures continued to wear them, but the kings adopted the new vogue for dainty sandals. The omission of hieroglyphic labels identifying the gods from the picture surface of the orthostats (Pl. 22a) is another aspect of the new stylization. The use of hieroglyphics continued, however, in monumental inscriptions.

The ninth century saw a great flowering of Assyrian power and culture. Assurnasirpal II (883–859) strengthened the internal organization of the realm. As 'King of the Four Quarters of the Earth', Shalmaneser III (854–824) accomplished the greatest extension of Assyria. In fact, only in the reign of this king did Assyrian art gain its far-reaching influence over the styles of neighbouring countries. As has been suggested, the process of Assyrianization began in Neo-Hittite art about the middle of the ninth century. A strong new wave of Assyrian influence may be observed in the time of Tiglath-Pileser III (745–727). Consequently, the middle Neo-Hittite phase, which shows only isolated and fairly modest Assyrian influences, must come somewhat earlier, about 850–750 B.C. Thus the main development of the middle Neo-Hittite phase falls naturally into the obscure period of weakness of the Assyrian empire that lasted from 824 to 750.

Neo-Hittite hair style   Despite the above-mentioned traditional features and the concomitant foreign borrowings middle Neo-Hittite style strikes a special note of its own. Its leading characteristic is a new hair style that is specifically Neo-Hittite. Typical of this are the corkscrew curls, often forming a knot at the nape of the neck (Figs. 62, 66, 83). This bundle of locks is made up of a mass of hair of which the lower end is rolled up so that a twist occurs (Fig. 83). This hair style is normal for male heads of the

FIGS. 53–57 (from left to right) – *Fig. 53: Capital depicted on a relief from Tell Tainat. After AJA, vol. 41, 1937, Fig. 12. Second half of 8th century B.C. Cf. p. 89. – Fig. 54: Bronze head-piece of a cauldron base. Found at Olympia. Late Neo-Hittite (Aramaeanizing Hittite) style. Second half of 8th century B.C. Cf. note 319 and p. 88. – Fig. 55: Small capital with shaft end from Carchemish. 8th century B.C. Cf. note 323 and p. 89. – Fig. 56: Capital from Tell Halaf. Basalt. After Naumann, Architektur Kleinasiens, p. 139, Fig. 151. Second half of 8th century B.C. Cf. note 327 and p. 90. – Fig. 57: Small sandstone capital. 8th century B.C. British Museum. Cf. note 330 and p. 90.*

middle Neo-Hittite period. It persists in Neo-Hittite art until the middle of the eighth century, to be displaced only in the second half of the eighth century by the Assyrian-Aramaean spiral curls. The above-mentioned mass at the nape of the neck, which appears in all male heads of the second traditional style, seems to have developed from the hair volute at the nape of the neck in the early Neo-Hittite style (Fig. 62, right). The creation of the rolled hair at the nape during the early Neo-Hittite style probably took place under the influence of the comparable Assyrian treatment. It is clearly discernible on many reliefs from various sites. At Zincirli, in addition to the open type of hair mass at the nape of the neck, we also find closed volute rolls that already give the appearance of a knot (Fig. 61–65). This round hair knot is one of the characteristic traits of the middle Neo-Hittite style. On Assyrian reliefs of the ninth and eighth centuries it serves to identify people of the hill country.[350] Towards the end of the eighth century the knots were replaced by the Sargonid arrangement (Pl. 3).

The concentric composition of the head locks is a Neo-Hittite innovation of the middle phase (Fig. 83), which probably owes its origin to Phoenician models. A later ivory box in the British Museum shows examples of this hair style (Pl. 41). As a Neo-Hittite feature it persists into the seventh century (Fig. 93).

The simple long tunic worn by the male figures is a characteristic feature of dress in the early and middle Neo-Hittite phases. The tassels hanging from the belt (Fig. 62) seem rather to be an Assyrian fashion, as the figures on the Black Obelisk of Shalmaneser III suggest.[351] The wide metal belt, with a rounded edge above and below, is another characteristic of the middle Neo-Hittite phase. It occurs only in male figures (Figs. 61 ff., 79 ff.). Quite novel is the woman's cloak that appears on carvings of the middle Neo-Hittite phase. It runs up over the head, covering all but the face, and extends down the body as far as the feet. Otherwise, women wear the same long and simple tunic as men, secured by a belt at the waist. This belt consists of thick, twined cords arranged parallel fashion (Pl. 22b); wealthy ladies would have had their belts covered with gold and silver. These belts,[352] which were already known in the second millennium, also appear on the figures of a drum discovered in the Idaean Cave in Crete.[353] It recurs on some female ivory figures of Syrian manufacture.[354]

Now we must examine some facets of the middle phase that are represented at individual sites. A lion-hunting relief and a genius relief from Malatya are worth mentioning.[355] With its animal and chariot depictions the lion scene goes back to Assyrian models. The genius figure wears a Neo-Babylonian feather crown and has wings of Assyrian type. Moreover, the attributes the genius holds in his hands are borrowed from Assyrian art. Since the chariot scenes of Assyria on

Neo-Hittite costume

Works from Malatya

99

FIG. 59 – *King Tuthaliya IV, protected by the god Sarruma. Yazilikaya. Second half of 13th century. Cf. note 337 and pp. 95, 209.*

which the Malatya chariot carving depends themselves belong to the first half of the ninth century, the Malatya sculptures must have been executed at the earliest in the middle or during the second half of the ninth century.[356]

MIDDLE NEO-HITTITE SCULPTURE FROM ZINCIRLI (832–810 B.C.)

The chronological position of the Zincirli works may be fixed with some certainty. We have a considerable number of examples of the middle Neo-Hittite style from this site: orthostat reliefs from the southern city gate (Figs. 64, 65)[357] and from the outer citadel gate (Figs. 61–63, 66)[358], two portal lions from the inner citadel gate (Figs. 71, 72),[359] lions from gate building Q (Fig. 73),[360] the great statue with paired lions (Fig. 74)[361] and the stone block with the relief of the storm god.[362]

Criteria for dating chariot scenes

The chariot and lion depictions provide criteria for firm dating. As has been indicated, the Assyrian models of the Neo-Hittite chariot carvings were first created in the time of Assurnasirpal II (883–859). The war chariot from Zincirli,[363] which is carved on one of the orthostats of the outer citadel gate, certainly derives from examples of the Classical style (Fig. 66). A comparison of the best Neo-Hittite examples, the chariots depicted at Carchemish (Fig. 86), with any Assyrian chariot carving (Pls. 1, 8) makes it unmistakable that the Neo-Hittite works are defective copies of the splendid Assyrian models. Consequently, the chronology of the Assyrian development is decisive for dating the chariots of the middle Neo-Hittite style. Compared with the above-mentioned best examples of the middle Neo-Hittite style (Fig. 86), the Zincirli chariot carving (Fig. 66) is rather mediocre. The sculptor has quite misunderstood the details of the harness. The link of the horse to the shaft and the shaft to the chariot is only clear in the relief: the artist has not taken much trouble with these important features. It is certain, however, that he modelled his work mainly on chariot reliefs of the Neo-Assyrian Classical style (Pls. 1, 8). We find the small chariot box with the quivers set criss-cross fashion, as well as a shield attached to the back of the chariot box with a lion head

FIG. 60 – *The storm god killing the serpent Illuyanka. Malatya. After Akurgal, Kunst der Hethiter, Pl. 104, below. Early Neo-Hittite style. 1050–850 B.C. Cf. p. 95.*

as decoration. The head-dress of the horse with a plume in the form of a brush, set atop a horseshoe-shaped clamp and trailing two fluttering streamers, is derived from similar Assyrian models (Fig. 4).[364] That the chariot box of Zincirli has the axle not at its rear edge but at the centre is evidence not of an early date, but of the clumsiness of the provincial master. Revealing is the fact that the griffin protome, which ought to have decorated the shaft-end, has been mistakenly attached to the reins. The upper front end of the chariot box seems to be connected to the end of the shaft with a thick cord. At this point chariots of the type in question usually have a richly decorated band (Pls. 1, 2, 8). The sculptor may have also misunderstood this feature and shown only the upper edge of the band (Fig. 66).

The griffin protome represented on the chariot relief of Zincirli suggests that the carver knew better Neo-Hittite models which he was copying. In fact shaft-heads in the form of a griffin protome recur on a chariot relief of Carchemish as well as on the chariots of the orthostat slabs of Tell Halaf. It may be, as the Hittite look of the griffin head suggests (Fig. 79), that this emblem was a feature of the Neo-Hittite world. In any case, such griffin protomae seem foreign to Assyrian art. In a splendid alabaster orthostat of Assurnasirpal II in the Staatliche Museen in Berlin,[365] the shaft-end has an animal head that cannot be clearly identified (Pl. 8). Our stylistic analysis clearly shows that the Zincirli chariot depiction arose in direct or indirect imitation of Assyrian models. The above-mentioned orthostat block and with it the oldest works from Zincirli are consequently to be dated in the middle of the ninth century at the earliest.

Thus the southern city gate, the citadel gate and the works of sculpture connected with them may come from the reign of Kilamuwa's father, King Haya (*ca.* 850–832). It must be admitted, however, that this oldest group of sculptures may just

Dating

as well come from the time of Kilamuwa himself (832–810). Kilamuwa, who set up a building inscription with a relief of himself[366] in the Aramaean style at the entrance to Palace J, may have had sculptures in Hittite style erected on the city and citadel gates to show respect for the indigenous people of his kingdom. In an inscription[367] he emphasizes that he overcame disputes between the Mushkabim (probably the local Luvian-Hittite population) and the Ba'ririm (Aramaeans) and that he was 'father and brother' to the local people, unlike earlier kings who had been accustomed 'to treat them like dogs'. Kilamuwa, who was known as Bar TM (x) in Aramaic, deliberately adopted a Luvian name.[368] Thus it may well be that the Zincirli works executed in the middle Neo-Hittite style all come from his time.

At first glance the reliefs from the southern city gate (Figs. 64, 65) have an old-fashioned look, but if one compares them with the sculptures of the outer citadel gate (Figs. 61–63, 66) it is only the difference in quality that is apparent. The two groups are identical in style and iconography. Coiffure, dress, and belts with their pendent tassels are directly anticipated in the reliefs of the outer citadel gate (Fig. 62),[369] together with the griffin-man type (Figs. 63, 65) and the sword shape (Figs. 61, 62). It should be noted that the city fortifications are probably contemporary with those of the citadel. Of course it may be that the two sculptural groups mentioned came from two different workshops, both active in the Sam'al kingdom in the last third of the ninth century.

It has already been noted that the lion figures known from the time of the empire

FIGS. 61–65 (from left to right) – *Fig. 61: Storm god. From outer citadel gate. Zincirli. After AiS, p. 218, Fig. 114, Pl. 41a. Middle Neo-Hittite style. 832–810 B.C. Cf. p. 99 and above. – Fig. 62: Orthostats from outer citadel gate. Zincirli. After AiS, p. 215, Figs. 105–107, Pl. 37. Middle Neo-Hittite style. 832–810 B.C. Cf. p. 99 and above. – Fig. 63: Griffin demon. Orthostat*

continued unchanged in both the early and the middle Neo-Hittite style. The portal lions of Malatya (Fig. 67), like all the middle Neo-Hittite lions at Zincirli (Figs. 70–74) and Carchemish (Pl. 21; Figs. 68, 69), are essentially variants of the same pictorial type, which can be described as follows.

The head and face always have a cubic shape. The ear takes a round form when it projects (Pl. 21), a heart shape when it lies flat (Figs. 73, 78). The button-like thickenings that appear by the upper part of the ear upon the roll of the mane (Pl. 21; Figs. 68, 69) are a typical Hittite feature. The neck fold that borders the lower part of the face generally takes the form of a roll. If the roll-like fold is lacking, a circle of mane usually serves to set off the face. The auricle is generally bounded by the roll of the mane (Figs. 68, 73, 78). The upper part of the nose, which often shows folds of skin at the root (Figs. 71, 72), is straight. The tip of the nose is often provided with folds of skin (Figs. 68, 72). The high cheek bones are generally bounded by a semi-ellipsoid roll (Figs. 68, 72). Folds of skin beneath the eyes never occur. Although the mouth is usually wide open (Figs. 68–72), it may also be firmly closed (Fig. 67). Especially characteristic is the tongue protruding and depressed against the lower lip. It may even appear this way in lions shown with the mouth closed (Fig. 67). The mane is rarely stylized. In reliefs the paws are generally schematized as claws (Figs. 70–74, 78).

Middle Neo-Hittite lions

The middle Neo-Hittite lions of Zincirli are somewhat mediocre, but iconographically they are faithful examples of the type. There are the relief lions of the southern gate (Fig. 70), the portal lions of the inner citadel gate (Figs. 71, 72), the lions of

Zincirli lions

from outer citadel gate. Zincirli. After AiS, p. 218, Fig. 116, Pl. 42b. Middle Neo-Hittite style. 832–810 B.C. Cf. pp. 99, 102. – Fig. 64: Griffin and sphinx. Orthostat from southern city gate. Zincirli. After AiS, p. 206, Fig. 97, Pl. 34. Middle Neo-Hittite style. 832–810 B.C. Cf. p. 102. – Fig. 65: Griffin demon. Orthostat from southern city gate. Zincirli. After AiS, p. 205, Fig. 95, Pl. 34. Middle Neo-Hittite style. 832–810 B.C. Cf. p. 102.

Gate Building Q (Fig. 73) and the paired lions with the standing figure of the deified king (Fig. 74). The much finer paired lions and the portal lions of Gate Building Q agree in almost all details, forming a closed group that departs considerably from the style of other middle Neo-Hittite lions from this site. The difference between the portal lions of the inner citadel gate (Figs. 71, 72) and the relief lions of the outer citadel gate (Fig. 70) is especially evident in the soft and rounded treatment of the bodies. It is hard to tell whether this stylistic discrepancy reflects a difference in date or simply a change in approach. It is very likely, however, that the Gate Building Q was erected at the same time as Building J. Plans and photographs of the north-west sector of the citadel clearly show that both these structures were built in the same project (Figs. 19, 20).[370] The paired lions supporting statues were outside the gate near the south-east corner of Building J (Fig. 19; indicated St).[371] The sculpture was probably set up during the erection of Building J or shortly after its completion. Recently W. Orthmann has clearly demonstrated that the standing figure represents a deified king.[372] The circumstances may have been as follows. Kilamuwa, who had embellished the interior of the north-west sector with Aramaean works (Fig. 10), wished to pay some flattering attention to his native subjects. So he erected a royal statue in Hittite style outside his Aramaean palace in accordance with the custom of the land. This was understood, I believe, not as portraying a particular king, but as the image of the deified ruler in a general sense. On the thirteenth-century reliefs of Yazilikaya the image of a deified king is represented behind the moon and sun gods, but without the addition of the ideogram of a particular king.[373] This was possibly a case of circumspect piety. Any local person who was confronted by a ruler figure with divine emblems would be tempted to regard it as portraying his own powerful deified king. Thus suggestion was preferred to direct statement. In this way the statue with its divine emblems represented a deceased and consequently

FIG. 66 – *War chariot. Relief from outer citadel gate. Zincirli. After AiS, p. 211, Fig. 102, Pl. 39. Middle Neo-Hittite style. 832–810 B.C. Cf. p. 100.*

deified king, but since it bore no name inscription and did not embody any particular king, it could also pass as the statue of the reigning monarch. The lions of Gate Building Q and the paired lions with the statue of the deified king are in any case works of the Kilamuwa era. This gives us another point of reference to buttress the dating of the middle Neo-Hittite sculptures of Zincirli in the period of *ca.* 832–810.

In the following period the Hittite art tradition seems to have fallen more and more into abeyance. In sculpture at this site it continued only in lions and griffins, although with ever diminishing force. Yet lions of the middle Neo-Hittite type are known from various sites in Syria and Phoenicia (see below). The lions of the Tell Halaf sculptures (Pl. 23a; Fig. 89) and of the Luristan bronzes (Fig. 132) also belong to this type.

The lion figures from Hama are especially important because they are datable by *Hama lions* the circumstances of excavation.[374] P. J. Riis[375] and E. Fugmann[376] have shown that the great lions of Hama must be dated before 800, probably about 825. The resemblance of the lions from Hama to the Zincirli lions of the inner citadel gate is astonishing. The cubic shape of the face and body, the outstretched tongue resting on the lower lip, the projecting round ears and the furrows of the nose, the special modelling of the cheek bones all accord with the features of the Zincirli lions. Thus they provide a useful confirmation for the view that the Zincirli works should be ascribed to the last third of the ninth century.

At Tell Ain Dara in northern Syria Feisal Seirafi[377] has excavated a colossal portal *Tell Ain Dara lions* lion of outstanding quality (Fig. 75), which he has convincingly dated in the ninth-eighth centuries. This lion provides a good parallel to the colossal lions of Hama, for the cubic shape of the face and body, the outstretched tongue resting on the lower lip, the pronounced cheek bones and the projecting round ears found there recur in the Tell Ain Dara lion. The latter piece shows a stylized roll on the legs recalling that on the Hama lions.[378] The volute shape of the claws and the thick enclosing folds are stylistic features that are also found in the lions of Malatya[379] and Carchemish.[380] The lion from Tell Ain Dara is thus representative of the middle Neo-Hittite style. It may have been carved at the end of the ninth or in the first half of the eighth century.

The ivory lion statuette from Al Mina (Pl. 21c, d; Fig. 77) is a characteristic example of the middle Neo-Hittite style (p. 181). With its palmette-like folds beneath the eyes and its round ears, however, the ivory lion head from Samos (Fig. 76) belongs to the late Neo-Hittite style (p. 180).

The middle Neo-Hittite style created a griffin-head type that is peculiar to it. *Middle Neo-Hittite* Hittite art proper has the griffin-head type only in combination with a human *griffin head* body (Figs. 63, 65, 79). But in our period griffin figures with lion bodies are also known; examples have been found at Carchemish,[381] Zincirli[382] and Tell Halaf.[383] Characteristic of the Hittite griffin-head type are the eagle head with horse's ears and the big hair curl spiralling at the top over the head and again beneath the neck (Pl. 21a). The big lock and the horse's ears appear only in Hittite, Aramaean-Hittite, and later in Greek and Etruscan art.

FIGS. 67–69 – *Above, Fig. 67: Detail of portal lion. Malatya. After Akurgal, Späthethitische Bildkunst, p. 46, Pl. 35. Early Neo-Hittite style. 1050–850 B.C. Cf. p. 103. – Below, left, Fig. 68: Lion base. Carchemish. (Cf. Fig. 48.) After Akurgal, Späthethitische Bildkunst, p. 47, Fig. 39. Early to middle Neo-Hittite style. Second half of 8th century B.C. Cf. p. 103. – Below, right, Fig. 69: Lion base. Carchemish. (Cf. Pl. 21a, b.) Early to middle Neo-Hittite style. Second half of 8th century B.C. Cf. p. 103.*

MIDDLE NEO-HITTITE SCULPTURE FROM CARCHEMISH

Carchemish was one of the most important centres of the middle Neo-Hittite style. From this site the following middle Neo-Hittite sculptures should be mentioned: mythological scenes (Figs. 78, 79),[384] procession reliefs (Fig. 81),[385] warrior figures (Fig. 80),[386] musician scenes, [387] victor reliefs (Fig. 86),[388] the sculptures of the royal gate,[389] a great relief of the moon and sun gods,[390] the relief of Katuwas (Fig. 83),[391] paired lions with the statue of Atarluhas (Pl. 21a, b; Fig. 69),[392] paired lions with the statue of a deified king,[393] column lions (Figs. 26, 68),[394] a bull base[395] and other isolated works.

Although these carvings are characteristic examples of the middle Neo-Hittite style, they display two different trends. To the first belong the mythological scenes, the procession reliefs, the warrior and musician scenes, as well as many

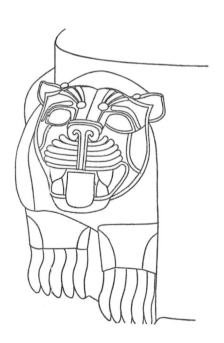

reliefs from the royal gate and the stair gate. These form a homogeneous group. The second trend, which is due to another workshop, includes the Katuwas relief, the orthostat series with victory scenes, the seated image of Atarluhas[396] and the head of the statue of the deified king.[397]

The first group is mainly characterized by a strong dependence on the Anatolian Hittite tradition. The two-headed sphinx (Fig. 78) and the griffin-men supporting the heavens (Fig. 79) are hybrid creatures of mythological type that stem from the Hattusa repertory. The horned cap of the gods, the long queue that reaches as far as the elbows and curling at the bottom, the elongated wedge-shaped beard and the sword sheath curving at the end are other features linking the mythological scenes of Carchemish to the carvings of Malatya and Hattusa. Most of the orthostat slabs under discussion show a preference for flat surfaces. Another peculiarity of this workshop is the reluctance to use the middle Neo-Hittite hair curl. It does appear on a number of pieces of the group (Figs. 84, 85), but so inconspicuously that it can only be recognized after careful scrutiny. It seems that the sculptors of the old school followed the new fashion unwillingly. One of the masters stylizes the manes of his horses with this hair curl, but he omits it in his figures of gods and heroes. He also avoids showing the Assyrian hunting chariot, preferring his own idiosyncratic chariot box.[398] The products of the traditional workshop enjoyed greater popularity, and reliefs of this same type are also found in Til Barsib.[399] Hallmarks of the workshop are the strong projection of the chin bones (Figs. 78, 80, 81; Pl. 22b) and the stylization, in the form of two or three pearls (Fig. 78), the claws on the lion's paw in the foreground. These two features recur in the works from Til Barsib mentioned above (Fig. 82).[400] All the lions created in the middle Neo-Hittite style at Carchemish must be regarded as products of this workshop. The lion bases (Fig. 68, 69; Pl. 21a) may also belong to this group, though the statues they support should be attributed to the other school of sculptors.

The statues—the seated figure of Atarluhas,[401] the head of the deified king,[402] the Katuwas relief (Fig. 83) and the orthostat reliefs with scenes of victory (Fig. 86)[403]—make up a separate stylistic group. The connecting link is the middle Neo-Hittite hair style, and the best examples of this found anywhere are among these works.

Anatolian Hittite features

H. G. Güterbock has rightly emphasized the close relationship between the mythological scenes and the victory reliefs.[404] The reason for this similarity is probably that both series belong to the middle Neo-Hittite style. It is clear, however, that despite the close stylistic relationship they follow two different trends. The carvers of the victory reliefs, that is the sculptors of the second trend, are artists representing a new current in Neo-Hittite culture. They show a predilection for Assyrian motifs, such as severed heads[405] and hands, and depict Assyrian war chariots being driven over the bodies of slain enemies (Fig. 86). Even when they present warrior figures in the early Neo-Hittite manner, they do not hesitate to place a miniature figure or the severed head of a defeated enemy in the hand of the victor.[406] This grim practice would have been unthinkable in the

Two different style trends

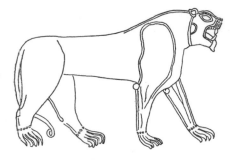

traditional middle-Neo-Hittite style or early Neo-Hittite style. Yet in Zincirli, where the native population was subject to a ruling caste of Aramaean origin, there was no purely Hittite workshop. As we have seen, in this city the Assyrian and Aramaean mentality dominated the approach to art from the beginning. Despite the differences in approach and the clearly divergent stylistic tendencies, the two trends of the middle Neo-Hittite style of Carchemish described above were contemporary. One of the finds gives proof of this. As H. G. Güterbock has indicated,[407] the second warrior figure from the right on the orthostat with the warrior scenes is unworked in the lower section because it was covered by the base and therefore invisible to the observer. The paired lions and the statue resting on them (with a splendid head[408] in the style of the Katuwas relief) were thus erected in the same building campaign as these fine examples of the more traditional tendency. The warrior figures, like the reliefs with the mythological scenes, have the same prominent jaw-bone and the same long queue with a curl at the bottom reaching as far as the elbow.

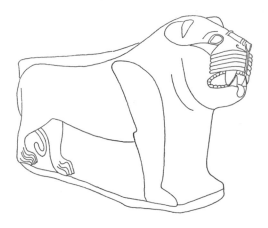

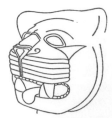

FIGS. 71, 72 – *Portal lion from inner citadel gate. Zincirli. After AiS, pp. 230–4, Figs. 138–40, Pl. 46. Early to middle Neo-Hittite style. 832–810 B.C. Cf. pp. 100, 103.*

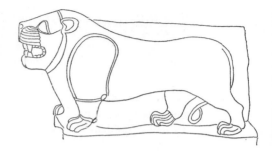

FIG. 73 – *Lion from Gate Building Q. Zincirli. After AiS, p. 244, Figs. 151, 152; p. 271, Fig. 177; p. 369, Pl. 65. Middle Neo-Hittite style. 832–810 B.C. Cf. pp. 100, 103.*

As W. Orthmann has aptly demonstrated,[409] the statue mentioned depicts a deified king. I believe that one can draw the same conclusions in this instance as at Zincirli (p. 103). The Carchemish statue must also be a generic representation of the deceased and therefore deified king with a specific allusion to Katuwas. Katuwas, who commissioned all the sculptures of the middle Neo-Hittite style at Carchemish from two workshops, must also have erected this statue of a deified ruler. It forms a pendent to the cult image of the storm god Atarluhas which was set up in front of the inner royal portal.[410]

It is worth while to attempt to date the inception of the middle Neo-Hittite style at Carchemish (and consequently of the reign of Katuwas) with the aid of the archaeological material. The only certain *point d'appui* for dating is the chariots shown on the victory reliefs (Fig. 86). The Carchemish sculptor created his war chariots chiefly on the basis of Assyrian models in the Classical style (Pls. 1, 8).[411] The horses' head-dress derives from similar Assyrian sources; the plume in the form of a broad tuft is set in a horseshoe-shaped holder bedecked with two cords or bands (Fig. 4). In the Carchemish horses the bands or streamers are replaced by a bundle of hair fluttering in the wind. There is no doubt that this is a modification of Assyrian motifs. This modified type seems to be a middle Neo-Hittite speciality, for the warrior reliefs of the traditional type have the same shape (Fig. 80). The band that connects the shaft-end with the upper front edge of the chariot box is also a typical feature of the Assyrian chariot scenes in the Classical style (Pls. 1, 8). The small chariot box and the shield attached at the back with its boss decoration which serves as a clasp, are important characteristics of the Assyrian chariot relief in the Classical style. Only the treatment of the sides of the chariot box at Carchemish points to Assyrian models in the transitional style (Pl. 2). We have seen above (p. 38) that the embellishment of the chariot box with rosettes or similar motifs first appears in the time of Tiglath-Pileser III (745–727). Consequently all the sculptures of the middle Neo-Hittite style at Carchemish (and the reign of Katuwas) must date after 745. But how can this dating be reconciled with Assyrian sources indicating that in the period 745–717 a king named Pisiris was reigning in Carchemish? Some years ago I tried to solve this problem in my book *Späthethi-*

Use of chariot scenes for dating

tische Bildkunst, where I assumed that the shift in Assyrian art—at least so far as the chariot types are concerned—may have taken place not in the time of Tiglath-Pileser, but somewhat earlier.[412] But the Assyrian sculptures we have from the so-called weak period of the Assyrian empire (824–745) continue the Classical style unchanged, as we have seen (p. 32). Therefore I now believe that in this period chariot renderings did not undergo any transformations of style and type. For intensive research in the Neo-Hittite period confronted me with a new problem. I was struck by the fact that until now hieroglyphic scholars have nowhere found evidence of the name of King Pisiris. How could it be possible that this king who was in power for twenty-eight years (745–717), if not even longer, did not leave a single inscription in hieroglyphics, when the Neo-Hittite kings were notoriously eager to boast of their achievements and works? I therefore

Katuwas = Pisiris   asked myself whether Katuwas and Pisiris could not be two names for the same king. I. J. Gelb[413] and after him H. G. Güterbock[414] have shown that many Hittite kings bore double names. So it is quite possible that Katuwas, who named himself with this style in the hieroglyphic monuments, was known to the Assyrians under his personal name of Pisiris. This hypothesis not only serves to open the way to the dating suggested above, but it frees us from the unlikely assumption that the last king who reigned in Carchemish from 745 to 717 erected no monuments. If Pisiris was identical with Katuwas, we can attribute all the middle Neo-Hittite sculptures of Carchemish to the third quarter of the eighth century. Naturally it is possible that some of the work was continued until 717 when Carchemish was conquered by Sargon. At that time Araras dismantled some of Katuwas' sculptures to replace them with work of his own (Fig. 93).

FIGS. 74, 75 – *Left, Fig. 74: Lion base of standing image of the deified king. Zincirli. After Akurgal, Kunst der Hethiter, Pls. 126, 127. (Cf. AiS, pp. 363 ff., Figs. 262–9.) Middle Neo-Hittite style. 832–810 B.C. Cf. pp. 100, 103. – Right, Fig. 75: Colossal portal lion at Tell Ain Dara, northern Syria. Middle Neo-Hittite style. 8th century B.C. Cf. note 377 and p. 105.*

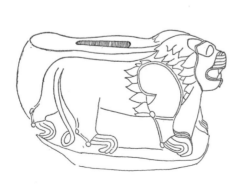 

FIGS. 76, 77 – Left, Fig. 76: Lion's head. Ivory. Found on Samos. After Buschor, Altsamische Standbilder, vol. III, Figs. 214, 215. Aramaeanizing Hittite style. Late 8th century B.C. Cf. pp. 105, 180. – Right, Fig. 77: Lion statuette from Al Mina. Ivory. (Cf. Pls. 21c, d.) Middle Neo-Hittite style. Second half of 8th century B.C. Ashmolean Museum, Oxford. Cf. pp. 105, 181.

SCULPTURE
FROM TELL
HALAF

A noteworthy workshop of middle Neo-Hittite sculpture was active in Tell Halaf. A homogeneous style that can be termed middle Neo-Hittite can be seen in the small orthostats[415] which decorated the southern outer wall in the southern part of the west wall and east wall of the *hilani* building (Fig. 87), in the big orthostats[416] which were built into the niche walls right and left of the *hilani* entrance (Pls. 88, 89), and also in the figures in the round from this site (Pls. 23, 24).[417] In form and content the basic features of the sculpture of Tell Halaf are clearly middle Neo-Hittite. The two-headed sphinx,[418] the scene of a man slain by two others,[419] the animal-men with peaked horned caps that appear either without attributes (Fig. 87) or else bear the winged sun disk,[420] the boomerang held in the hands of gods,[421] or of heroes,[422] the couple in which the man appears to the woman's right[423]—all these are pictorial ideas and motifs that belong to the early and middle Neo-Hittite styles. As G. Loud has shown, the demons with double lion heads[424] and the running hero with bent knees and raised hands[425] from Tell Halaf appear on an ivory relief[426] of the late second millennium from Megiddo that bears the impress of strong Hittite influence. The Megiddo piece suggests that the spread of these motifs in the Near East is due to the impetus of Anatolian Hittite art. Of course it is also possible that the Hittite features mentioned reached Tell Halaf by way of Phoenician art, since (as will be shown) the Tell Halaf sculptures betray close links with Phoenician culture. But many Hittite motifs at Tell Halaf, such as the triad consisting of the sky god, the great mother and the divine sun (Pl. 23a), seem to come directly from Hattusa.[427]

The long tunic with short sleeves, simple belt and fringe at the bottom[428] tallies with Katuwas' costume at Carchemish (Fig. 83). Similarly, the short apron with a vertical fold in the middle, the simple belt and the hem without a fringe correspond to the pattern of male dress in the early and middle Neo-Hittite styles (Figs. 60–65, 79–83). Without exception, the bearded figures appear in the Hittite fashion with the upper lip shaven (Figs. 87, 88). The mythological figures that were taken over in Neo-Hittite art[429] wear long queues curled up at the bottom as in the Carchemish sculptures. The chariot shaft ending in the form of a griffin protome[430] shows that the chariot type does not come straight from Assyrian models, but

*Middle Neo-Hittite
traits in Tell Halaf
sculpture*

from Neo-Hittite intermediaries. This terminal feature is absent in Assyrian art. Note that as in the Zincirli chariots the Tell Halaf sculptor has mistakenly placed the griffin head on the reins (Fig. 66). Moreover, the form of the head-dress of the horses and the cross-hatching of the rope connecting the chariot box to the shaft-end are derived from Zincirli, along with the chariot type as a whole. The lion type offers a true parallel to the early and middle Neo-Hittite works. The lions of Tell Halaf appear with mouths wide-open, outstretched tongues pressing on the lower lip, the stylized ear heart-shaped, the tip of the nose furrowed, the small curl of the mane and the face in cubic shape (Fig. 89; Pl. 23a). These are faithful imitations of early and middle Neo-Hittite figures as seen at Malatya, Carchemish and Zincirli (Figs. 67–74). However, there are also many interesting stylizations in the manner of Syro-Phoenician animal figures. The griffin heads of Tell Halaf[431] have spiral locks on the neck and the beaks closed. It is certain that these two features are characteristic traits of the middle Neo-Hittite griffin type. A big bird's head from Tell Halaf[432] shows the same two large locks on the neck and the same 'hem' on the lower part of the neck as in the griffin heads of Carchemish. More-

FIGS. 78–83 (from left to right) – *Fig. 78: Chimaera. Carchemish. After Woolley, Carchemish, vol. I, Pl. B 14a. Middle Neo-Hittite style. Second half of 8th century B.C. Cf. pp. 100, 107, 188. – Fig. 79: Griffin demon. Carchemish. After Woolley, Carchemish, vol. I, Pl. B 12. Middle Neo-Hittite style (traditional school). Second half of the 8th century B.C. Cf. p. 101. – Fig. 80: Warrior. Carchemish. After Woolley, Carchemish, vol. I, Pl. B 2a. Middle Neo-Hittite style (traditional school). Second half of 8th century B.C. Cf. p. 107. – Fig. 81: Ibex bearer. Carchemish.*

over, the alternating use of basalt and limestone in the orthostats is Neo-Hittite; it is also found at Carchemish.

Assyrian influence was marked, for the Aramaean kings of Tell Halaf adopted the Assyrian script and language. Apart from the chariot reliefs,[433] which copy Assyrian models without real understanding, Assyrian features appear in the coiffure, dress and weapons.[434] The cloak worn by the gods is also Assyrian, as well as the thick shock of hair diagonally placed at the neck, the pointed helmet, the round shield and the short sword.

Assyrian traits

Very close links existed with Syro-Phoenician culture. Phoenician models not only inspire the palmette-tree[435] that appears in late Hittite art, but also the vegetable filler motifs[436] on the small orthostats (Fig. 112). Special mention must be made of the small orthostat slab showing a man climbing to the top of a palm-tree on a ladder,[437] a scene that seems foreign to this area and was probably suggested by Syro-Phoenician models. The ship scene[438] may also be attributed with certainty to Syro-Phoenician influence. Entirely Phoenician is the motif of a winged man fighting a lion (and in one instance a hybrid creature).[439] The pose with arm bent

Syro-Phoenician traits at Tell Halaf

After Woolley, Carchemish, vol. I, Pl. 22b. Middle Neo-Hittite style (traditional school). Second half of 8th century B.C. Cf. p. 107. – Fig. 82: Storm god. Til Barsib. After Thureau-Dangin, Til Barsib, Pls. 9, 10. Middle Neo-Hittite style, Carchemish workshop (traditional school). Second half of 8th century B.C. Cf. p. 107. – Fig. 83: King Katuwas (Pisiris) of Carchemish. After Woolley, Carchemish, vol. II, Pl. A 13d. Middle Neo-Hittite style (modern school). Second half of 8th century B.C. Cf. pp. 107, 110.

back aiming the sword is characteristically Phoenician; it appears on Phoenician ivories of the late second millennium,[440] recurring on Phoenician bowls of the eighth and seventh centuries B.C.[441] The embellishment of the *poloi* (cylindrical caps) of the gods with alternating rosettes and palm-trees[442] is a feature of Syro-Phoenician architectural ornament known to us from Hama.[443]

In the context of these close links with the south the concentric arrangement[444] of the curls of hair and the hair mass, which is overlaid with a square pattern of incised lines suggesting a net,[445] must be due to the influence of Phoenician works, which provide the best examples of this linear stylization of hair (Figs. 103–111). The Phoenician character of the stylization of the bodies of the Tell Halaf animals (Figs. 87–89) has recently been demonstrated by R. D. Barnett.[446] Together with Barnett's statements the following schematizations can be found: (1) flame-like forms on the thigh of the rear leg; (2) diagonally incised lines running parallel to the silhouette of the back from the root of the tail to the shoulder and commonly bounded at either end by a series of short strokes; (3) abdominal hair with zigzag stripes forming hatched triangular fields; (4) V-shaped mane tufts; (5) ankles in the form of lozenges with horizontal double lines.

All five elements of stylization are common to the animal bodies of the Tell Halaf sculptures and Syro-Phoenician ivories. The sculptors of Tell Halaf did omit the two or three pearls generally shown between the diagonal lines of the ankle in Phoenician ivories,[447] because basalt did not invite such detailed rendering (Figs. 87–89).

The Tell Halaf lion type (Fig. 89) has one feature that appears elsewhere only on the portal lion of Tell Ain Dara. This is a thick diagonal or horizontal line leading beneath the ear from the roll of the mane to the edge of the eye (Fig. 75). The lion from Zincirli (Fig. 13), which comes from the time of King Sargon, has a similar cord-like fold that runs from the ear to the palmette stylizations beneath the cheek bone. This may represent a variant of the stylization found in the lions of Tell Halaf.

Dating
(730–700 B.C.)

The links connecting the main features of the Tell Halaf sculpture with the middle Neo-Hittite style indicate a date within the period 850–750/730 B.C. However, a number of stylistic features suggest that within this span the works originate from the very end, and even betray traces of the late Neo-Hittite style. Before entering into this question, it should be pointed out that the small orthostats (originally numbering over 200) form a group apart. It has long been recognized that the small orthostats were re-employed on the *hilani* building and that many earlier inscriptions on the slabs were erased by Kapara to make way for his own. A. Moortgat[448] has dealt with this question in detail, concluding that the small orthostats must belong to the older building erected before the time of Kapara. He has also pointed to a number of stylistic differences that distinguish the small orthostats from the other carvings, but which (as he states) must be regarded as differences in quality.[449] At this point it is worth noting several features of style and costume in the large orthostats and in the sculptures in the round that do not appear on the small orthostats and which may serve as criteria

for dating. The figures of gods (Pl. 23a) and the hunter figures (Fig. 88) on two large orthostat reliefs in a niche of the *hilani* façade wear Assyrian costume, which first appears in Neo-Hittite art in the demons of Sakçegözü (Pl. 15a). The garments consist of a short tunic and a long cloak. Characteristically, the seam of the cloak exposes the forward leg, leaving it free. This fashion was current in Neo-Assyrian art from the ninth century onwards. In the second half of the eighth century, however, it took on a modified form that differs in cut from the examples of the Classical style. In the ninth century[450] the almost straight outer edge of the seam of the cloak starts well above the belt, which it leaves almost free and runs almost straight to the ankles. But in the sculpture of the time of Sargon the outer edge of the cloak's seam begins below the belt; from this point it trails down in a buoyant curve (Pl. 3). The demon reliefs of the Sakçegözü orthostats (Pl. 15a) have the same costume as seen in the examples mentioned of the time of Sargon. This type persisted in the transitional style of Neo-Assyrian art (p. 32), for a very similar instance occurs from the time of Tiglath-Pileser III.[451] It appears that the demons of the Sakçegözü reliefs derive from models of the Tiglath-Pileser period, while the Tell Halaf examples in turn depend on models such as those found at Sakçegözü. We have seen above that the chariot carvings of Tell Halaf come not from Assyrian but from Neo-Hittite prototypes (p. 112).

Some genius figures of the small orthostats of Tell Halaf[452] have the same costume in its older Assyrian form. The costume as well as the iconography of the genius figures goes straight back to Assyrian works. The big shock of hair on the nape of the neck also comes from Assyrian models in the Classical style, whose influence persisted into the middle of the eighth century. In any event, the costume of the hunter and god figures (Pls. 23, 24; Fig. 88) is much closer to examples from Sakçegözü than to the costume of the small orthostats from Tell Halaf. This comparison demonstrates that the makers of the large orthostats and figures of gods knew later Neo-Hittite features that were unfamiliar to those who carved the small orthostats. One decorative feature, which at first sight might seem trivial, the triple zigzag or wave motif, which may be seen on the fore ankle of the lion figure of the *hilani* entrance (Pl. 23a),[453] attests the strength of the late Neo-Hittite-Aramaean current. This decorative motif appears for the first time in the lions of Sakçegözü (Fig. 14) and in Hilani III at Zincirli (Fig. 12)[454] from about 730. No decoration of this kind may be seen on any of the older lions belonging

Carvings from Tell Halaf

FIG. 86 – *War chariot. Carchemish. After Woolley, Carchemish, vol. III, Pl. B 42a. Middle Neo-Hittite style (modern or advanced school). Second half of 8th century* B.C. Cf. pp. 107, 109.

Anklets   to the middle Neo-Hittite style. The goddess[455] wears four anklets on each leg.[456] Similar anklets recur in a late Neo-Hittite work, the female figure of a couple from Maraş (Pl. 26). It is clear that these were understood as real circlets because the Tell Halaf goddess wears two further sets of four as bracelets. It is noteworthy that on many Syrian ivories also the ankles are adorned with four circlets. The fashion of wearing four anklets may have been current in Syria during the last quarter of the eighth century.

Coiffure   The long spiralling locks of the woman in the Tell Halaf couple extended in the round[457] recall the hair style of the demons of Sakçegözü (Pl. 15a). The same coiffure recurs in two Syrian ivories found at Toprakkale (Fig. 111), which date from the time of Rusas II (685–645). It is found again in the human-shaped Urartian cauldron attachments (Pl. 45), belonging to the last quarter of the eighth century. All these comparisons show that the large orthostats and the sculptures in the round of Tell Halaf were made in the last third of the eighth century.

Some years ago I dated the Tell Halaf sculptures—which are discussed here for the sake of comparison—to the ninth century at the earliest.[458] But an exhaustive stylistic analysis shows, as we have seen, that these sculptures are really late works. The artists of Tell Halaf adopted the style of Syro-Phoenician ivories for their

FIG. 87 – *Winged lion with human head. From the series of small orthostats. Tell Halaf. After Tell Halaf, vol. III, Pl. 87a. Middle Neo-Hittite style. 760–730* B.C. Cf. pp. 111, 114.

animal figures. The flame-like stylization on the thighs and the other stylizations of the animal bodies certainly appear on Phoenician ivories as early as the end of the second millennium. We now know, however, that ivories with the same animal body stylizations were also produced in the last quarter of the eighth century. Through his successful excavations at Nimrud (Kalkhu), M. E. L. Mallowan has demonstrated that a number of the finest ivories may be ascribed to the end of the eighth or indeed to the seventh century.[459] Moreover, R. D. Barnett has repeatedly affirmed a dating at the end of the eighth or the beginning of the seventh century.[460] M. E. L. Mallowan has also spoken in favour of a late dating for the Tell Halaf sculpture. To be sure, he admits that the carvings might be as early as the last quarter of the ninth century,[461] but does not exclude the possibility that some orthostats might have been extended later.

Flame-like stylization

The genius drawing his sword with a backward thrust of the arm, in a very characteristic gesture, to meet a threatening lion is a motif that appears on Phoenician bowls of the eighth and seventh centuries, as has already been noted (p. 114). Other features all point to a late dating, possibly to the last third of the eighth century. It is not necessary to rehearse these arguments here, for there is another important criterion that definitively resolves the question of dating.

A tomb in the north-west part of the *hilani* area secreted a cache of gold and bronze objects with style elements that provide reliable criteria for dating the Tell Halaf buildings and sculptures. According to the excavators the well-lined underground chamber lay below the front of the terrace of the *hilani*; consequently it belongs to the time of Kapara, to the so-called old building period (p. 119).[462] This means that the *hilani* building and the sculptures in the entry niche are later than the cache material. Of the many funerary gifts recovered from the tomb only a few may be mentioned here: a half-oval plaquette in gold (Pl. 25),[463] three bronze

Small finds as elements in dating

FIGS. 88, 89 – *Left, Fig. 88: Hunting scene. From the series of large orthostats on the façade. Tell Halaf. After Tell Halaf, vol. III, Pl. 103. Middle Neo-Hittite style with late Neo-Hittite traits. 730–700 B.C. Cf. pp. 111, 114. – Right, Fig. 89: Lion. From the series of large orthostats on the façade. Tell Halaf. After Tell Halaf, vol. III, Pl. 106. Middle Neo-Hittite style with late Neo-Hittite traits. 730–700 B.C. Cf. p. 114.*

vessels (Figs. 90–92)[464] and three gold ear-rings.[465] The gold plaquette, which
B. Hrouda claims was a piece of jewellery for the front of a head-dress, has a
scene that certainly recalls the depictions on the small orthostats, although it is
in a somewhat different style. The stylization on the thighs of the rear legs may
be a simplified version of the flame-like notchings. But it may also be interpreted
in terms of the M-shaped scheme found on animals of the Neo-Hittite style
(Figs. 5j, 12, 13), for the other four stylizations that we find in animal bodies of
the small reliefs are lacking (Fig. 87). Yet as A. Moortgat has shown,[466] the tree
is almost the same as in the reliefs in question. Then, too, the parallel lines of the
goats' necks recur on many animal figures of the small orthostats.[467] The gold
plaquette may come from a Syrian goldsmith's workshop that had close links
with the art centres of northern Syria and Anatolia. The imbricated pattern
suggesting a hilly landscape on which the palm-tree stands also comes from the
Anatolian Hittite sphere. The coloured enamel inlay originally filling both the
cells of the palmette and imbricated pattern is a technique that was at home in
Syria.

Two of the bronze vessels are entirely Phrygian in style (Figs. 90, 91). The
cauldron has the specifically Phrygian knuckle-bone handle[468] and an overall shape
that recalls the bronze cauldrons of the *deinos* type from Gordion.[469] The pitcher
(Fig. 91) with its vertical and tall handle placed at a right angle to the elongated
tubular spout follows a characteristic shape of Phrygian art.[470] These two vessels
date from the last third of the eighth century at the earliest. In any event this type
of Phrygian pitcher was very popular in the Near East. One of the finest ceramic
examples has come to light at Carchemish.[471] Similar Phrygian pitchers are depicted
on a Carchemish relief[472] and on an orthostat from Karatepe (Pl. 32).[473] The two
Phrygian bronze vessels from the Tell Halaf cache thus provide a reliable criterion
for dating the *hilani* and its carvings to the last third of the eighth century—a
dating that has already been established on the basis of other stylistic comparisons
in architecture (pp. 73, 87) and carvings (p. 115). Moreover, Tell Halaf has
yielded a small sherd in the old Phrygian style.[474] It is only a tiny fragment, but
there is no doubt that it is a typical Phrygian product, which belongs to the third
quarter of the eighth century[475] and thus confirms our dating.

The bowl with the lotus-star handles (Fig. 92) speaks for the same dating. B.
Hrouda has set forth the close parallels for this vessel in finds from Til Barsib,
Cyprus, Olympia and Nimrud.[476] One may also cite a piece from Gordion (Fig.
148),[477] a fragment in the Metropolitan Museum in New York (Fig. 147)[478] and
finally ceramic copies from the Kerameikos cemetery in Athens (Fig. 144).[479]
The Phrygian bowl may be placed at the end of the eighth century at the earliest.
The Phrygian and Greek imitations indicate that in the last quarter of the eighth
century the oriental originals were very much in demand. In this way we have a
further confirmation of the fact that the buildings and sculpture of the Kapara
era may be dated to the period *ca.* 730–700.

A. Moortgat has convincingly attributed the gold ear-rings to the ninth century.[480]
It is not particularly surprising that this jewellery is several generations older than

the other objects deposited in the cache. Items of jewellery, notably ear-rings,
were given by parents and especially by grandmothers to their children and
grandchildren. They ought not to be used in dating the cache in question. Since
we have dated the large orthostats (Figs. 88, 89), the sculptures in the round
(Pls. 23, 24), and consequently the *hilani* building (Fig. 25) of Kapara in the last
third of the eighth century, we ought to date the older building and the small
orthostats (which are fairly close to the large orthostats in time) approximately to
the second third of the eighth century. The carvers of the small orthostats were
modest stonemasons. The master who executed the large orthostats was probably
trained in the same workshop in which the small orthostats were made. The
highly gifted artist who carved the sculptures in the *hilani* recess must also have
belonged to this workshop, since he employed the same iconographic and
stylistic repertory as all the other sculptors of Tell Halaf. He was highly sophisti-
cated and his artistic innovations show him to be a master of unusual stature. To
him we owe the transformation of the small supporting figures of the Syrian
minor arts into monumental creations. He invented the pictorial motif of the
'caryatids',[481] a happy blend of sculpture with architecture (Pls. 23, 24).

As a result of the constant pressure of Assyrian and Aramaean influences the
traditional Hittite features of the art of southern Anatolia and northern Syria were
gradually obliterated. These two foreign influences, combined with those of other
neighbouring countries, generally appear in mixed form in the carvings of the

*Period of small
orthostats
(760–730 B.C.)*

LATE NEO-
HITTITE STYLE

PLATE 26 – Funerary stele of a couple from Maraş. Late Neo-Hittite
stylistic phase (Aramaeanizing Hittite style). Late 8th or early 7th century
B.C. *Archaeological Museum, Adana. Overall height 1 m. Cf. p. 127.*

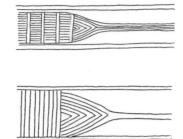

models of the time of Tiglath-Pileser III as from those of Sargon (p. 37). But the nape hair of some officers of the Araras slabs[495] and especially the hair of the two princes (Fig. 93) is vertically arranged and lies on the shoulders, so that the work can only have been carved during or after the Sargonid era (Pl. 3). The plastically formed lock ends and the round nape shocks are done in completely Sargonid style. In some figures of the Araras orthostats, the way in which the neck hair is arranged in loose overlapping locks (Fig. 94) closely recalls the neck hair of the Gilgamesh figures of Sargon.[496] The features shared with the Sakçegözü reliefs— the cloak with the end held in one hand (cf. the mother with the child and the animal), the vertical rear folds of the sandal type and the stylization of the front legs of the goat-like animal (Fig. 97)—suggest a date after 730. The belt (Figs. 95, 96), which is a creation of the Sennacherib period, also indicates a date towards the end of the eighth century. Since the Araras reliefs appear in place of the Assyrian middle Neo-Hittite reliefs of Katuwas (i.e., Pisiris; see p. 121), they must have been executed after the conquest of the city of Carchemish by the Assyrians in 717 B.C. Assyria did not maintain a regular governor in the city; only two governors are mentioned, in 691 and 646, as active in Carchemish in the name of the Assyrian kings. Consequently, the usurper Araras[497] and his son Kamanas may have reigned in the interval between 717 and 691. A later ascription to a date during the first third of the seventh century is possible, but the comparisons adduced above point rather to the period from 717 to 691.

B. Landsberger has clearly shown that in the Anatolian provinces Assyrian power declined in the period between 705 and 685 B.C.[498] He believes that for a time the provincial capital of Sam'al could not be held for Sennacherib. He 'had to go to great trouble just to keep a part of the Anatolian legacy of his predecessor, except for the province of Tabal-Hilakku, which was lost for ever, probably as early as the end of Sargon's reign.'[499] Under these political conditions it is possible that Araras was able to ascend the throne, claiming a modest degree of independence for Carchemish.

Some hieroglyphic specialists date the Araras reliefs before 750. But the basis of their dating is uncertain. I have studied the problem with the friendly assistance of the hieroglyphic scholar F. Steinherr.[500] One of the chief arguments for this dating depends on the identification of certain hieroglyphic signs on the Araras reliefs with the name of the Assyrian king Assurdan (771–745). But this group of signs

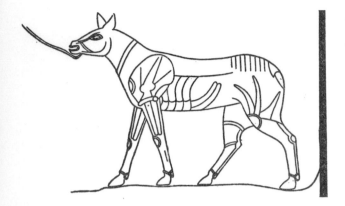

FIG. 97 – *Animal figure from the great relief of Araras. After Woolley, Carchemish, vol. I, Pl. B 8. Late Neo-Hittite style. 717–691 B.C. Cf. pp. 122, 125.*

can just as easily be interpreted as Essarhaddon (680–669). Hieroglyphic specialists have decided in favour of the reading Assurdan because they assume that Araras could not have reigned after 717, that is after the Assyrian conquest of the city of Carchemish. However this may be, the identification does not seem to be correct. I must recall here the critical remarks of J. Friedrich,[501] who has shown Th. Bossert's Carchemish interpretations to be without foundation. E. Laroche interprets the hieroglyphs anonymously as simply 'an Assyrian king'[502] and thus also seems to disagree with Th. Bossert's view.

Further supporting evidence advanced by hieroglyphic scholars is the reading of the Urartian name 'Sasturis'. But anyone who has carefully studied Th. Bossert's article[503] must be convinced of the impossibility of this identification. For his interpretation also involves the names Midas and Muski.[504] If these readings are valid, however, the identification with Assurdan cannot hold. Midas, who is mentioned in the Assyrian annals between 717 and 709 as king of Phrygia, cannot easily be a contemporary of Assurdan. All this shows that these decipherings are far from providing certain criteria for dating.

FIG. 98

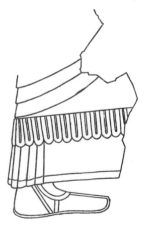

FIGS. 98, 99 – *Above, Fig. 98: Back pleats of chiton and sandals on the Araras relief. After Akurgal, Späthethitische Bildkunst, p. 37, Fig. 20. Cf. Fig. 93 and p. 122. – Left, Fig. 99: Back pleats of chiton and sandals on a relief from Sakçegözü. After Akurgal, Späthethitische Bildkunst, p. 37, Fig. 19. Aramaean style. About 730 B.C. (and later). Archaeological Museum, Ankara. Cf. p. 122.*

stele from Maraş,[509] in which the woman sits on the man's right side. But the mediocre quality of this piece suggests that the sculptor was unfamiliar with Hittite practice. In our slab the boy seems to be the deceased person. His mother holds him on her lap, for he evidently died at a fairly early age. The two knuckle bones beneath his left hand may, if they do really represent knuckle bones, indicate that the son was not an adolescent, but still depended on his 'mother's' (or nurse's) guidance. Studying the original in the Louvre, I believed that the bobbin-shaped object beneath the boy's left hand consists of two knuckle bones. But now, looking at the photograph, I have the impression that the bobbin-shaped object is attached to the end of the cord in order to prevent it slipping out of his hand. Anyhow the fact that the boy is standing on the woman's lap indicates his youth. Yet the boy had learned to read and write. He is holding the stylus in his right hand between the thumb and index finger as if ready to write. At the top of the slab are five characters in Hittite hieroglyphics that may be read as 'Tarhunpiya'.[510] This was the dead boy's name. One of his favourite games in life must have been catching birds. This was an aristocratic diversion among Near Eastern magnates and wealthy men until recent times. That the boy had wealthy parents is proved by his training in reading and writing and the jewels. Although he is wearing a simple Hittite belt, the collar of his long tunic is decorated with elegant embroidery. His upper arm and wrist are adorned with bracelets, and his neck displays a torque. Both ends of the bracelets terminate in lions' heads, the ends of the torque in ducks' heads. These five pieces of jewellery were probably made of gold. Love of luxury is seen also in the adornment of the ear with fine jewels. Apart from the pendents on the ear lobes, we note—as on the female figure of the large funerary stele from Maraş (Pl. 26)—decorative pieces around the auricle, which were probably worked with pearls or precious stones. Like all the other figures of the Maraş funerary stelae, the boy is wearing elegant sandals. The 'mother' is dressed in the same fashion as the two female figures of the funerary stele with the couple and their daughter (Pl. 28). Her cloak is cut in exactly the same way as the garment of the mother on the relief under discussion with the difference that the lower part of her tunic has no folds, but hangs down smoothly. In our relief, the woman's tender embrace of the child recalls the woman with the child on the Araras relief[511] and the mother with daughter in the previously described relief from Maraş (Pl. 28). In the Maraş stele mentioned above, published by M. Kalaş,[512] the same motif recurs, in which the child is depicted in an upright standing position. Some years ago, following F. von Luschan, I identified the slabs we have been discussing as funerary stelae.[513] Another *Funerary stelae* funerary stele from Maraş, which is now in Paris (Fig. 100),[514] shows a man holding a balance in his right hand. This seems to characterize him as a merchant. He has the same coiffure with spiral curls as is found in the reliefs under discussion. Another funerary stele from Maraş, now in Adana, shows a man with a stylus[515] and a writing tablet, who is therefore a scribe (Fig. 101).

All these slabs featuring figures with tools and objects from daily life do not—as *Attributes of* some scholars believe—depict gods, but should rather be interpreted as images of *various professions* deceased persons who are commemorated with the tools of their profession. Recently Mustafa Kalaç[516] has published a slab depicting a storm god which clearly indicates that in Maraş and the neighbourhood cult stelae following the Hittite-Luvian tradition were also produced. However, in this case the god, who has a beard with Aramaean spiral curls, is shown in the usual way with the horned conical cap, trident and hammer. A winged sun disk on the god's head probably indicates that he is to be understood as the figure of a deified king. However this may be, from this stele it is clearly evident that Hittites and Luvians also lived in Maraş and that the cult stelae are to be distinguished from funerary stelae through such unmistakable divine attributes as the horned cap and the trident. If the figures on reliefs we have classified as funerary stelae were actually divinities the artists would have provided them with the appropriate emblems, as in the case of the relief showing the storm god.

Dating of funerary stelae

The funerary stelae from Maraş and vicinity belong to the same period and radiate the same spirit. The fine spiral forms that are modelled in high relief on the hair lock ends of the boy's head on the Paris stele (Pl. 29) follow the Sargonid fashion (Pl. 3). They have the same natural curl effect and volumetric fullness as in the reliefs of the time of Sargon. Both the Sargonid and Aramaean spiral lock ends have a knob-like thickening in the centre. The lock ends of the wine merchant from Maraş (Pls. 26, 27) are executed in the same high relief. This close dependence on Sargonid work, which is reflected especially in the hair style, suggests that the funerary stelae from Maraş should be dated to the end of the eighth century. The close relation with the Sakçegözü reliefs, which is noticeable in the Aramaean treatment of the folds, also speaks in favour of a dating towards the end of the eighth century. The mother and daughter of the Maraş stele (Pl. 28) have garments with thick masses of folds, probably following Aramaean models, e.g. the costume of the Zincirli princess (Pl. 13). Since the funerary stele of the princess of the Barrakab period was executed about 730 B.C. (p. 56), the Maraş funerary stelae may have been made in the last third of the eighth century or slightly later, about 700. It is possible, however, that the custom of erecting richly carved funerary stelae continued into the seventh century in Maraş and vicinity.

In the above-mentioned book I have pointed out that none of the stelae of Maraş, which lack divine attributes, are orthostats; rather are they monuments intended to stand alone. In their undamaged state they had a lower projection that served to fix them in the ground or in a stand. Thus these stelae should be understood as funerary stelae (Pls. 26, 29, Figs. 100, 101). With their scenes of family life, captured in a touching and lively idiom, they herald the Attic funerary stelae of the Greek Classical style.

PLATE 31 – Gate sphinx at Karatepe. Late Neo-Hittite stylistic phase (Aramaeanizing Hittite style). About 700 B.C. *Cf. pp. 129, 137.*

An important question still remains to be discussed. The funerary stelae of Maraş are the creations of the subsequently settled Aramaean population, but the objects the figures hold in their hands are derived from the indigenous tradition. The ears of grain (Pl. 28) appeared previously in the middle Neo-Hittite figures of Carchemish (Pl. 22b). As we know from Hittite texts, the spindle and the mirror are attributes of Hittite women. The banqueting or drinking scenes with a seated figure and an adorant before represent an old motif of the mountain people of Anatolia,[517] which may be noted at Kültepe[518] as early as the beginning of the second millennium B.C. The Aramaeans transferred these cult scenes to funerary stelae. Moreover, the flat loaves and meat patties on the table are local fare still common today in southern Anatolia and northern Syria.

Rock relief at Ivriz

The great relief of Ivriz is a splendid example of the Aramaean Hittite style (Pl. 30).[519] The god's cap and the spiral locks of the two figures are Aramaean features. Then too the placement of the horns on the god's cap occurs earlier in the case of the Hadad from the time of the Aramaean king Panamuwa[520] (p. 55). The king is consistently garbed in the new fashion, with a richly adorned tunic and an Assyrian cloak, recalling the one seen in the reliefs of the Barrakab period from Zincirli and Sakçegözü (Pl. 14). His headgear is unusual and recurs, as Poulsen and Barnett have noted,[521] in an ivory priestess figure from Ephesos (Pl. 66). The profiles of the two figures with their strongly curved noses further suggest that this is an Aramaean work. Noteworthy is the fact that the king is wearing certain Phrygian items of personal adornment. The belt and the fibula are similar to the metal belts and fibulae found at Gordion. A similar belt recurs in a Samian ivory statue in the form of a lyre handle made about a century later (p. 215).

Hittite elements

A great many iconographic and stylistic features attest to the persistence of the Hittite tradition. The god appears in a gesture of homage, as was usual in the art of the empire.[522] The dress and attitude of the god are almost purely Hittite. As on the Hittite reliefs (Pl. 22a) the seam of the kilt swings up over the knees.[523] The position of the arms and hands follows the pattern set in works of the empire period.[524] The character of the scene makes it clear that the Aramaean donor erected this monument for his Luvian-Hittite subjects. The hieroglyphs, which were not usual among the Aramaeans, who had their own script, were intended for the benefit of the indigenous population. The inscription indicates that the king represented was Warpalawas, who is known to us from Assyrian sources as Urballa from 738 B.C.[525] It seems, therefore, that the relief was executed about 730. The sculptures found by Th. Bossert and his associates (Pls. 31–35) at Karatepe north of Adana are among the latest exemplars of the Aramaean Hittite style.[526] Hitherto the most important conclusions to be drawn from these works have been presented by Bahadir Alkim[527] and Halet Çambel.[528] Recently Paolo Matthiae has

KARATEPE SCULPTURES

PLATE 32 – Musical scene. Orthostat relief from the south portal at Karatepe. Basalt. Late Neo-Hittite stylistic phase (Aramaeanizing style). About 700 B.C. *Cf. pp. 136, 138.*

published a detailed monograph.[529] Shortly to be issued is the final publication by the archaeologist Halet Çambel, who has been closely concerned with the finds for many years and who erected a remarkable museum on the site. In expectation of this publication we must confine ourselves here to some of the main problems of these carvings. The sculptures of Karatepe are Aramaean Hittite works[530] showing considerable Phoenician influence. Such themes and *Phoenician style* motifs as Bes (an Egyptian demigod), monkeys, palms and ships, which otherwise *elements* do not appear in Anatolian sculpture, point to the close links between the Karatepe region and the Semitic centres of the south.[531] The apron worn by the sphinxes of Karatepe[532] is another motif from the Syro-Phoenician repertory (Pl. 31). The epaulettes found on these sphinxes[533] are also a Phoenician style element.[534] The costume of the genius figures and the form of the winged sun disk are further proofs of the links between the Karatepe sculptures and the south. The conical cap worn by the king and some other figures seems more Phoenician than *Nursing mother with* Aramaean, since it is somewhat elongated. Noteworthy is the long tunic of the *child* nursing mother, which is grooved in parallel folds from top to bottom (Pl. 35). Although a similar fold treatment is common in Hittite art,[535] the Karatepe reliefs seem rather to have been inspired by Syrian and Phoenician models.[536] The iconography of the relief—the theme of the mother nursing a standing boy—is entirely Phoenician-Egyptian. Egyptian models are discernible not only in the unusual motif of nursing, but also in the way in which the boy grasps the arm of his mother.[537] However, the sculptor has taken the theme not directly from Egyptian work, but from versions produced by Phoenician masters, for it is encountered on Phoenician bowls of the eighth and seventh centuries (Fig. 102).[538] In somewhat different form the same motif is known at Ras Shamra[539] as early as the second half of the second millennium. The scene showing King Asitawata eating while attended by musicians also points to southern influence. In the Phoenician-type reliefs of the Syrian ivories the same pictorial theme appears (p. 153). We must mention another important feature of the Karatepe reliefs that comes from Phoenician art. Many orthostats of Karatepe show figures with rubbery arms and legs. The rear feet and legs of the kneeling figures are wound about like snakes' bodies (Pl. 34b). Similar rubbery limbs appear on the kneeling figures of the Phoenician tridacna shells (Pl. 36d). The use of a characteristic representational device of this kind can hardly be an accident: it undoubtedly points to close links between Karatepe and Phoenicia. Our examination of the Tell Halaf sculptures has established that they too show perceptible Phoenician influence. But the Karatepe carvings, which employ Phoenician inscriptions and a considerable number of southern motifs, have advanced much further in assimilating Phoenician culture than the sculptures of the kingdom of Kapara found at Tell Halaf (Pls. 23, 24).

Two styles Halet Çambel's careful studies of the Karatepe sculptures have permitted her to ascribe them to two different masters.[540] Master A executed the large slab with the king enjoying a festive meal (Pl. 33) and Master B the adjoining orthostat with the musicians and servants bearing food and drink (Pl. 32). Moreover Halet Çambel has rightly perceived that the two masters had collaborators who shared

FIGS. 100, 101 – *Left, Fig. 100: Man with a balance. Funerary stele from Maraş. After Vieyra, Hittite Art, Pl. 73. Aramaeanizing Hittite style. About 700 B.C. Paris, Louvre. Cf. p. 131. – Right, Fig. 101: Scribe. Funerary stele from Maraş. After Akurgal, Späthethitische Bildkunst, Pl. 42b. Aramaeanizing Hittite style. Late 8th century B.C. Cf. p. 131.*

in the work. Especially the orthostats that she attributed to the circle of Master B show two hands that are quite distinct in the quality of their work. Master A also seems to have had assistants, but these were more nearly up to his own level of quality. Consequently, we will deal with the sculptures of Karatepe not in terms of two masters, but of two groups. A great many carvings (Pls. 33–35) show a Phoenicianizing style (Group A), while the rest of the sculptures (Pl. 32) stand more or less in the tradition of the Aramaean Hittite art of Zincirli and Sakçegözü (Group B).

Phoenician group

The orthostat slabs,[541] which have a monopoly on the Phoenician style features we have mentioned above, form a separate group. Furthermore, the racial type of the figures shown on these slabs is homogeneous. These are men of a particular ethnic group, probably Phoenicians, who may be recognized by a strongly curved nose (Pls. 33–35). By comparison with the Phoenician type of the Karatepe reliefs the nose shape of the Aramaean figures (Pls. 12–15) is less pronounced. None the less the Karatepe works do not show a true Phoenician style, but a strongly Phoenicianizing one. A number of style elements of these slabs are Assyrian or Aramaean, even Hittite. The warriors wear Assyrian pointed helmets of the eighth and seventh centuries.[542] The helmet tipped forward like a 'Phrygian cap' by some of the Karatepe warriors finds its closest parallel in Assyrian art of the late eighth and seventh centuries.[543] Only the trailing plume, which recalls Greek representations, is not found in Assyrian art. The sword[544] carried by some figures

FIG. 102 – *Mother with child. Detail of Egypto-Phoenician bowl. From Praeneste (Palestrina), Italy. After Frankfort, AAAO, p. 200, Fig. 97. Cf. p. 136.*

at their sides (Pl. 34a)[545] is very similar to the weapon seen on the Zincirli statue on two lions. Moreover, the belts of some figures on these slabs (Pl. 34a) correspond closely to middle Neo-Hittite examples from Zincirli and Carchemish (Figs. 61–65, 79–83).[546] The way in which a hero of Karatepe carries a calf on his shoulder (Pl. 34a) is a middle Neo-Hittite pictorial motif (Fig. 31). We find the musical instruments in the middle Neo-Hittite and Aramaean reliefs of southern Anatolia and northern Syria: the double flute (Pl. 32) appears in Carchemish and the elongated lyre (Pl. 34d) in Zincirli[547] and Tell Halaf.[548] As A. Dessenne has shown,[549] the end of the sphinx's tail on the Karatepe reliefs in the form of a water bird's head is a Hittite motif found in Carchemish, Zincirli (Figs. 64, 78)[550] and Sakçegözü (Pl. 15b).

Expressionistic work with humorous overtones

The markedly expressionistic scenes of the Phoenician group are animated by a gayer approach that seems almost comical. The monkey under the king's dining table, the scene with birds of prey and a hare, the bear dance, the warriors displaying their weapons as well as the Bes with two monkeys on his shoulder, are merry scenes of burlesque that reveal the strength and special charm of this provincial but attractive sculpture. These carvings imbued with a Mediterranean spirit of gaiety should not be regarded as formal reliefs of a great palace, but rather as the capricious decoration of a summer residence. The mother nursing her child is a masterpiece of its kind, not because of the beauty of the execution or the naturalism of the volumes, but because of the unique expressiveness of the naive method of narration (Pl. 35).

Aramaean Hittite group

The other orthostat slabs belong to a style apart that would be unthinkable without the influence of the sculptures of the Barrakab period at Zincirli and Sakçegözü. I should like to suggest that the fine slab with musicians (Pl. 32) was by one master and the other reliefs[551] of the same group were made by assistants in the workshop. It is unlikely that reliefs so different in quality could stem from a single hand. This master and his assistants clearly continue the tradition of the sculptural schools that created the works of the Barrakab period in Zincirli and Sakçegözü. The figures of these groups have a similar hair knot on the nape of the neck with the same plastically formed lock ends as were produced in the Aramaean centres (Pls. 26, 30). Moreover, the stylization of the mass of hair of the figures (Pl. 32) in diagonal lines is known from carvings of the Barrakab period (Pl. 14). From the carvings of Sakçegözü we are familiar with the cloak that leaves the advanced leg free (Pl. 15a). The sandal-like shoes with turned-up toes and thongs to fasten them at the ankles have appeared in the Ivriz god and king (Pl. 30). The pitcher with the long spout and the high handle, which the

PLATE 33 – King Asitawata at a festive meal. Orthostat relief from the south portal at Karatepe. Basalt. Late Neo-Hittite stylistic phase (Phoenicianizing style). About 700 B.C. *Cf. p. 136.*

138

V. PHOENICIAN AND SYRIAN ART REGION

The study of art works from Zincirli, Sakçegözü, Tell Halaf and Karatepe clearly shows that in the late ninth and throughout the eighth centuries much of northern Syria and southern Anatolia underwent strong influence from the Semitic south. The vital centre of this Semitic expansion lay in Phoenicia. Perhaps the most important debt of the late Neo-Hittite style to the Semitic peoples was the tectonic shaping of the columnar order with base and capital brought by the Aramaeans who had immigrated from the south (p. 80). The elaboration of the palace type called *hilani* may also be linked to the new approach to architecture introduced by the southern immigrants (p. 69). Also significant were influences in the field of building ornament, especially plant motifs of Syro-Phoenician origin (p. 83). Widespread were Syro-Phoenician fashions in hair styles and in men's costume, and influences from this source appeared in the choice of themes and the stylization of animal figures (pp. 113, 122). In this chapter we shall examine the Phoenician and Syrian originals that lay behind these developments.

From the middle of the second millennium B.C. Phoenician art occupied a special place in the Near Eastern world. Admittedly it had a largely eclectic approach, but from Egyptian, Mycenaean and Hittite style elements Phoenician artists successfully created original art works that enjoyed wide popularity in the Near East and throughout Mycenaean Greece in the late second millennium B.C. In the ninth, eighth and seventh centuries the Phoenician art centres of the first millennium still mainly continued the tradition of the second millennium, so that the persistence of such motifs as the sphinx and griffin figures of the Minoan-Mycenaean type is actually due solely to the continuity of Phoenician art.[554]

The Phoenician artists of the ninth-seventh centuries produced works in ivory, metal, faience and glass, which were exported to all countries of the then civilized world.[555] But they must have maintained workshops in several places in the Mediterranean, for art works (including many metal bowls and faience pieces) have come to light that have not yet been paralleled among the material recovered in Phoenicia itself. In his basic publication the archaeologist E. Gjerstad has classified the bowls found in Cyprus on the basis of stylistic observations,[556] identifying a number of them (which he terms Cypro-Phoenician)[557] as products of Phoenician artists settled in Cyprus.

Works that show a strongly Egyptianizing style may also be claimed as Phoenician products. The genius figures with the Egyptian double crown[558] and other figures wearing a conical cap in the form of a reduced Upper Egyptian crown[559] are characteristic of the Egyptian style of Phoenician art. Also the hair stylized in the form of short but thick rods[560] is a faithful imitation of Egyptian prototypes. As in the figures of an ivory plaquette from Nimrud[561] and another from Samos,[562] the hair is often schematized in the Egyptian manner with long thin rods—a version of an Egyptian wig. In these two plaquettes the shape of the face, the

PHOENICIAN
ART
Eclecticism

EGYPTIANIZING
STYLE

placement of the hands and arms as well as the costume are entirely in the Egyptian style. Moreover, Egyptian hieroglyphs have been added to the Nimrud plaquette. The seats as well as the sceptres the seated figures hold in their hands are further Egyptian motifs. Yet the execution is clearly Phoenician. Without exception the ivory carvings found in Arslan-Taş[563] and Khorsabad[564] belong to this style. Also a series of female figures[565] among the ivory carvings of Nimrud, which have been regarded as Syrian, must be ascribed to this style on account of their Egyptian wigs and the eyes, which are treated entirely in the Egyptian fashion. The Nimrud ivories that have been labelled 'Syrian' include some that I would regard as Phoenician works because of their strongly Egypto-Phoenician traits.

It seems, however, that artists of the first rank were at work in Assyria or Syria who were not Phoenicians, but who produced outstanding ivories in the Egyptianizing style of Phoenician art. In M. E. L. Mallowan's excavations at Nimrud some heads in the Egyptianizing style have been found that in the modelling of facial forms are clearly distinct from other Phoenician-Egyptian heads. I would mention particularly two splendid works, the 'Mona Lisa' and the 'Woman at the Window', both in the Baghdad Museum.

Baghdad 'Mona Lisa'   The 'Mona Lisa' head[566] wears her hair in the Egyptian-Phoenician manner; she has a well-formed oval face with modelled features (Pl. 37). The triangular mouth is slightly open and seems to smile. The same joyful expression is radiated by the vital almond-shaped eyes. M. E. L. Mallowan, who had the good fortune to find this fascinating work, has aptly compared it with the smiling maidens of the Athenian Acropolis and of the cities of Ionian Anatolia, which were made five or six generations later.[567]

'Woman at the Window'   The second head, that of the 'Woman at the Window',[568] stands much closer to Phoenician works than the 'Mona Lisa' in the rendering of the hair and ears (Pl. 38). But the formation of the lips and the modelling of the mouth area and the chin clearly distinguish it from the other Phoenician ivories of Nimrud and Arslan-Taş which show the same theme. The faint smile with the deeply sunk, angular mouth is achieved with the same fine expressiveness as is found in the sculptures of the archaic Ionian world of the sixth century. The motif of the woman at the window is linked with the cult of Aphrodite Parakyptousa. This cult flourished in Cyprus[569] and Babylon.[570]

Aphrodite cult in Babylon   Herodotus[571] tells a somewhat unlikely story about this cult: 'The most infamous of their customs is one that obliges every Babylonian woman once in her life to go and sit in the temple of Aphrodite and allow a strange man to have intercourse with her. And many women who, being proud of their wealth, disdain to mix with the rest, are brought to the temple in covered carriages drawn by teams, and there take their places attended by a great retinue of servants. But for the most part they sit in a great crowd, wearing a cord around the head in the precinct

PLATE 36 – Tridacna shell found at Assur. Phoenician work. First half of the 7th century B.C. *Staatliche Museen, Berlin. Overall height 16.4 cm. Cf. pp. 150 ff.*

36 a

36 b

36 c

36 d

36 e

of the goddess, whilst some come and others go; straight gangways are left clear passing in all directions between the women, and along these the strangers walk and make their choice. And a woman who has once sat down there will not leave and go home until a stranger has thrown a silver coin into her lap and lain with her outside the temple. After throwing the coin the man must say: 'I demand thee in the name of the goddess Mylitta', for so the Assyrians call Aphrodite. Whatever the value of the coin, she will not refuse it, for that would be unlawful, for the coin is hallowed. She goes with the first man who throws and rejects none. By having intercourse she has discharged her duty to the goddess and she goes away to her home; thereafter she is not to be won by any gift however great. Those women who excel in beauty and stature are soon released, but such as are ugly have to wait long before they can comply with the custom, sometimes as much as three or four years. In some parts of Cyprus there is a custom of the same kind'.

The cult described by Herodotus in such highly coloured terms surely existed in Babylon, but the cuneiform texts indicate that it was neither obligatory nor generally practised.[572] The 'women at the window' were the acolytes who in emulation of their mistress would show themselves in order to entice men from the street and unite with them in the service of the goddess. The cord that Herodotus mentions seems actually to have been worn by the prostitutes around the head, for it is found in examples from Arslan-Taş and Khorsabad[573] comparable to the Nimrud piece.[574]

The ivories from Arslan-Taş have been dated to the second half of the ninth century because among the finds are three fragments of an ivory box with the name Hazael, who had the box made.[575] The owner has been identified with King Hazael of Damascus,[576] whose reign falls in the second half of the ninth century.[577] But the circumstances in which they were found in Khorsabad and Nimrud and the stylistic criteria of the ivory carvings do not agree with this dating. Among the pieces from Arslan-Taş preserved in the Louvre is a lion head in the Assyrian style with three palmette-leaf skin folds under the eyes. It has already been shown that this lion type appears first in the time of Sargon (Fig. 9). Like the bull heads (Pl. 12a), the lion heads belong to the decoration of furniture. It seems likely that in the course of time the projecting ornaments were sometimes broken off and the old heads replaced with new ones. But it ought not to be assumed that a bed was in use in a princely house for a century. Consequently, the Egyptianizing ivory plaquettes, like the lion head mentioned, probably come from the time of Sargon (720–705). The surviving fragments of the Hazael box may not be adduced as comparative material for dating since they show neither figurative scenes nor decorative motifs. The pieces probably came from a jewellery box which was made in the ninth century, but which was preserved for a long time in the princely

Ivories from Arslan-Taş

Lion type of Sargonid style

PLATE 37 – 'Mona Lisa'. Woman's head. Ornament on a piece of furniture. From Nimrud. Phoenicianizing style. Early 7th century B.C. *Iraq Museum, Baghdad. Height 16.1 cm. Cf. pp. 129, 144, 214.*

house as a precious gift or prize of war. One should note, however, that the name Hazael was not borne exclusively by the Aramaean king of Damascus. A. Dupont-Sommer has already pointed out this difficulty, remarking that the ivories of Arslan-Taş might come from Damascus 'if it were certain that the name Hazael, which appears on the box fragments from Arslan-Taş, actually refers to the king of Damascus.'[578]

Khorsabad ivories The ivory carvings from Khorsabad,[579] which probably come from the same workshop as those from Arslan-Taş, are firmly dated, for the palace of Khorsabad was built by Sargon on a virgin site that was to be abandoned again after his death (p. 39). M. E. L. Mallowan has convincingly shown that some of the ivories in the Egyptianizing style which he discovered come from the time of Sargon, while the rest were produced as late as the seventh century.[580] I would prefer to assume that the fine Assyrian works in the Egyptianizing style were made in the seventh century. In the chapter on Assyrian art we have seen that from the time of Esarhaddon onwards (680–669) Egyptian influences made themselves felt in Assyrian works (p. 43). So it is understandable that Phoenician ivories in the Egyptianizing style or Assyrian adaptations of them should be in use in the first half of the seventh century. A. Parrot[581] has shown that several of the Nimrud ivories could have been sent to King Esarhaddon as tribute. Moreover, the appearance of this style in such Greek centres[582] as Samos, Crete and Rhodes, as well as in Etruria, indicates that the artists responsible for it were active far into the seventh century. A plaquette of this type, which has plant ornament only, has come to light in the Erythrai excavations, which I recently began with H. Gültekin, director of the Izmir Museum. This piece was found in the temple débris, which contained works from the years 670–545 B.C. A number of Phoenician and Syrian ivory workshops were active until the end of the seventh century. The Ionian art of ivory-carving probably grew up in imitation of Phoenician-Syrian models (p. 219). The animal figures in the Phoenician Egyptianizing style also show distinct Egyptian influences. For example, the lion faces are always done in the Egyptian manner, without folds and with the mouth closed. But the lions from Beisan,[583] with their open mouths, outstretched tongues and pronounced cheek bones, follow Hittite precedent. The sphinxes always wear Egyptian double crowns. Yet the epaulettes are probably a Phoenician invention. H. Kantor has also derived the apron found on Phoenician sphinxes from Egyptian models.[584] The griffins[585] usually continue the Hittite-Mycenaean version of the Phoenician prototypes developed in the late second millennium.[586]

OTHER PHOENICIAN STYLES
Kerameikos bronze bowl
Apart from the Egyptianizing fashion, other stylistic currents existed in Phoenicia. At present, however, it is not possible to distinguish Syrian products from wares that might have been made in Phoenicia itself. But the bronze bowl that has come to light in a tomb of the late ninth century in the Kerameikos[587] in Athens (Pls. 39, 40; Fig. 30) certainly belongs to Phoenician art. The manner of its surface composition and some stylistic details very closely recall the figural scenes on the bowl from Idalion (Fig. 104).[588] Common to both are the rosette in the centre of the interior of the bowl with a bulge at the ends of the petals which are bordered

FIG. 103 – *Phoenician bronze bowl. Found in a tomb of the Kerameikos, Athens. Late 9th century* B.C. *Cf. Pls. 39, 40 and p. 148.*

by a plaited band, and the wide pictorial frieze framed by a plaited band at the top and bottom. Moreover, the figures of the two bronze bowls have similar folds on the garments and a related linear stylization of the hair. The blossoms borne by the figures on the Kerameikos bowl recur in the right hand of the enthroned woman of the Idalion bowl. The hatched rendering of the hair found on the figures of the Kerameikos bowl, which is nothing more than a linear translation of the Egyptian hair fashion, is typical of Phoenician art. The figures of the tridacna shells also display this device (Pl. 36). The Kerameikos bowl is the only Phoenician work that can be dated with any precision. On the basis of Greek material associated with it in the burial (including clay vessels of the early Geometric style), K. Kübler has placed the bronze bowl in the last quarter of the ninth century,[589] thereby happily confirming the dating E. Gjerstad proposed for the Idalion bowl. With the help of the Cypriot vase types depicted on it, E. Gjerstad has dated the Idalion bowl in the eighth century.[590] As K. Kübler has rightly

FIG. 104 – *Detail of Idalion bowl. After KiB, p. 104, Fig. 3 and p. 107, Fig. 5. Cf. p. 148.*

indicated, the Idalion piece must have been made somewhat later than the Kerameikos bowl.[591]

Nimrud bronze bowl A bronze bowl from Nimrud showing a lion hunt with a chariot[592] may be claimed as a Phoenician work. The sphinx with the Egyptian double crown and the use of a bird motif as filler point to Egyptian influence. But the kneeling lion hunter with the linear stylization and the concentric arrangement of the hair as well as the checkered clothing ornamentation is shown in the Phoenician style. The figures on the tridacna shells have a similar clothing decoration (Pl. 36). The lion has a long horizontal back line and abdominal hair, two characteristic motifs found on the animal figures of the Syrian ivory reliefs and the Tell Halaf sculptures (Figs. 87–89). The three parallel stripes on the thigh of the rear leg are possibly a transformation of the flame-like stylization that appears at the same spot on the above-mentioned Syrian ivories. The face and the body of the animal show a strongly Assyrianizing style of Hittite derivation. The lion has rather pronounced cheek bones, but the other features follow the Assyrian lion type. The two skin folds of the palmette-leaf type beneath the eyes and chin bones indicate that the bronze bowl belongs to the second half of the eighth century at the earliest. The body stylization mentioned, however, suggests an origin towards the end of the eighth century. A bronze bowl from Olympia[593] may be ascribed to the same category as the previously mentioned Nimrud bowl.

Tridacna shells The tridacna shells are authentically Phoenician in style. A splendid example from Assur shows figures that must be regarded as typically Phoenician because of their hair style and dress as well as the lavish use of palmette and lotus (Pl. 36). W. Andrae has provided a careful description and fine interpretation of this work:[594] 'The thick hinge of the shell has been sculpturally modelled into a human (female) head, and the outer surface of the shell is engraved to show an ornately

PLATE 38 – 'Woman at the Window'. Ivory plaque from Nimrud. Phoenicianizing style. Early 7th century B.C. *Iraq Museum, Baghdad. Height 6.8 cm. Cf. pp. 144, 214.*

FIG. 112 – *Phoenician ivory plaquette. Found at Arslan-Taş. After Thureau-Dangin, Arslan Tash, Pl. 36 (no. 61). Second half of 8th century. Cf. Fig. 113.*

Sargonid hair knots, which appear on some other ivory boxes in the Syrian style,[613] agrees well with this dating. A golden 'crown', now in the Walters Art Gallery, Baltimore,[614] has been ascribed to the Syrian style by C. Watzinger (Pl. 42).[615] He asserts that the winged sun disk with the star in the middle (this appears on the back of the crown),[616] as well as the plant forms behind the ibexes and the stylization of the naked goddesses are Syrian. I have not seen this curious work in the original, but I am inclined to agree with C. Watzinger's attribution on account of the summarily executed eyes of the naked women,[617] which are the same as in the figures of the ivory box discussed above. Moreover, the wig-like coiffure is arranged in the manner of the Syrian ivories of the Phoenicianizing trend. A similar hair style is seen in the two musicians playing psalteries on the Nimrud ivory box (Fig. 41). To my knowledge, however, a truly identical arrangement of the wig is not found among the published art works of the ancient Near East.[618]

A masterpiece of particular elegance is the well-preserved ivory head of a woman now in the British Museum (Pl. 43).[619] The piece shows the head of a young woman with a fine low *polos* and long hair, stylized into several thick tresses. The tresses fall vertically and are rolled into spirals at the ends. The slightly open mouth gives the head a vitality that, together with the full and round forms of the face, makes an attractive contrast to the austere linear handling of the eyes and the hair strands. The carver must have been one of the most accomplished artists of the period. For vital expressiveness his work ranks immediately after the fascinating 'Mona Lisa' of the Baghdad Museum (Pl. 37) as one of the finest creations of ancient Near Eastern art. The hair style of the head (cf. Fig. 111) may be dated to the last quarter of the eighth century at the earliest (p. 56). Thus this remarkable ivory may have been produced in the late eighth or indeed in the early seventh century.

At this point we must mention two splendid ivory works that were recently found at Gordion, plaques that formed part of an ensemble of horse-trappings.[620] One plaque depicts a nude, winged 'mistress of the beasts' standing on a bull's head. On the other plaque is a chimaera. Before it is a lion's head, and at the height of the shoulders a human head appears frontally. The two plaques belong to an eclectic style that must be localized in northern Syria. The position of the 'mistress of the beasts' on the bull, her *polos* adorned with rosettes, and the tails of the sphinxes

Finds at Gordion

with birds' heads at the end are specifically Hittite traits. As we have shown above (note 343) the chimaera is a Hittite invention. Furthermore, the details of the lion's head of the chimaera, the open mouth with the tongue protruding over the lower lip, the stylization of the chin bones in the form of a half-ellipse and the furrowing of the tip of the nose are unmistakable characteristics of the Hittite lion (Pl. 21; Figs. 68–74). The cubic forms of the lion's head also bespeak the Hittite character of the work. Yet other details of the two Gordion plaques show that these Hittite traits were combined with forms of Syrian art. The facial features of the human heads are worked entirely in the Syrian fashion, and the shape of the eyes, the incised eyebrows, the big locks at the ear, as well as the turn of the head to one side towards the spectator are characteristic features of the Syrian artistic attitude. Since the plant ornament of the plaque with the chimaera appears in similar forms on other Syrian art objects, we are justified in regarding these ivories as Syrian work dependent on a strong Hittite tradition. These Syrian-Hittite imports found at Gordion are precious documents in determining the chronology of Syrian ivories. At Gordion they were found at a level[621] that belongs to the late eighth century at the earliest.[622] This gives us a criterion for further study of the dating problem.

IRANIAN SPHERE In order to complete our panorama of Near Eastern culture in the first half of the first millennium, we would have to examine the products of the Urartian and Iranian spheres (cf. Pls. 44–47). But since the art of the Iranian regions has already been discussed in another volume of the ART OF THE WORLD series,* we shall be content simply to mention this theme below in the framework of Near Eastern contacts with Greece (pp. 192, 197); for other aspects we refer the reader to Professor Porada's excellent monograph.

* E. Porada, *Ancient Iran*, London, 1965. See also E. Akurgal, *Urartäische und altiranische Kunstzentren*, Ankara, 1968.

PART TWO

Greece

VI. EARLY GREEK ART AND ITS CONNECTIONS
WITH THE NEAR EAST

First encounter between East and West

The first encounter between East and West about which we are well informed historically and archaeologically took place towards the middle of the second millennium B.C. This confrontation took place as a result of Mycenaean expansion. C. Schaeffer's successful excavations at Ras Shamra in Syria have clearly shown that this period saw a fruitful exchange in art between these two poles of world culture.[623] It is evident that the Mycenaeans played the donor role in this encounter. It would surely have led to other fruitful exchanges if disturbances in the Aegean world about 1200 B.C. had not put an end to the favourable situation. There followed a dark age in which Greece,[624] Anatolia and some other parts of the Mediterranean world reverted to a primitive stage of existence. Since culture had been limited to a thin upper crust among the Mycenaeans and Hittites, the fall of political power sealed the doom of that once flourishing intellectual life. In Greece the knowledge of writing disappeared and with it the whole intellectual heritage. What remained was simply a practical acquaintance with techniques required for the accomplishment of daily tasks. Only through the intermediary role played by Phoenician and Syrian workshops were a few motifs and style elements of Mycenaean art preserved for the following age. The Aegean migration also ruined the cultural life of Anatolia,[625] where the Hittites had maintained a great independent culture for almost 800 years.[626] After the fall of the Hittite empire central Anatolia sank into a period of stagnation lasting almost 400 years. It was left to the southern Anatolian and northern Syrian principalities to continue the cultural heritage of the Hittite world. In Syria also, as W. F. Albright has shown,[627] the traditional culture was able to unfold further without interruption. It must have been about the middle of the ninth century that the Greeks were able to follow in the footsteps of their Mycenaean ancestors by making their appearance in the *entrepôts* and colonial cities of the Near East. Although they had already begun to found cities in western Anatolia about 1000 B.C.,[628] the

Earliest Greek finds in Near East

earliest Greek finds that have come to light at various sites in the Near East can scarcely be earlier than the beginning of the eighth century. As V. Desborough has recently demonstrated,[629] these comprise exclusively *skyphoi* (drinking vessels) in the late Protogeometric style of Cycladic origin; Desborough dates them within the period between 900 and 750.[630] These *skyphoi* were not export wares, for by this period the Greeks possessed much better works which they could send to the East. Consequently, these pieces must be everyday vessels used by Greek merchants from the Cyclades active in the Near East. Greek exports to the eastern lands of the Mediterranean began only much later, not before the seventh century. The *skyphoi* that have been found must have belonged to individual Greeks resident in Near Eastern cities. These immigrants were pioneers of the future Hellenic trade colonies in the Near East, of which the oldest (as we shall see) was founded towards the middle of the eighth century.

influenced by the religion and mythology of the Near Eastern peoples. Every seaman or merchant from the Near East could tell the Greeks something about the venerable gods and the wonders accomplished by the legendary heroes of that strange world. Then too the Greeks who began to travel in the Levant in the ninth century learned by hearsay to know the gods and myths of this fabulous world. The Near Eastern religions and myths that the Greeks knew through word of mouth were probably the earliest influences of the East on the West. At the end of the eighth century at the latest the mythical elements of eastern origin in the works of Homer and Hesiod had already taken on a stable Greek form, so that the period of their acquisition from the Near East must go back a long way beyond the middle of the eighth century. From the legends which the Greeks took over orally from the Phoenicians and other peoples they slowly built up their own world of mythology. Some examples of the epic tales that reached the Greeks from the Near Eastern peoples in the first half of the eighth century have survived. Especially noteworthy are the Illuyanka myth and two epic works, the legends known as the 'Heavenly Kingdom' and the 'Song of Ullikummi'. According to the Illuyanka myth, 'The dragon Illuyanka defeated the storm god, taking his heart and eyes. The storm god sought to revenge himself. He took the daughter of a man named Arm as his wife and begat a son. When the son was grown he married the daughter of the dragon Illuyanka. The storm god commanded his son: "If you go into your wife's house, ask her for my heart and eyes." When he then went to ask for the heart she gave it to him. Later he asked her for the eyes, and she gave them to him. He took them to his father and so restored his father's heart and eyes to him. After his person had regained its former state the god went to the sea to do battle. In the struggle he came close to defeating the dragon. But the storm god's son took the loser's side. And he cried aloud to his father: "Include me! Don't spare me." Then the storm god killed the dragon Illuyanka and his own son.' An orthostat relief from Malatya has a scene from the Illuyanka myth (Fig. 60).[632]

This old Anatolian myth kept its popularity into the days of Classical antiquity. A story of the battle of Zeus and Typhon, which forms the basis of a description by Apollodoros in the Roman period,[633] reproduces the main features of the Illuyanka myth. In the Typhon myth Zeus loses not only his heart and eyes in the fight with the monster but also the sinews of his hands and feet. In the Illuyanka myth the lost organs were recovered with the help of the storm god's son and his wife, the dragon's daughter. In the Typhon story it is Hermes who purloins the sinews while his companion Aigipan distracts the dragon's daughter who has been charged with looking after them. The Anatolian origin of the Typhon legend is evident from the geographical names in the myth. The mountain that is mentioned, Mount Cassius, stands on the Syrian coast just south of the river Orontes. The Korikian Cave where Typhon lives lies on the Cilician coast, as the myth has it. Aeschylus and Pindar also place the Typhon myth in Cilicia. Thus the version of the Typhon legend that appears in Apollodoros' work certainly derives from ancient Anatolian models. Greeks may often have heard the myth when they

Religion and mythology the first imports

Illuyanka myth

Origin of Typhon myth

encountered Levantine peoples at Al Mina towards the middle of the eighth century (see below).

The rendering of the Illuyanka myth in art, of which we hitherto know only the Hittite example from Malatya mentioned above (Fig. 60), seems to have provided the model for the Hydra as represented in Greek art (p. 95). One must assume, however, that apart from Hittite representations of Illuyanka the Greeks knew other Near Eastern dragon-battle scenes, instances of which are found in Mesopotamia.

Source of Hesiod's Theogony

The epic known as 'The Heavenly Kingdom' is a theogony presenting three generations of gods:[634] Anu, Kumarbi and the storm god. Anu is the Babylonian sky god and Kumarbi represents the Hurrian name of a god who corresponds to the Sumerian deity Enlil. Kumarbi emasculates Anu by ripping out his genitals with his teeth. He swallows the semen, but then spits it out again when Anu tells him that otherwise he will be pregnant with three terrible deities. 'You are pleased at having swallowed my manhood. But don't be pleased over your insides. I have given you three fearful gods as the fruit of my body. You will come to the point when you will finally dash your head . . . against the rocks of the mountains.'

The earth became pregnant from the seed Kumarbi spat out. The following very fragmentary section of the clay tablet probably described how the earth gave birth to the storm god and two other deities. From other parallel texts it is evident that the storm god became king in place of Kumarbi. It has long been known that Hesiod's *Theogony* derives from this Hurrian myth. Hesiod also tells of three generations of gods: Ouranos, Kronos and Zeus successively ruled the heavens. Here too the first god was emasculated by his son. Hesiod relates that in the night, while Ouranos was entwined in love around his wife Gaia, Kronos cut off his father's private parts with an enormous sickle and threw them behind him. From the bloody drops the earth brought forth the Giants. From the private parts, however, which were carried by the waves far over the sea, arose the foam-born Aphrodite.

The 'Song of Ullikummi' tells[635] how Kumarbi created the monster Ullikummi out of diorite in order to regain the kingdom of heaven with his help from his son, the storm god Tesup. After a long struggle the storm god defeated the stone monster to remain the king of the heavens for all time. This epic also seems to have influenced Greek mythology. In Hesiod's *Theogony* we learn how Zeus, after his victory over Kronos and the Titans, was again attacked by the monster Typhon. The sequence of events is the same. Moreover, the scene of the epic is the same in both versions[636]—once more Mount Cassius on the Syrian coast, where the Greeks founded their colony of Al Mina about the middle of the eighth century.

Adoption of Phoenician alphabet

The Greeks' adoption of the Phoenician alphabet, which they improved by introducing signs for vowel sounds, is the most important result of the meeting between East and West. The rise of Greek script, of which the earliest piece of evidence is a famous Attic prize amphora of about 730, probably occurred in the first half of the eighth century, as W. F. Albright has cogently argued.[637]

Near East.[644] Then such art centres as Olympia, Corinth, Boeotia, the Cyclades, Samos and Miletos must have been outstanding entrepots for the maritime traffic of the age. At all these sites art works have been found that either come from the Near East or show Near Eastern features and motifs.

Quite possibly the Geometric style accomplished its shift from flat, abstract ornament to figural representation mainly through the impact of Near Eastern forms. Greek contact with the Near Eastern world began when the Geometric style had passed its peak and was on the point of entering a new phase, a phase that spelled the displacement and breaking up of the geometric character from which it takes its name. A great number of vessels, which are decorated with small lines or stripes and with dots, clearly show that a phase of decline had already begun.[645] If the figural innovations of the ripe and late Geometric styles had not appeared, Geometric art would probably have been condemned to complete degeneration.

Not only did Near Eastern artists have exotic animals and mysterious legendary creatures to hand on as models, but they practised a kind of art resting upon a venerable tradition, and within its bounds they were able to work with a free hand. Under the influence of the eastern examples Greek vase-painters were able to free themselves from compass and ruler[646] as well as from the oppressive discipline of compositions in metopes and strips. It is a striking fact that with the rise of the figural style lions (Fig. 114), griffins, sphinxes, Centaurs, animal combat groups and grazing animals (Fig. 113)—themes and motifs that heretofore had been entirely lacking in Greek art—suddenly appeared on gold plaquettes, in vase-painting and on bronzes.

The emergence of the new Greek style after 750 occurred at a time in which the whole Near East was undergoing a great upsurge. Before 745, that is before the beginning of the reign of the great Assyrian king Tiglath-Pileser III, there was little substantial cultural and artistic activity in the Near East. Great movements of art generally occur in times of political upswing; this may be seen almost everywhere in the history of world civilization. The renewed strength of the Assyrian empire after an obscure period of weakness lasting some seventy years stimulated the rise of active artistic centres in the Neo-Hittite Aramaean and Syro-Phoenician principalities, which began to supply the great Assyrian palaces and to export their products throughout the civilized world.

The numerous Near Eastern works of art that appeared in many places in Greece show clearly that the new stylistic trend was stimulated by these prototypes.

But Greek artists did not take as their models all Near Eastern works found in Greek sanctuaries. Votive gifts presented by Easterners living or travelling in Greece might not necessarily correspond to Greek taste, and these form an exception. Assyrian and Egyptian products held little interest for the Greeks. Figures of deities with horns and other outlandish Near Eastern attributes found no favour, nor did figures with elaborately dressed hair. An examination of the earliest Greek sculptures shows that they are usually close to works of the Hittites and Syrians. The strongly Phoenicianizing products also look quite strange next

Escape from tyranny of compass and ruler

to Greek works. We shall see that in Greece only those Egyptian and Phoenician style elements that were modified in northern Syrian centres found acceptance. The Greek creations have a particular affinity with Hittite art. The calligraphic contours of the figures and the cubic animal bodies of Hittite art (Pl. 21; Figs. 68, 69, 78–85) are in fact quite close to the Geometric and linear approach of the eighth-century Greeks. We shall also show that the formal idiom of Greek animal figures of the seventh century was mainly shaped by the employment of Hittite style elements.

Near Eastern imports, known from the late ninth century only in isolated examples (Pl. 39, 40; Fig. 103), multiply astonishingly after the middle of the eighth century. The common appearance of Near Eastern motifs on ripe and late Geometric vases is a clear reflection of this. For the present we may therefore ascribe the upper chronological time limit of the Orientalizing influence to the middle of the eighth century. But of course the Orientalizing style proper did not come into full vogue until the beginning of the seventh century. Yet it is noteworthy that the trend gradually emerged towards the middle of the eighth century, and became increasingly important during the second half of the eighth century. As has been noted, the first signs are the appearance of grazing animals in vase-painting[647] and gold plaquette work.[648] In the second half of the eighth century there followed lions, animal combat groups, sphinxes, griffins and Centaurs—figures inhabiting an entirely new world.

Rise of Orientalizing style

In the course of the ensuing discussion we shall see that Near Eastern motifs appear for the first time in art works produced in mainland Greece, especially in Attica. The islands and Ionia followed after a considerable time lag. The process of orientalizing was a Greek fashion trend that spread slowly from west to east. If the Orientalizing style begins in the mainland as early as about 750, it appears on the Cyclades and on Rhodes only about 700, as Schiering has rightly noted.[649] Its flowering in Ionia came still later, about 650 at the earliest. While it was obsolete on the mainland as early as about 625, it enjoyed a kind of Indian summer in the East Greek world which lasted until the middle of the sixth century. The following paragraphs will treat in detail the earliest Near Eastern influences in mainland Greece.

New York bronze group

A work of outstanding merit stands at the head of the phase of Greek art that begins about the middle of the eighth century: the bronze group in the Metropolitan Museum, New York (Pl. 48).[650] This piece ranks as one of the earliest Greek works to be influenced by the mythology and sculpture of the Near East. According to E. Buschor's perceptive suggestion[651] the group shows Zeus fighting the primeval monster Typhon for the mastery of the world. Typhon, who is known to us from Hittite mythology, was a monster made of diorite (p. 165). In Hesiod[652] and later in Pindar he is a creature with one hundred heads. In Greek art of the sixth century he appears as a snake with the upper body of a man. If Buschor's hypothesis is correct, we must assume that for the Greeks at the beginning many pictorial motifs had not yet acquired final form. As the German scholar rightly observes, until the first quarter of the seventh century 'Centaur' contribution to the rise and expansion of the Greek Orientalizing style. In recent years this question has given rise to considerable discussion among archaeologists. F. Matz has emphasized the close links of the 'Daedalic' style with the Near East.[656] E. Homann-Wedeking[657] and D. Ohly[658] have noted common features shared by early Greek sculptures and Syrian ivories, and Dunbabin has also sought prototypes in Syria.[659] In the following section we shall discuss this important question in the light of the results obtained in the first part of this book.

Syrian and Phoenician ivories have been found throughout the Greek world.[660] The ivory carvings that have come to light on Crete, Samos and Rhodes[661] belong to the same stylistic group as that from which the Nimrud ivories derive (Pls. 37, 38, 41, 43). Dunbabin has singled out two Syrian products found in Corinth.[662] One is a matrix in Corinthian clay, but shows a pronounced Syrian style, the other a clay statuette, which Dunbabin regards as a Syrian import.[663] Both pieces give clear evidence of the popularity of Syrian products in Greece. Hitherto the soil of Attica has failed to yield Near Eastern ivory objects comparable to the Nimrud pieces. However, some Greek ivory statuettes, which come from a tomb in the Dipylon cemetery at Athens,[664] show that the artists were inspired to a great extent by Syrian originals. Two of these are illustrated here. One of them, the larger, is a masterpiece of early Greek art (Pl. 49). The smaller is a work of lesser quality (Pl. 65a–d). The standing position, the arms closely pressed against the body, as well as the *polos*, are all features of Syrian prototypes that recur in Attic statuettes. The Syrian originals wear tall, medium or low *poloi*, such as we find in Greek works. The Greek carver of the smaller ivory statuette (Pl. 65a–d), which comes from the same tomb[665] keeps the leaf ornament of the Syrian *poloi*,[666] but the carver of the larger piece has replaced this motif with a meander, the leading ornamental motif of Greek Geometric art.[667] The hair style seems to be a reworking of the Syrian fashion. The mass of hair, which consists of long closely packed locks, actually recalls the forms of Syrian ivories. Yet the way in which the hair is merely bound together in a mass at the back, and not allowed to appear in individual tresses at the front, is not paralleled in Syrian art. The severely rectangular mass of hair is also un-Syrian. The herring-bone pattern of stylization does of course appear in Syrian art (Pl. 43),[668] but in its present strong and simple form it corresponds to the type represented in the decoration of Greek Geometric vases.

Still more important, however, are the differences evident in the body structure of the ivories from Syria and Attica. Anyone would be struck by the powerful dynamism of the Greek works, which achieves an impressive power in the sharp profile of the faces and the engaging accentuation of the volumes of the body. The Greek statuette has a true freshness of appearance, but at the same time it seems somewhat harsh in comparison with the idealized beauty of the female figures of the Near Eastern ivories (Pls. 37, 38, 43). The Syrian models represent the last flowering of a refined courtly art depending on an old tradition, while the Attic statuette may be regarded as a milestone in the rise of a young and vigorous Greek art. The statuette with the leaf-pattern *polos* breathes the same Greek

Dipylon statuettes

spirit (Pl. 65a–d). It shows comparable face and body forms and has the same rectangular hair mass as the statuette with the meander *polos*. That the effect is less lively and that the buoyant accents of the body structure are lacking, are due to its master, who was probably not one of the leading ivory carvers. As D. Ohly has justly remarked,[669] he created a 'work that was strongly dependent on the Near East'.

As long as thirty years ago R. Hampe published subtle stylistic observations placing the Dipylon statuette (Pl. 49) in the line of development of late Geometric sculpture.[670] He clearly demonstrated the 'more flowing' and 'recent' character of the late Geometric pottery associated with the statuette in the tomb, and thus convincingly dated it to the end of the eighth century.[671] In some penetrating remarks Alscher has recently stressed the advanced style of the Athenian ivory statuette and the late type of the associated pottery, confirming Hampe's dating.[672] This conclusion accords with the results of our earlier researches on the Syrian and Phoenician ivories found in what was once Assyria. I believe that I have proved that these Near Eastern carvings come from the time of Sargon (721–705; p. 160). Since the small Dipylon statuette faithfully reproduced the leaf-pattern *polos* of the Syrian carvings, it seems to belong—together with the other statuettes of this tomb—to the same period that gave rise to its models.

Syrian crowns Syrian art works in the manner of the ivory pieces from Nimrud and the gold crown in Baltimore (Pl. 42) served early seventh-century Greek artists as prototypes. Following models of this kind they produced their 'Daedalic' human figures, thereby creating a homogeneous style, which might be called pan-Hellenic, since it dominated all parts of the early Greek world at that time. The overwhelming majority of seventh-century Greek statuettes shows a hair style that has been called the 'stepped-wig' coiffure. The useful monograph by R. J. H. Jenkins collects almost the entire available corpus of material. In these figures we find hair of medium length cascading down with horizontal waving. This coiffure is a Syrian invention, although in Syrian art the hair usually has a vertical articulation (Pl. 36a). However, the Nimrud ivories also include examples with hair following the horizontal scheme.[673] The nude goddesses of the Syrian gold crown show a similar stepped arrangement of the hair (Pl. 42). Whether it is waved horizontally or vertically, in some Syrian examples the hair leaves the ears free, and these project forward in a rather unnatural way (Pl. 38).[674] The same markedly projecting ears recur in a number of early Greek examples.[675] It is exceptional that the goddesses of the Syrian crown wear crowns over the hair, since the other Syrian examples have no head-dress. In the Cretan statuettes[676] and in some Spartan ones[677] the stepped-wig coiffure is generally combined with the *polos*.[678]

Syrian origin of the stepped-wig coiffure The early Greek hair style of the stepped-wig type is distinguished from Syrian prototypes only by the fact that it usually shows short pearl or spiral locks at the hairline on the forehead.[679] In some pieces small circles appear at this point. The forehead locks are lacking in the Syrian prototypes. None the less, this detail too may derive from Near Eastern models, for in other Syrian ivories and in some[680]

FIGS. 118, 119 – *Left, Fig. 118: Pegasos. After Frank-fort, Cylinder Seals, Pl. 35c. Middle Assyrian style. Last quarter of second millennium B.C. Cf. below. – Right, Fig. 119: Pegasos on a Urartian bronze plate. After T. Özgüç, Belleten, vol. 25, 1961, p. 290, Fig. 24. Cf. below.*

no griffin type of their own: they were content to render faithful imitations of the griffin figures of late Neo-Hittite art.

The fine head from Olympia reproduced here (Pl. 57) belongs to H. Jantzen's monumental group,[718] and was made about the middle of the seventh century by a Greek metalworker.

Another Near Eastern hybrid, the sphinx,[719] appeared at about the turn of the *Sphinx* eighth to the seventh century in Greek art of Crete and the mainland. Apart from the comprehensive and useful monograph of A. Dessenne,[720] we have discussions by F. Matz[721] and H. Walter[722] of this mythical creature,[723] which played a con-siderable role in Greek religion. Once more objects from Syrian workshops may be cited as the closest prototypes, for the female sphinx is a creation of Syrian art centres (Fig. 11). Other evidence for this is provided by the side-burns, the short spiral locks and the stepped-wig coiffure, three Syrian features that recur in the sphinxes depicted on Protocorinthian vases of the second black-figured style.[724] The other hybrid creatures serving as motifs in early Greek art, which appear towards the end of the eighth century, may be mentioned here briefly, for E. Kunze has treated them in a basic work entitled *Archaische Schildbänder*. So I shall limit myself to pointing out the Near Eastern prototypes of a few of the imported hybrid creatures.

The best collection of material illustrating early Greek mythology is found in a remarkable book by K. Schefold, *Myth and Legend in Early Greek Art*, in which new ideas about Greek mythology are presented.[725]

We have already met the sirens[726] on attachments on Urartian cauldrons and among angel figures on Phoenician tridacna shells (Pl. 36). The figure of Pegasos[727] *Pegasos* seems to be a creation of Assyrian art (Fig. 118). Later it became very popular in Urartian art (Fig. 119), whence it may have come to Greece. The Centaur[728] *Centaur* was often depicted in the Near East on Babylonian boundary stones. Greek artists may have begun to imitate it towards the end of the eighth century, following examples on imported Babylonian textiles. The Gorgon's head[729] *Gorgon's head* derives from Syrian prototypes, as H. Kantor has recently shown.[730] The chi-maera[731] first occurs in Greek art on Protocorinthian vases in two different *Chimaera* pictorial types. In one[732] it has a hybrid lion and human head (Fig. 116); in the

FIGS. 120, 121 – *Left, Fig. 120: Herakles struggling with the lion. Shield-buckle relief. After Kunze, Archaische Schildbänder, Pl. 53. About 600 B.C. Cf. below. – Right, Fig. 121: Theseus struggling with the Minotaur. Shield-buckle relief. After Kunze, Archaische Schildbänder. About 600 B.C. Cf. p. 189.*

other[733] a lion and goat head. The second chimaera type became standard in the following period; it was also known to Hesiod.[734] The first type is a faithful rendering of a middle Neo-Hittite archetype (Fig. 78).[735] The chimaera with the lion-goat head is probably a version elaborated by early Greek artists.

The more one studies the question of origins the more one finds that some Greek divinities either betray close links with the Near East or represent direct borrowings. Herodotus tells us that the cult of Aphrodite found on Cyprus and on the Greek island of Cythera was transplanted from Ashkelon in Palestine.[736] The unpleasant account of the goddess's birth found in Hesiod (p. 166) suggests a close connection with the Near Eastern Ishtar (p. 147).

Artemis as 'Mistress of the Beasts' The nature goddess Artemis,[737] when she appears in the iconographic type known as 'Mistress of the Beasts' (Pl. 50), is a creation of the Near Eastern world. The Artemis of the Olympian pantheon seems to be only partially derived from this Near Eastern archetype. N. Yalouris has shown that Athena too in her guise of 'Mistress of the Horses' derives from this motif.[738] Moreover, he has demonstrated that the goddesses Artemis, Hera and Demeter occasionally appear as 'Mistress of the Horses' as well. He has rightly stressed that the goddesses took up the age-old theme of 'Mistress of the Beasts', but that this motif gradually lost its Near Eastern character.[739]

E. Bielefeld has recently shown that the iconographic type of Apollo Philesios is of Anatolian Hittite origin.[740] A cult image of this god holding a stag in one hand stood in the sanctuary of Apollo at Didyma about 500 B.C. It was made by the Sicyonian sculptor Kanachos. E. Simon[741] has published careful studies together with a collection of the known evidence regarding this work, which was taken to the Persian capital of Ecbatana shortly after the battle of Lade, to be returned to its original home 200 years later.

Herakles According to Herodotus Herakles came from Phoenicia.[742] As F. Brommer[743] has pointed out,[744] at least three of Herakles' deeds are of Near Eastern origin: the Stymphalian birds, the struggle with the Nemean lion and the slaying of the Hydra. The scheme of Herakles' struggle with the Nemean lion (Fig. 120) is a Greek reworking of the Near Eastern battle motif associated with the name of

PLATE 58 – Warrior. Bronze statuette found at Olympia. Late 7th century B.C. *Olympia Museum. Height 17.3 cm. Cf. p. 190.*

the hero Gilgamesh (Pl. 47). Theseus' struggle with the Minotaur also appears in this fashion (Fig. 121). Herakles himself is a Greek manifestation of the universal hero of the Near East, Gilgamesh.[745] We have noted above that on the Malatya relief (Fig. 60) the storm god is accompanied by his son in his struggle with the Hydra-like monster. This accompanying figure recalls Iolaus, Herakles' faithful comrade, who supports him in his battle with the Hydra. H. Goldman has drawn attention to this dependence on Near Eastern archetypes, citing other common features that link the Greek hero with his Mesopotamian precursor.[746] In a careful study F. Dirlmeier has recognized Anatolian and Near Eastern elements in the myth of King Oedipus.[747] H. Kantor has drawn attention to a

Theseus and Minotaur

Myth of King Oedipus

number of Near Eastern motifs of mythical type adopted in Greece.[748] There is still much to be said about Near Eastern influences in the realm of religion and mythology.[749] I believe, however, that a reasonably clear picture has emerged, so that we can curtail discussion of these problems, which really extend beyond the bounds of our subject, in order to continue our investigations into art history. In conclusion it must be emphasized that the deities imported from the Near East as well as the religious and mythological features were soon fully accommodated in both form and iconography to the Greek character. In his monograph on early Greek legends Karl Schefold has said: 'One concept, at any rate, which is typically Greek is seen in the fact that all the antagonists are descended from the same mother, the Earth, whose children also include men. Thus the ancient oriental dualism, which divided the world into a light and a dark side, collapsed.'[750]

Warrior figures   Five splendid bronze statuettes from Olympia[751] that form a separate group[752] reveal some late Neo-Hittite influence. They are helmeted figures shown naked down to the belt around the waist; in their hands they must have carried weapons— probably spears and shields. As E. Kunze has explained, the five statuettes must have been made at intervals over a long period.[753] Here we illustrate one of a pair (Pl. 58), which together form the last link in the chain. Although these two pieces belong to the end of the seventh century, they follow the very same pictorial type[754] as the earliest statuettes, which are datable to the beginning of the seventh century. According to E. Kunze's fine interpretation, they represent the youthful Zeus; the form was repeated throughout the century in the Altis (Olympia's sacred precinct).[755] The wide belt, which appears both in these two later pieces

Hittite belt   (Pl. 58) and also in the earliest statuettes, is familiar to us from Hittite art. It is found on female figures of the middle and late Neo-Hittite styles (Pl. 22b; 26–28) and on many male and female figures of Assyrian and Syrian reliefs. It seems to have been a kind of sash, which was made of fine material and wound around the body. It made its way into Greece as early as the end of the eighth century along with the Orientalizing tendency. The same may be said of the helmets of the statuettes, although this type of helmet is only found in complete form in a specimen from the middle of the century, the so-called 'Steiner' figure;[756] this form too goes back to the Near East. This helmet type, with its plume projecting forwards, often occurs on Assyrian reliefs of the second half of the eighth century (Fig. 122). In somewhat modified form it recurs in the warriors of the orthostat reliefs of Karatepe (Pl. 34b).[757] The Urartian attachments in the form of a double head from Vetulonia in Etruria (Fig. 126)[758] help us to visualize the Near Eastern pieces which must have served Greek artists as models. However, Near Eastern objects featuring the above-mentioned helmet type must have been known in Greece as early as the last quarter of the eighth century, for the fragment of the upper end of a tripod leg in Olympia[759] shows a relief with two warriors, one of whom wears the same kind of helmet (Pl. 59).[760] The helmet of the other warrior has a different shape, which is also of Assyrian origin (Fig. 123).[761] The form of the plume of a bronze helmet in the Geometric style from Argos (Fig. 125)

PLATE 59 – Tripod leg found at Olympia. The struggle over the
Delphi tripod, with Herakles on the right and Apollo on the left.
Bronze. Late 8th century B.C. *Olympia Museum. Height of figures about
10 cm. Cf. p. 191.*

is a faithful rendering of the helmet plumes found on the reliefs of Tiglath-Pileser III (Figs. 123, 124).

Aramaeanizing Hittite hair style

In this connection it seems appropriate to ask whether any statuettes of the early seventh century, which have long cascading hair with dense thick locks, do not owe their coiffure to Near Eastern models. One might refer to a bronze statuette from Olympia[762] and another in the Athens National Museum.[763] Both have a hair style that closely recalls that of the late Neo-Hittite-Aramaean reliefs (Pl. 15; Figs. 11, 111). That there was no lack of late Neo-Hittite bronze objects in Olympia is proved by a bronze relief showing a man with an Aramaean nose (Pls. 12–15) and Aramaean dress. His cloak,[764] which winds diagonally around the body and is held at the tip by one hand, is also found on reliefs from Zincirli and Sakçegözü (Pl. 14). As on the reliefs from Sakçegözü (Pl. 14) and Zincirli, the figure on the Olympia relief also wears a chiton with the back part enlivened by a cluster of vertical pleats (Figs. 98, 99). Moreover, the hair of the head and beard is stylized in the Aramaean fashion, except that the execution is less careful than on the Sakçegözü relief. The Aramaean bronze relief from Olympia, which comes from the last quarter of the eighth century, demonstrates afresh that even in this early period Greek artists had models in the shape of Near Eastern originals from the southern Anatolian and northern Syrian areas. But the Greeks imitated only those Near Eastern objects and traits that suited their own tastes and experience. Objects such as the bronze relief from Olympia seem to have had no appreciable effect.

Aramaean origin of chiton

The close links of early Greek art with the Near East that have been indicated above suggest that the origins of many other stylistic features of Greek sculpture in the seventh century are to be sought in this quarter as well.

The word chiton, which ultimately derives from the old Akkadian language, was transmitted to the Greeks by the Aramaeans.[765] It may be that chitons were imported as fabrics made in the Near East. The long tunic worn by the Nikandre figure, the Auxerre statuette[766] and other seventh-century works is a simple garment, that is found throughout the world without need for positing foreign influence. But the belt appearing on the two pieces mentioned and on most of the figures of the seventh century points strongly to the dress of the middle Neo-Hittite figures (p. 95; Pls. 21, 22; Figs. 79–82). Such comparisons are sufficient to show that the long body tunic (together with its name and belt) derives from the Near East.

Urartian influences

Near Eastern influences from the Urartian and Iranian art spheres must have reached Greece as early as the end of the eighth century. Urartian attachments in the form of human figures were the most popular export objects of the Near

FIGS. 122, 123 – *Above, Fig. 122: Assyrian helmet. After Barnett and Falkner, Sculptures of Tiglath Pileser, Pl. 36. Second half of 8th century B.C. Cf. p. 190. – Below, Fig. 123: Assyrian helmet. After Barnett and Falkner, Sculptures of Tiglath-Pileser, Pls. 50, 51, 62. Second half of 8th century B.C. Cf. p. 190.*

FIGS. 124–6 (from left to right) – *Fig. 124: Assyrian helmet. After Barnett and Falkner, Sculptures of Tiglath Pileser, Pl. 73. Second half of 8th century B.C. Cf. p. 192. – Fig. 125: Greek helmet. Found at Argos. After Demargne, Naissance de l'art grec, p. 360, Fig. 473. Late 8th century B.C. Cf. p. 190. – Fig. 126: Urartian attachment from Vetulonia, Etruria. After Akurgal, Kunst Anatoliens, p. 46, Fig. 26. Early 7th century. Cf. p. 150 and below.*

East after the late Neo-Hittite griffin attachments, which have been discussed above. Urartian cauldron attachments (Pl. 45) have been found at Olympia, Delphi and many other Greek sites. An attachment showing a bearded figure, which has come to light at Olympia,[767] is a companion piece to the attachment from Vetulonia[768] in Etruria (Fig. 126). Both again closely parallel the bearded head from Gordion reproduced here (Pl. 45). Figures of this kind were eagerly imitated in the great centres of the late eighth and early seventh centuries. More than thirty years ago E. Kunze published a fundamental study of the entire corpus of material.[769] Here we reproduce three photographs of two bird creatures from Olympia that formerly adorned the rims of two bronze cauldrons (Pls. 60, 61); Kunze has convincingly explained them as reworkings of foreign models produced by 'already mature, purely Greek' artists.[770] Although the Urartian pictorial type of bird creature has been continued faithfully and the equally Urartian ornament on the chest has been retained, it is clear that the idiom of the forms and ornament has a strongly Greek stamp. 'The organic fusion of the parts, the firm buoyant contours, the treatment and articulation of the hair,' the angular formation of the face and the projecting pointed nose are characteristics of early Greek art of the late eighth and early seventh centuries.[771] That many of these Greek versions of Urartian models originated only in the first quarter of the seventh century or even later has been irrefutably shown by R. Hampe.[772] Above (p. 181) we have tried to demonstrate that Near Eastern griffin and lion attachments were enthusiastically imitated well into the beginning of the second half of the seventh century.

Greek vase-painting of the first half of the seventh century shows a wealth of motifs that may be traced to Urartian and Luristan bronzes. The lions of early Attic (Pl. 41), as well as those of the earliest Protocorinthian vases[773] (Pl. 114), recall in their general appearance the lion figures of Luristan bronzes.[774] The buoyant diagonal movement of the running animal figures in early Greek vases (Figs. 115, 116) corresponds to a scheme that had been developed earlier in the art of eastern Anatolia and Iran (Fig. 127). A characteristic feature is the abdominal line, which is continued directly by the wide outstretched and superimposed forelegs, so that from the thigh to the tip of the fore feet a single diagonal line runs straight through. The earliest examples of this scheme in the Greek world appear on Attic,[775] Protocorinthian[776] (Fig. 115) and Cycladic (Fig. 128) vases. It is likely that Corinthian artists also took up some Urartian motifs. Whether the early Protocorinthian dot-rosettes are derived from the very similar decorative motif in Urartian art (Fig. 129) is not clear to me. But the half and quarter rosette of the animal frieze style derives from Near Eastern models, as R. D. Barnett has proved.[777] Apart from the examples Barnett cites, we meet these rosettes especially on Luristan bronzes.[778] It is revealing that the rosettes and ornamental circles appearing on the thighs of the human figures of an early Attic krater[779] (Fig. 130) and on those of a bronze statuette of the first quarter of the seventh century from Olympia,[780] recur in Luristan in the thighs of animal figures (Figs. 131, 132). The heart-shaped stylization of the shoulder blades as found among the animals depicted in Cycladic vase-painting (Pls. 54–56; Fig. 133) was a standard device among artists working in metal.[781] However, the use of the same scheme for the thigh of the rear legs is characteristic of painters of the animal frieze style (Fig. 134). In various Near Eastern countries this part of the animal was often stylized in the form of a special muscle configuration (Fig. 5). The S-spiral which appears on the thighs of the horses depicted on the Cycladic vase in the British

Other influences from Luristan bronzes

PLATE 60 – Bird creature. Cauldron decoration. Bronze. Found at Olympia. Greek work after Urartian models. Early 7th century B.C. *Olympia Museum. Height 6 cm. Cf. p. 193.*

PLATE 61 – Bird creature. Cauldron decoration. Bronze. Found at Olympia. Greek work after Urartian models. Early 7th century B.C. *Olympia Museum. Height 14 cm. Cf. p. 193.*

Museum (Pls. 54–56, Fig. 133), may also derive from Luristan bronzes, since metal-workers there were accustomed to adorning animal thighs with similar motifs (Figs. 131, 132). In their schemes for the thigh area Near Eastern artists always proceeded by stylizing the muscles as found in nature (Fig. 5). The Phrygian frieze plaques (Figs. 135, 136) then took over this motif from vase-painting in the animal frieze style.[782]

FIGS. 127–9 (from left to right). *Fig. 127: Lion from a silver horse-trapping. Ziwiye. After A. Godard, Le Trésor de Ziwiyè, p. 124, Fig. 109. Mannaean art. Early 7th century B.C. Cf. p. 194. – Fig. 128: Cycladic lion on a Naxian amphora. After Matz, Geschichte der griechischen Kunst, Pl. 175. Second quarter of 7th century B.C. Cf. p. 194. – Fig. 129: Urartian attachment from Toprakkale. After Akurgal, Kunst Anatoliens, p. 40, Figs. 18, p. 303; Appx. Fig. 9. Late 8th century B.C. Cf. Fig. 9, p. 194.*

The S-spiral depicted on the thighs of Cycladic horses recurs as a decorative motif on the same area of the body in an ivory lion from Artemis Orthia[783] and in Etruscan art (Fig. 137).[784] It was also used in a similar way as filler in animal bodies depicted in the animal-frieze style (Fig. 138).[785] The only example of an S-spiral used as body ornament that I have been able to find in the Near East appears on the glutei represented on a bronze statuette[786] from Kazbek (Fig. 139) and on the shoulders of the ibexes of a silver bowl from Ünye near Samsun in Anatolia (Pl. 67). But it may be assumed that this device must have been familiar as a body ornament on Luristan bronze animals, for the Greek and Etruscan

FIG. 130 – *Detail of an early Attic krater in Berlin. After CVA, Berlin, Pl. 20. Cf. p. 194.*

196

PLATE 62 – Row of men, one of whom holds a phorminx. Detail of a late Geometric Attic oinochoe from the Dipylon. Second half of 8th century B.C. *Archäologisches Institut, University of Tübingen*. *Cf. p. 204.*

examples mentioned can only be derived from artistic centres of the Iranian plateau such as those of Luristan. Luristan artists may have brought the motif with them from their homeland in the Caucasus, where the S-spiral had been very popular from the Bronze Age onwards.[787] The 'harmless strolling lions',[788] of the kind found in East Greek vase-painting, appeared earlier on Toprakkale shields.[789] The lower lip curling into a volute shape, which appears in many north Ionian lions (Fig. 140), need not reflect an accidental similarity, but may depend on the influence of Urartian models (Fig. 141).[790] The stylistic trends of the Orientalizing period led the Greeks to take up various shapes of vessels. K. R. Maxwell-Hyslop has indicated the important role of Urartian art in the transmission of Near Eastern vessel forms to Greece and Etruria.[791] Towards the end of the eighth century the new Orientalizing fashion was so powerful that the Urartian cauldron type and its accompanying base ousted the traditional Greek tripod together with the

Further Urartian influences

FIG. 131

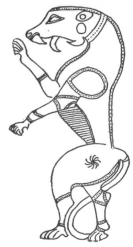

FIG. 132

FIG. 133

FIG. 134

FIG. 135

FIG. 136

FIG. 137

FIG. 138

FIG. 139

FIG. 140

FIG. 141

FIGS. 131–41. – *Fig. 131: Luristan bronze. After Godard, Bronzes du Louristan, Pl. 42. Early 7th century* B.C. *– Fig. 132: Lion from a bronze plate from Luristan. After Ghirshman, Perse, p. 70, Fig. 91. Early 7th century* B.C. *– Fig. 133: Horse depicted on a Cycladic griffin oinochoe from Aegina. After P. Bocci, Studi miscellani, 2, Pl. 9. (Cf. Figs. 54–56.) – Fig. 134: Boar depicted on an oinochoe in the animal-frieze style from Bayrakli (Old Smyrna). After Akurgal, Kunst Anatoliens, p. 179, Fig. 126. – Fig. 135: Lion depicted on a terracotta revetment from Pazarli. After Akurgal, Phrygische Kunst, Pl. 52b. Second half of 6th century* B.C. *– Fig. 136: Ibex depicted on a terracotta revetment from Pazarli. After Akurgal, Phrygische Kunst, Pl. 54b. Second half of 6th century* B.C. *– Fig. 137: Horse on a Bucchero oinochoe. Late 7th century* B.C. *After Studi Etruschi, vol. 30, 1962, Pl. 24, Fig. 2. – Fig. 138: Lion on a plate from Nisyros, Rhodes. After Kardara, Rhodiake Angeiographia, Pl. 270; Clara Rhodos, vols. VI–VII, pp. 506–8, Pl. 1. – Fig. 139: Bronze figure from the Kazbek Treasure in the Caucasus. After Bossert, Kunstgewerbe, vol. IV, p. 10, Fig. 2. – Fig. 140: Lion from a vessel in the animal-frieze style. After Schiering, Werkstätten, Pl. 14, 2. – Fig. 141: Urartian lion type. After Akurgal, Kunst Anatoliens, p. 302, Fig. 6. Cf. pp. 194f. (Figs. 131–8), 196 (Fig. 139), 197 (Figs. 140, 141).*

199

cauldron with ring handles. Early Attic and Protocorinthian vase-painters liked to show the new cauldron with its animal protomae and conical base.[792] Elsewhere I have shown that the base of the bronze cauldron from Praeneste in Etruria is a Near Eastern work in the style of the Sakçegözü reliefs.[793]

The Near Eastern shapes of metal vessels were even imitated in clay by early Attic potters. Attic foot cauldrons and foot kraters from the Kerameikos (Fig. 142), from the Athenian Agora and the road to Piraeus (Fig. 143)[794] are Greek versions of Near Eastern models. R. Hampe has recently pieced together several vases from hundreds of small early Attic sherds he acquired on the art market. They are now exhibited in the Schönborner Hof, Mainz (Fig. 144). Similar cauldron shapes and conical feet were often depicted on Assyrian reliefs (Figs. 145, 146).[795] Moreover, the plastically formed lotus blossoms (Fig. 147), which were attached to the cauldron rim in the manner of animal protomae, often occur as decorative ornament on vessels in the northern Syrian and Anatolian art spheres. Above we have encountered vessels with similar ornament from Tell Halaf (Fig. 92), Til Barsib, Cyprus and Nimrud[796] (p. 118). The last example, in ivory, shows a type of lotus bud very close to examples found in early Attic ceramics. Another piece with a handle decorated with a lotus blossom (Fig. 147) is in the Metropolitan Museum, New York. Like the piece found at Nimrud it must have come from a Syrian workshop. The early Attic imitations may have been inspired by Near Eastern metal vessels resembling that in New York. As R. Hampe has recognized,[797] Tumulus III at Gordion, excavated by German archaeologists, has yielded a

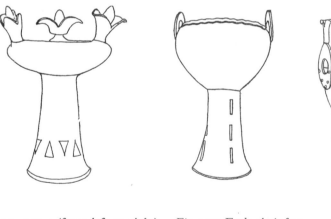

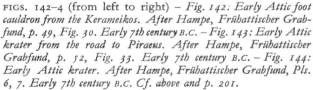

FIGS. 142–4 (from left to right) – *Fig. 142: Early Attic foot cauldron from the Kerameikos. After Hampe, Frühattischer Grabfund, p. 49, Fig. 30. Early 7th century B.C. – Fig. 143: Early Attic krater from the road to Piraeus. After Hampe, Frühattischer Grabfund, p. 52, Fig. 33. Early 7th century B.C. – Fig. 144: Early Attic krater. After Hampe, Frühattischer Grabfund, Pls. 6, 7. Early 7th century B.C. Cf. above and p. 201.*

FIGS. 145–7 (from left to right) – *Fig. 145: Assyrian krater from a relief of the Sennacherib period. After Maxwell-Hyslop, Iraq, vol. 18, 1956, p. 153, Fig. 15. – Fig. 146: Assyrian krater from a relief of the Sennacherib period. After Maxwell-Hyslop, Iraq, vol. 18, 1956, p. 153, Fig. 4. – Fig. 147: Handle of a vessel with a lotus blossom. After Perrot and Chipiez, Histoire de l' Art, vol. III, p. 797, Fig. 557. Metropolitan Museum, New York. Cf. p. 200 and below.*

bronze cauldron[798] showing the same lotus blossoms on the handles (Fig. 148). But the handles are not ring-shaped as in the early Attic cauldron in Mainz (Fig. 144); instead they are semi-circular as in the New York piece (Fig. 147). The Gordion object may be an import from the Near East. Ornaments like lotus blossoms are foreign to the nature of Phrygian art. Therefore this vessel cannot have been made in central Anatolia.[799] Furthermore, a bronze basin has been found at Gordion which, with its ring handles (Fig. 149), is a version of the Greek tripod cauldron.[800] Tumulus III at Gordion,[801] from which the bronze basin with lotus-blossom handles comes, may be dated about 700. Therefore the Near Eastern pieces that served the Attic potters as models were exported to Attica about 700. That these foot cauldrons were popular at this time is shown by the Karatepe reliefs. The main scene of these reliefs (Pl. 33), as K. R. Maxwell-Hyslop has perceived,[802] has a foot cauldron of the type under discussion standing on a little table of its own between the man with a fan and the dining-table. Although the rendering leaves much to be desired, it cannot be doubted that it shows a foot cauldron of our type.

This observation is important, in as much as the dating of the Karatepe reliefs about 700 or at the earliest to the end of the eighth century (p. 141) is virtually certain. Of course the Greek vases are often modified versions with their own note of originality. Lotus blossoms are sometimes replaced by ring handles (Fig. 143), a characteristic feature of the Greek Geometric tripod cauldron. In some instances Near Eastern blossoms have been combined with Greek ring handles (Fig. 144). Moreover the proportions of the cauldrons and their conical bases are often, as Hampe has aptly noted,[803] adjusted to the Greek feeling for form. But the close dependence of the Greek works on their Near Eastern models (Figs. 145–148) is unmistakable.[803a]

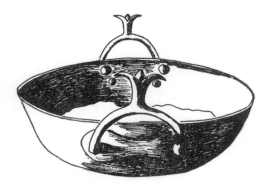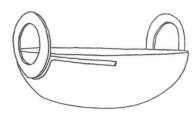

FIGS. 148, 149 – Left, Fig. 148: *Bronze basin with lotus-blossom handles. Found at Gordion. After Körte, Gordion, p. 72, Fig. 50. About 700 B.C.* – Right, Fig. 149: *Bronze basin with ring handles. Found at Gordion. After Körte, Gordion, p. 72, Fig. 52. About 700 B.C. Cf. p. 201.*

Towards the end of the seventh century the Orientalizing style was replaced in sculpture by monumental sculpture and in vase-painting by the black-figured style. However, the Near Eastern style elements continued to be taken over by the Greeks, though to a decreasing extent, of course. R. M. Cook has pointed to an important Near Eastern influence upon the technique of the black-figured style: 'Geometric artists had occasionally incised a zigzag line to relieve a dark band, but the systematic use of incision probably came from the engraving of metalwork, a process introduced into Greece from the East; this would account for the unnecessary incising of outlines in earlier black-figure work.'[804]

Orientalizing style in the Cyclades

The fine Melian amphora[805] of the second half of the seventh century in the Athens National Museum (Fig. 152a) displays a wealth of Near Eastern motifs, which appeared somewhat later in the Cycladic islands than on the mainland.

The main scene seems to show an important event from the legend of the sanctuary of the Delian Apollo:[806] with the Hyperborean maidens the god returns from the far north to be received by his sister Artemis. The ceremonial grouping of the Hittites, whereby in divine and royal couples the female figure always stands at her male consort's left (p. 127) has been consciously followed here. The two deities on the Melian amphora are shown at the moment of meeting, as in the main scene at Yazilikaya (Fig. 27). The maidens raise their hands in greeting. Since in both instances the scenes are to be regarded as directed towards the observer, the god stands on the goddess's right on the amphora and at Yazilikaya. Zeus and Hera[807] (Pls. 64, 65), Menelaus[808] and Helen (Fig. 150), Paris[809] and Helen (Fig. 151) were all shown in the same way.[810] Especially the wooden piece from Samos attests that in early Greek art, just as in the comparable late Neo-Hittite Aramaean couple from Maraş (Pl. 26), the female figure follows Hittite usage in always appearing to the left side of her partner, whether seated or standing. The goddess on the amphora appears in a simplified and altered version of the Near Eastern theme of 'Mistress of the Beasts'.[811] The wings, which show the horse to be a divine steed, have the early Neo-Hittite sickle shape, which the Greeks took over from the Luristan bronzes.[812] The small rosette, which adorns the thigh of the left-hand warrior in the combat scene on the neck of the amphora,[813] points to influence from Luristan bronzes (p. 194; Figs. 131, 132). The griffin protome appearing at the end of the chariot shaft is a Hittite motif known to us from chariot senes at Zincirli (Fig. 66), Carchemish and Tell Halaf (p. 111). In Greek art it first appears on this amphora. Later the motif occurs in Ionian sculpture[814] and vase-painting[815] as well as on architectural reliefs in terracotta[816] of East Greek art. The long trailing garments worn by Artemis and the maidens as well as by the women on the neck of the vessels recall the dress of figures on Hittite reliefs (Pl. 22a). They appear in similar form on Syrian and Phoenician reliefs from Nimrud (Figs. 107, 110). The long tunic with its pointed train was usual in these Syrian reliefs. The lattice pattern of the garments of the Melian figures is a favourite motif (p. 154) of Phoenician (Pls. 36, 39) and Syrian[817] (Pl. 41; Figs. 107, 108) art. Since Syro-Phoenician ivories were exported to Greece until

PLATE 63 – Chiot cup (detail). Found at Çandarli (Pitane). About 560 B.C. *Archaeological Museum, Istanbul. Cf. p. 183.*

FIG. 150 – *Menelaus courting Helen. Shield relief. After Kunze, Archaische Schildbänder, Pl. 11. Early 6th century* B.C. *Cf. p. 202.*

Earliest lyre representations

the middle or even until the end of the seventh century (p. 148), it is not difficult to accept the possibility of influence by Syro-Phoenician art. The women's heads depicted on metope registers around the foot of the amphora[818] also speak in favour of links between Melian vase-painters and Syrian art, for they recall the theme of the 'Woman at the Window', a favourite motif of Syrian ateliers (Pl. 38). The lyre in the god's hand (Fig. 152b) has a very similar form to that of the phorminx on a late Geometric oinochoe from the Dipylon,[819] which is now in Tübingen (Pl. 62). Both derive from Near Eastern models, for the lyre shown on the Karatepe reliefs (Pl. 32, Fig. 153) has almost the same form as that on the Greek vase. None the less the Melian lyre presents a novelty of great importance: it has seven strings. Lyres of similar shape with the same number of strings are represented on two sub-Geometric vessels of the second quarter of the seventh century. They came to light in excavations at Old Smyrna[820] (Fig. 154) and at Pitane (Fig. 155). These two vessels and the Melian amphora constitute the earliest known representations of the seven-stringed lyre. The phorminx, the instrument of the Homeric age, has four strings.[821] The early Greek lyres of the mainland possessed between three and five strings. Near Eastern lyres, however, generally had many strings, in some instances reaching the figure of twenty-three.[822] Neither the Near Eastern nor the early Greek lyres from the mainland represented in art show a standard number of strings; this begins only in the examples painted on the Melian vases and the two vessels from Old Smyrna and Pitane. It is probably no accident that the earliest representations of the newly invented lyre with seven strings first appear on vessels of East Greek origin. It must have been just at the beginning of the second quarter of the seventh century that Terpander of Lesbos became acquainted with Anatolian music at Lydian banquets, as a fragment of Pindar relates.[823] Perhaps it is due to this contact of Greek singers with Lydian and Phrygian music that the sequential transition from the four-stringed phorminx to the seven-stringed lyre took place. The impulse to increase the strings came from outside, but the seven-stringed instrument is a Greek achievement. Henceforth it became standard on all lyres, providing the basis for the European musical scale.

PLATE 64 – Sacred marriage of Zeus and Hera. Wood carving from the Heraion of Samos. Last quarter of 7th century B.C. *Lost. Height 19.1 cm. Cf. pp. 207 ff.*

65 a

b

c

d

e

f

g

The Melian amphora is not the only object that reveals the multiple Near Eastern influences current about the middle of the seventh century in the Cyclades. We have seen above that the Cycladic oinochoe in the British Museum (Pls. 54–56; Fig. 133) also shows a great many style elements that derive from Near Eastern models.[824]

The relations of the East Greek world, especially its Ionian areas, with the Near East began only about 650. Although Samos was one of the Greek centres that imported and imitated Near Eastern works towards the end of the eighth century (p. 180), the Hellenic East failed to play a role in the development of early Greek art.[825] Samos, like the whole of western Anatolia, seems to have undergone a period of stagnation in the first half of the seventh century.[826] After the middle of the seventh century, with the founding of colonies, a great upsurge under Milesian leadership is evident in all areas of the Ionian world.[827] At this time most parts of the Greek East came into direct contact with the Near East. But the results of this contact were entirely different from those produced by the meeting of the Greek mainland with the Near East in the course of the eighth century. At that time the Greeks were still inexperienced and could only profit from the Near East in restricted fields. But now, when Hellenism found itself at a much more advanced stage of cultural development, the East Greeks were able to use their Near Eastern contacts to deal with fundamental questions of spiritual and intellectual life. For this reason the birth of philosophy and the exact sciences occurred not on the Greek mainland, but in the Greek cities of the west coast of Anatolia. At this time the mainland had left behind its Orientalizing phase, and had begun to concern itself with the consolidation of its social structure and the development of intellectual life, using native Greek components. After the middle of the seventh century the Near East and especially the newly discovered Egypt seem to have become the goals of Ionian Greeks in search of new knowledge and experience. Thales of Miletos travelled extensively as a merchant, visiting Egypt and acquiring a wide background in various fields. Another Milesian, Anaximander, who designed a world map and a chart of the heavens, probably studied the ancient astronomical lore of the Near Eastern peoples in some great centre such as Babylon. The Ionian natural philosophers received manifold impulses from the Near Eastern lands, but in an astonishingly short time they discovered the method of scientific research, thereby raising intellectual activity to an altogether different level, one on which the foundations for the western spirit could be built.

Eastern elements are evident in the Ionian world in all realms of cultural activity. We shall discuss this matter first in relation to sculpture. The fine wood carving of the late seventh century from Samos (Pls. 64, 65) is an East Greek creation,[828]

Orientalizing style in Ionia

Origin of philosophy and exact sciences

Wood carving from Samos

PLATES 65a–d – Ivory statuette from the Dipylon, from the same tomb as the piece shown in Plate 49. Late 8th century B.C. *National Museum, Athens. Height 10.8 cm. Cf. p. 174.*

PLATES 65e, f – Zeus and Hera (see Plate 64).

PLATE 65g – Funerary stele of Dermys and Kittylos. Limestone. Found at Tanagra. Late 7th century B.C. *National Museum, Athens. Overall height 2 m. Cf. p. 209.*

FIG. 151 – *Marriage of Paris and Helen. From a Corinthian krater. After Schefold, Früh-griechische Sagenbilder, Pl. 70a. Cf. p. 202.*

revealing a great number of Near Eastern traits. On account of the eagle visible between the heads of the figures the couple may be identified unmistakably as Zeus and Hera. This attribute also confirms that this piece with its markedly Near Eastern aspect is actually a Greek product.

Hieros gamos In this carving Zeus and Hera are shown in a sacred marriage scene. A very similar *hieros gamos* scene is found on the short side of a steatite pyxis[829] of northern Syrian-Aramaean origin belonging to the late eighth century (Fig. 156). Just as in the Samian carving, the male figure holds the breast of his consort, who stands on his left flank.

The *hieros gamos* scene reflects the alliance concluded between the Indo-European storm god and the Mediterranean fertility goddess.[830] This link had already come into being at the end of the third millennium with the immigration of the Indo-European peoples into Anatolia. The main scene at Yazilikaya (Fig. 27) is the oldest known depiction of the alliance between the autochthonous Hattian goddess Wurusemu and the foreign storm god of the Hittites.[831] Since, however, in *Hittite pictorial* this league of equals the storm god was still the preferred partner, it follows that *motif* he should stand on the right side. In Hittite texts the right is expressly characterized as the place of honour.[832] This pictorial motif of the divine couple, with the god always standing to the right of his consort, has retained its validity from Hittite times down to the present. A number of examples are known from Neo-Hittite art (p. 127; Pls. 26–29). The Samian wood carving represents one of the many examples that could be cited from Greek Archaic times (p. 202). Later, the Jupiter Dolichenus reliefs re-echo the same theme.[833] During the Roman empire the ruler pair appear in the Hittite position on a series of cameos. Even in Naumburg Cathedral in medieval Germany the donor Eckhard stands on the right side of his wife Uta. And finally in state ceremonies of our own day the royal pair regularly follow the old Hittite scheme.

The wood carving from Samos shows another Hittite feature whereby each partner places his arm on the shoulder of the other. This attitude was already noted in the case of the Maraş couple (Pl. 26). It recurs in Greek art on the funerary stele of Dermys and Kittylos from the end of the seventh century (Pl. 65g).[834] The same motif also found favour in Egyptian art. In fact Phoenician and late Neo-Hittite sculptors took it from Egyptian models. The Greeks must have received it indirectly via Syrian or late Neo-Hittite works, since the Samian wood carving shows only traits of Near Eastern character.

As D. Ohly rightly says,[835] Hera's gesture of grasping Zeus' arm may be compared with the scene of Achilles and Priam in the *Iliad*,[836] where Achilles seizes the wrist of the old man's right hand, so as to 'take the fear from his heart'. Although this friendly and attractive gesture found literary expression in Homer, it must be noted that it is not exclusively Greek, but is a common custom of Mediterranean lands that can be traced in the Near East from very early times. On a Phoenician bowl one sees a goddess nursing the young king (Fig. 102). The latter holds the goddess's wrist, just as Hera does in the Samos carving. The god Sarruma, who is embracing King Tuthaliya, holds him by the wrist. Moreover, King Araras, who proclaims his son crown prince on a relief from Carchemish (Fig. 93), leads him by the wrist. This motif seems to be ultimately of Egyptian origin since it appears on wall reliefs there from the fifth dynasty onwards (p. 136).

Hand gestures

It is uncertain whether Hera's gesture is to be interpreted simply as a sign of agreement. Rather it seems likely that in this case, in accordance with the Mediterranean temperament of the Ionian Greek character, two contradictory feelings, affirmation and denial, are expressed simultaneously. The carving from Samos recalls a passage in the fourteenth book of the *Iliad* where the poet tells the charming story of the meeting between Zeus and Hera on Mount Ida in north-western Anatolia. In fact the Samian wood carving almost looks like a sculptural version of the love scene described by Homer. In the sculptural group Zeus holds Hera's breast; in the *Iliad* he enfolds the goddess in his arms in the sweetness of his desire. On the other hand the way in which Hera takes the wrist of her consort can signify, as we have said, both acceptance and refusal, paralleling her attitude in the epic poem, where she seems freely to reject the entreaty of love's embrace, while in reality she has come from afar to join her husband on the marital couch. Here is the passage from the *Iliad*[837] in the translation by R. Lattimore.

Love scene of Zeus and Hera

> But Hera light-footed made her way to the peak of Gargaros
> on towering Ida. And Zeus who gathers the clouds saw her,
> and when he saw her desire was a mist about his close heart
> as much as on that time they first went to bed together
> and lay in love, and their dear parents knew nothing of it.
> He stood before her and called her by name and spoke to her: 'Hera,
> what is your desire that you come down here from Olympos?
> And your horses are not here, nor your chariot, which you ride in.'
>
> Then with false lying purpose the lady Hera answered him:
> 'I am going to the ends of the generous earth, on a visit
> to Okeanos, whence the gods have risen, and Tethys our mother,
> who brought me up kindly in their own house, and cared for me.

FIG. 152a – *Artemis receiving Apollo at Delos. From a Cycladic amphora. Second half of 7th century B.C. Cf. p. 202.*

I shall go to visit these, and resolve their division of discord,
since now for a long time they have stayed apart from each other
and from the bed of love, since rancour has entered their feelings.
In the foothills by Ida of the waters are standing
my horses, who will carry me over hard land and water.
Only now I have come down here from Olympos for your sake
So you will not be angry with me afterwards, if I
have gone silently to the house of deep-running Okeanos.'

Then in turn Zeus who gathers the clouds answered her:
'Hera, there will be a time afterwards when you can go there
as well. But now let us go to bed and turn to love-making.
For never before has love for any goddess or woman
so melted about the heart inside me, broken it to submission,
as now . . .'

Then with false lying purpose the lady Hera answered him:
'Most honoured son of Kronos, who sort of thing have you spoken?
If now your great desire is to lie in love together
here on the peaks of Ida, everything can be seen. Then
what would happen if some one of the gods everlasting
saw us sleeping and went and told all the other immortals
of it? I would not simply rise out of bed and go back
again, into your house, such a thing would be shameful.

No, if this is your heart's desire, if this is your wish, then
there is my chamber, which my beloved son Hephaistos
has built for me, and closed the leaves in the doorposts snugly.
We can go back there and lie down, since bed is your pleasure.'

Then in turn Zeus who gathers the clouds answered her:
'Hera, do not fear that any mortal or any god
will see, so close shall be the golden cloud that I gather
about us. Not even Helios can look at us through it,
although beyond all others his light has the sharpest vision.'

So speaking the son of Kronos caught his wife in his arms. There
underneath them the divine earth broke into young, fresh
grass, and into dewy clover, crocus and hyacinth
so thick and soft it held the hard ground deep away from them.
There they lay down together and drew about them a golden
wonderful cloud, and from it the glimmering dew descended.

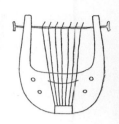

It should be remarked in passing that Homer's description contributes a small
detail to the question of Near Eastern influences. The lotus plant alluded to in the
concluding verses of the love scene points to the region of Syria and Phoenicia,
where older and probably rather different versions of the divine love scene may
have been sung.

D. Ohly has convincingly shown that the chiton of the god in the Samian wooden
carving is to be found on contemporary Greek reliefs, for example on a Laconian
ivory pinax.[838] But if we survey the field of Near Eastern models we will find the
same costume in even more striking form in Syrian art (Fig. 108). An almost
identical chiton is worn by the man of a Syrian ivory from the Barberini tomb at
Praeneste.[839]

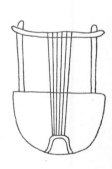

A critical examination of the faces of the two deities discloses un-Greek features,
especially in the supple, full forms, as well as in the curved, over-fleshy nose and
the thick lips. Yet the Samian piece is a Greek work; the free and lively attitudes
of the figures attest this. The goddess is clothed entirely in the Greek manner.
As Ohly has shown,[840] she wears a cape, such as is found also in the Auxerre
statuette and in the sculptures at Prinias in Crete. The same garment occurs in a
fine wooden statuette recently excavated on Samos.[841] The manifold Near Eastern
motifs cited are not simply imported elements: rather they are ingredients of a
new formal idiom that have already been modified and adjusted to suit Greek

FIGS. 152b–55 (from top to bottom) – *Fig. 152b: Lyre depicted on Cycladic amphora in
Fig. 152a. – Fig. 153: Lyre shown on a relief at Karatepe (cf. Pl. 32). – Fig. 154: Lyre shown
on a deinos sherd from Bayrakli (Old Smyrna). After Akurgal, Kunst Anatoliens, p. 15,
Fig. 3. Second quarter of 7th century B.C. – Fig. 155: Lyre depicted on a sub-Geometric krater
from Çandarli (Pitane). Unpublished. Cf. p. 204.*

FIG. 156 – *Steatite pyxis showing the hieros gamos (sacred marriage) theme. After Barnett, Nimrud Ivories, p. 130, Fig. 48. Aramaean work of northern Syrian type. Second half of the 8th century B.C. British Museum. Cf. p. 208.*

taste. The carver of the Samian group was an artist working in the Greek style, but he probably had a rather exotic name.

Ephesian ivories   As further creations of the Ionian area influenced by the Near East we may mention the ivories from Ephesos.[842] A spinning woman in ivory from the late seventh century, which comes from the Artemision at Ephesos (Pl. 66), still depends on the Near Eastern tradition in the formation of the incised eyebrows and eyelids; but like the related eunuch priest it is a work of Ionian ivory carvers. Elsewhere I have shown that the cylindrical form of the lower body, which is shaped in the fashion of the *xoana* (wooden cult images), and the motif of the spinning figure caught in a particular moment of action are Greek traits.[843] The non-Greek facial type suggests that we have here one of the Lydian maidens, who (as Aristophanes indicates in *The Clouds*) were instructed to hold the goddess Artemis in great honour.[844]

The spinner's jewellery—the heavy necklace made up of big pearls and especially the thick bracelets—has a Near Eastern look. One thinks involuntarily of the Aramaean female statuettes of late Neo-Hittite art, which have similar thick bracelets (Pls. 25–28). The spiral curl by the ear also recalls Hittite or Aramaean female figures. As F. Poulsen and more recently R. D. Barnett have emphasized,[845] the bonnet bedecked with pearls bears great similarity to that of the late Neo-Hittite King Warpalawas of the last quarter of the eighth century. I believe that it consists of a kind of head-dress that is known to us from Greek literary sources as the mitre. We know that Sappho wanted for her daughter a brightly coloured Sardian head-piece, but she could not buy it because Pittacus, Mytilene's ruler, had forbidden the import of luxury goods from abroad.[846] Here is the passage in a translation by Mary Barnard.[847]

Don't ask me what to wear

I have no embroidered
headband from Sardis to
give you, Cleis, such as

PLATE 66 – Priestess. Ivory statuette from Ephesos. Late 7th century B.C. *Archaeological Museum, Istanbul. Height 10.5 cm. Cf. p. 212.*

I wore
> and my mother
always said that in her
day a purple ribbon
looped in the hair was thought
to be high style indeed

but we were dark:
> a girl
whose hair is yellower than
torchlight should wear no
headdress but fresh flowers.

Two types of swastika motif

The unusual swastika motif (Fig. 157) that appears on King Warpalawas' long chiton (Pl. 30) links the Ivriz relief with the ivory carvings from Ephesos. In this swastika the arms do not originate from a single central point, as was normal in the swastikas of the Geometric style (Fig. 157); instead they start from two centres (Fig. 157). The swastika form mentioned appears in Phrygian art as an ornament in wood carvings. Phrygian artists must have acquired 'sub-Geometric' swastikas of this type from Near Eastern textiles, such as the garment Warpalawas wears on the Ivriz rock relief (Pl. 30). In later periods of antiquity the Phrygians were famous for their embroideries and cloths.[848] An ivory from Ephesos representing a eunuch priest[849] displays the same swastika found on the textiles (Fig. 157). The artist probably took the motif from Phrygian textiles.

Syrian origin of Archaic smile

Another essential feature the Greeks borrow from the Near Eastern world is the 'Archaic smile', which makes its appearance in Greek art about the middle of the seventh century, to remain dominant throughout the Archaic period.[850] It can hardly be an original invention of the 'Daedalic' artists, but must go back to Syrian models that were influential during the orientalization process of the first half of the seventh century. The 'Mona Lisa' of the Baghdad Museum (Pl. 37) and the other women depicted in Syrian ivories (Pls. 38, 43) are already shown smiling. It seems very likely that early Greek artists had a special predilection for this attractive Syrian ivory work. In any event the sudden appearance of the motif together with other Near Eastern elements speaks in favour of an eastern origin. The Syrian artists had been able to express the smile only by distorting the lips, and the eyes lacked any genuine radiance. The first examples from the Greek mainland also lack any smiling quality in the eyes. It was the accomplishment of Ionian artists that in the faces they created they were able to endow the eyes and the lips with an air of radiant happiness. The oldest example of an art object with smiling eyes may be the ivory eunuch priest from the Artemision at Ephesos.

FIG. 157 – *Swastika emblems. Above, in metal work and vase-painting; below, in textiles (cf. the costume of King Warpalawas at Ivriz, Pl. 30). Cf. above.*

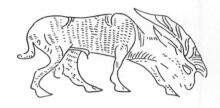

FIGS. 158a, b – *Above, Fig. 158a: Ibex depicted on a bronze mirror in Berlin. After Greifenhagen, Antike Kunst, vol. 8, 1956, p. 16, Pl. 5. East Greek work. First half of 6th century B.C. Cf. p. 216. – Below, Fig. 158b: Lotus anthemion from the same mirror.*

The spinning woman (Pl. 66), about a decade earlier, still lacks these gay eyes. Like the newly published ivory statuette of a man, now in Berlin (Fig. 166), this shows the smile only in the modelling of the mouth area. The Berlin statuette is strongly anchored to the Near East. In an informative article A. Greifenhagen has weighed all the possibilities in the light of clear stylistic and iconographic observations, rightly stressing the close connections with Syrian ivories. Yet he is justified in calling this fine ivory an Anatolian Greek work. Of course its creator may have been a carver of Syrian origin active in Ephesos who still worked predominantly in the style of the traditional Syrian school. With the long shoulder tresses, which jut forward in spiral fashion, the hair style of the sphinx serving as a base is quite Syrian (Fig. 166). The statuette is not captured in momentary action, as is the case with the spinning woman (Pl. 66). Rather the figure has a static attitude like that of the Syrian support figures from Nimrud. The gentle undulations of the body also appear in Syrian statuettes. As Greifenhagen has shown, the chiton folds resemble those of Syrian ivories. As has been indicated, the smile is not an exclusively Ionian characteristic; it can just as easily be a Syrian peculiarity. To be sure, the eyes are not almond-shaped as in the Nimrud statuettes, but almost the same eyes appear in a Phoenician statuette from Samos which A. Geifenhagen illustrates. As he points out, the only certain Greek element seems to be the disk ear-rings. Greifenhagen rightly shows that this fine statuette may belong to the end of the seventh century.

In addition to Near Eastern influences, the Ionian objects have features that derive from Phrygian art. A Samian ivory youth[851] of the late seventh century *Phrygian elements* wears a belt which may be seen in similar form on the Ivriz rock relief (Pl. 30) and especially in Phrygian metalwork.[852] N. Firatli[853] has correctly compared a Phrygian bronze belt with that of Warpalawas. Moreover, R. S. Young has correctly linked a bronze object from Gordion, which probably represents a belt, with that of the Ivriz king.[854] Finally, I may refer to the observations of J. Boardman,[855] which demonstrate that as late as the sixth century the Greeks were still importing and copying Phrygian belts. Elsewhere we have shown that a number of Phrygian products, such as the Phrygian fibula and the Phrygian plate with bobbin-shaped handles, made their way into Greek centres.[856] In addition we were able to prove that various style elements of Phrygian art were borrowed by Cycladic ateliers.[857] Recently I. Strom has contributed new observations along these lines.[858] The Greeks, especially the Ionians, must have been under strong influence from the indigenous Anatolian peoples. G. M. A. Hanfmann has rightly

PLATE 67 – Silver bowl from the Pontus. Late Cimmerian work. Late 6th century
B.C. *Archaeological Museum, Ankara. Diameter 15.5 cm. Cf. p. 218.*

spoken of the important role of the native peoples of Anatolia in the formation
of the Ionian spirit.[859] Thus the charm of Ionian art is partly due to the exotic
contribution of the indigenous people of Anatolia.[860]

In the seventh and sixth centuries B.C. Near Eastern influence clearly slackened.
It is found only in the islands and in Anatolia, with rare appearances on the
mainland.

Two interesting works may be cited from this last period that still show multi-
farious Near Eastern influences.

Ivory mirror   A. Greifenhagen has recently published an engraved bronze mirror, which he
rightly classifies as an East Greek work.[861] He compares this mirror (Fig. 158a, b)
with another mirror in the British Museum.[862] The London mirror[863] does indeed
show some reminiscences of Urartian art, such as the spiral locks on the neck
and abdomen of the ibexes (Fig. 161) and the griffins' tails terminating in the

shape of a shaving brush (Fig. 162). I believe, however, that this piece represents Median work. The stylization of the thighs of the animal figures, which consists of a curve and a hump, betrays the Iranian origin of the mirrors. This is well known to us from Median works and counts as an important component of Achaemenid art. The bulls' heads and palmettes of the London mirror recur (as R. D. Barnett and A. Greifenhagen have already noted) on a sword handle from Chertomlyk,[864] also a Median piece.

The stylization of animals' bodies with rows of dots and short lines is a metalwork technique that was also popular among East Greek vase-painters. The lotus anthemion on the Berlin mirror decorated with rows of dots (Fig. 158b) closely recalls the *rinceaux* and lotus ornaments (Fig. 159) of the Rhodian and Anatolian vases in the frieze style, which are also adorned with rows of dots.[865] Some animal figures in the frieze style also display the same type of adornment on the shoulders and legs.[866] I have connected this type of painting in the frieze style with Phrygian art,[867] and, moreover, I have shown that Cycladic vases revealing this technique (Fig. 128) were inspired by Phrygian models.[868] Recently C. Kardara has further developed these ideas in her illuminating study of Rhodian vase-painting, where the problem is discussed at length.[869] I believe, however, that the scope of Phrygian influence was limited. Some years ago K. Schefold proved that there was a connection between the white slip of Orientalizing East Greek vase-painting and Phrygian art.[870] Other neighbourly links with Phrygia could be pointed out. Yet the importance of all these various influences should not be exaggerated: one must not forget that after the first quarter of the seventh century the flowering of Phrygian art and culture was over and that in the time of the frieze style, after 650, the provincial Phrygian workshops themselves had fallen under strong Greek influence. I believe that R. M. Cook also shares this view.[871] Since this technique of using rows of dots and short lines is characteristic of vase-painting in the frieze style, we are justified in assuming that the same technique was also employed in East Greek metalwork. A bronze plate in the Louvre, which was recently published by F. Villard,[872] is an attractive piece of evidence in support of this assumption. F. Villard plausibly ascribes the bronze plate to the East Greek sphere.[873] The figures show a similar body stylization of rows of engraved dots (Fig. 160), recalling that of the Berlin mirror (Fig. 158a, b). I believe F. Villard is correct in assuming a Rhodian artist.[874] This technique may

Phrygian technique of painting

Louvre bronze plate

FIG. 160 – *Detail of a bronze plate in the Louvre. After Villard, Monuments Piot, 48, p. 48, Pl. 5. East Greek work. Cf. above.*

have been common also to other centres of the East Greek world. Thus the Berlin mirror—as A. Greifenhagen rightly assumes[875]—can be claimed as an East Greek work of the first half of the sixth century. A silver bowl placed by E. Gjerstad in his Cypro-Egyptian III group has a linear ornament of human and animal figures, which recalls the East Greek bronze works under discussion.[876] But the figures of the Cypro-Egyptian bowl are embellished with parallel lines without the rows of dots and short lines on the bronzes. Thus the two East Greek works seem to have followed the tradition of the Urartian style employing short lines.[877] The very late Urartian features of the London mirror that have been discussed above are clear evidence for this.

Silver bowl from Black Sea area

Finally I may return to a previously mentioned silver bowl (p. 196) recently found at Ünye east of Samsun on the Black Sea coast (Pl. 67). In H. Luschey's classification[878] this piece belongs to the type of Greek phiale showing a simple series of bosses. With its limitation to five bosses only it is a unique piece, since

FIGS. 161–4 – *Left, above, Fig. 161: Ibex depicted on a bronze mirror in the British Museum. After Antike Kunst, vol. 8, 1965, p. 17, Fig. 1. Median work. Cf. p. 216. – Left, centre, Fig. 162: Griffin shown on the same mirror as in Fig. 161. – Left, below, Fig. 163: Scythian animal figure from the axe of the Kelermes Treasure. After Piotrovsky, Vanskoye Tsarstvo (Urartu), Pl. 55. Second quarter of 6th century B.C. Cf. note 881 and p. 217. – Right, Fig. 164: Gorgon depicted on a Rhodian plate in the British Museum. After Arias and Hirmer, Greek Vase Painting, Pl. 29. Early 6th century B.C. Cf. p. 219.*

218

FIG. 165 – *Detail of a cuirass from Olympia. After Olympia, vol. IV, Pl. 59. See below.*

the boss vessels known up to now have at least six or eight, and often more, even-numbered bosses in a row.[879] Within this broad type the Ünye piece stands closest to the example from the Oxus Treasure in the British Museum,[880] which also has figures between the bosses. The ibexes of the Ünye bowl (as I have shown elsewhere)[881] betray close links with Caucasian-Iranian art centres. The S-spiral on the shoulders recurs in a lion depicted on an Orientalizing vase (Fig. 138), and on the Kazbek bronze statuette from the Caucasus (p. 196; Fig. 139). The stylization of the leg muscles, which consists of parallel ribs, is found in the same form in the Scythian figures[882] of the Kelermes Treasure[883] (Fig. 163). The curious 'wings' of the ibexes together with the palmettes with two volutes opposite one another, attached to the ends of the five-pointed star, link the bowl with Median and Achaemenid objects.[884] The stylization of the thighs in the form of a divided heart connects the piece with the series of terracotta plaques from Pazarli (Fig. 136). The thick pointed horn with its pronounced knobbing recalls the horns of ibexes depicted on objects from the Ziwiye Treasure[885] and those of the Luristan bronzes.[886] Moreover, the double-lined half-circles on the abdomen and shanks are ornamental features of Mannaean art.[887] The bowl may have originated as an offshoot of Cimmerian art in the second half of the sixth century.

The treatment of folds first found in Greece in Ionian sculpture may likewise be traced to Phoenician, Syrian (Pl. 39, Figs. 106–110) or Aramaean sculptures of the late Neo-Hittite style (Pls. 12–14, 26–28, 31–35). We have discussed this problem in detail elsewhere. Here I simply note that the first attempts towards a fold system of this type are found earlier in the vase-painting of Cycladic, Rhodian and Thasian ateliers. We have assumed[888] that Urartian works may have played a mediating role, since various ateliers seem to have been active in Toprakkale until the beginning of the sixth century. Phoenician and Syrian ivories (Figs. 107–110) may also have influenced Greek vase-painters, for these ivories were also exported to Greece until the middle of the seventh century (p. 148). It has already been noted that the trailing garments on Cycladic vases with their decoration in lattice designs or other linear patterns (Fig. 152) find their best parallel in Syrian ivory reliefs (Figs. 104–110). The costume of the Gorgon on a Near Eastern plate of the early sixth century from Rhodes, which is now in London (Fig. 164),[889] shows diagonal lines running from the belt to the seam at the bottom that are probably to be regarded as folds. The Syrian ivories just mentioned have figures wearing similar garments enriched by the indication of folds. The Rhodes Gorgon shares the trailing garment with figures deriving from Syrian workshops. A woman on a piece of armour from Olympia (Fig. 165) wears a garment identical with that found on tridacna shells.

Origin of Greek fold rendering

FIG. 166 – *Ivory statuette in Berlin. After Greifenhagen, Jahrbuch der Berliner Museen, vol. 7, 1965, p. 151, Fig. 32. East Greek work. About 600 B.C. Cf. p. 220.*

PLATE 68 – Architectural revetment from Düver near Burdur, south-western Turkey. East Greek-Anatolian work. Late 6th century B.C. *Cf. p. 222.*

The artists of Cycladic and East Greek Orientalizing vases may have used as their models works of Phoenician, Syrian and perhaps Urartian origin, which were on the market until the mid-seventh century and considerably later. With great hesitation, perhaps about 570, sculptors adopted the foreign method of rendering folds. It is characteristic that the earliest examples of fold treatment in sculpture consists of parallel vertical folds, and shows a kind of modelling that is also found in the Gorgon figure on the above-mentioned Rhodian plate (Fig. 164) and in the East Greek ivory statuette of the late seventh century in Berlin (Fig. 166). In Crete fold treatment seems to have been employed already in the second quarter of the seventh century even in small sculptures. Among the remarkable finds brought to light by D. Levi's successful excavations at Gortyna there is an early Greek terracotta relief showing the murder of Agamemnon.[890] In this relief Aegisthus wears a long gown, the skirt part of which has vertical folds resembling the vertical lines of the vase-paintings that have been discussed. Long garments with vertical folds are also worn by the figures on Melian vases of the early sixth century.[891] The garment of the 'Mistress of the Beasts' on a bronze relief from

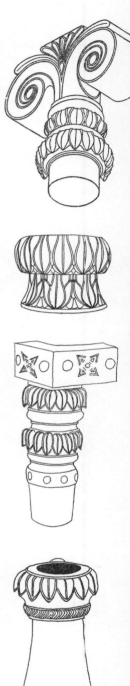

FIGS. 167–70 (from top to bottom) – *Fig. 167: Aeolic capital from Neandria (cf. Akurgal, Kunst Anatoliens, p. 285, Fig. 253). See below. – Fig. 168: Capital from Bayrakli (Old Smyrna). After Akurgal, Kunst Anatoliens, p. 282, Fig. 251. Late 7th century B.C. See below. – Fig. 169: Urartian piece of furniture (detail). Bronze. After Akurgal, Anatolia, vol. 5, 1960, Pl. 6. Early 6th century B.C. See below. – Fig. 170: Urartian piece of furniture (detail) from the Melgunov Treasure. After Barnett, Iranica Antiqua, vol. II, 1962. First half of 6th century. See below.*

Olympia seems to be arranged in comparable folds, although of a wavy type.[892] In the field of architecture the Ionians especially emulated the Near Eastern peoples. The Aeolic capital (Fig. 167) and more generally the first capital shapes of Ionian architecture were created after Near Eastern models. The foliate capital from Old Smyrna,[893] which dates from the end of the seventh century (Fig. 168), shows a circle of pendent leaves, which is found in the bases and capitals of late Neo-Hittite architecture of about a hundred years earlier (Figs. 33–35). Furthermore, the way in which the Smyrna capital is drawn in at the centre, and especially the finely curved profile of the circle of leaves, recalls some of the Zincirli bases (Figs. 33–35, 44, 45). The Near Eastern base and capital forms were carried throughout the Mediterranean world, including Ionia, by Syrian and late Neo-Hittite furniture in ivory (Figs. 44, 45) until the middle of the seventh century and probably later. Urartian bronze furniture with capitals and pendent leaf crowns (Fig. 169) have even been found in a Scythian tomb,[894] which K. Schefold has dated to the second quarter of the sixth century (Fig. 170).[895] The similarity between these Urartian pieces and Ionian work is startling. What distinguishes them is the buoyant profile of the Greek creations (Fig. 171), which is lacking in Urartian pieces, although the motif remains the same. It is particularly noteworthy that the Urartian models mentioned above originated at the same time as the Ionian works. The Smyrna capital shows that Ionian architects were capable of forming their building elements as early as the end of the seventh century. Apart from imported objects of the minor arts the Ionian builders must have seen various vase, column and capital forms at Near Eastern sites. It has been shown that in Assyrian art of the late eighth and the entire seventh century the late Neo-Hittite building forms were enthusiastically copied (p. 46). From such great monuments of this time, which stood *in situ* until the fall of the Assyrian empire in 606 B.C., Ionian artists may have taken their cue. The Smyrna capital represents one of the earliest experiments carried out by a Greek sculptor (Fig. 168). Similarly, the Aeolic capital (Fig. 167) developed towards the end of the seventh century after Phoenician models which Ionian artists could study both in imported objects of the minor arts and in the monuments themselves. But the Ionic capital, as I believe I have shown in my book *The Art of Anatolia*,[896] is an Ionian creation, representing a transformation of the Aeolic capital into a new shape in accordance with the Greek sense of form. In the repertory of Near Eastern capital forms there is not a single example that can be compared with the Ionic capital. The capitals on a relief from Khorsabad, which have been drawn so as to look like Ionic capitals, are really capitals with a crown of leaves.

The type of column-base found in Ionian architecture is largely dependent on Near Eastern models. In its general form the tectonic structure of the Ionic column-bases from the old Artemis temple in Ephesos (Fig. 171) was directly anticipated by late Neo-Hittite artists (Figs. 33–35, 44, 45).

All three components of the Ionic base—the plinth, the spira and the torus—are present in the column-bases of late Neo-Hittite buildings. The spira of the Ephesian example (Fig. 171) is made up of two deep grooves and three tori. A rectangular sphinx base, which was found at Nimrud, shows the same profile (Fig. 43). Astonishing similarities exist even in some details; thus we find the idea and the way in which the Ionic column necking is profiled with rings already in late Neo-Hittite examples (Figs. 44, 45, 49, 50). Still more important, however, is the general tectonic character which is found in antiquity in this pronounced form only in late Neo-Hittite and Ionian architecture (p. 86).

The lower parts of the columns modelled in relief, the *columnae caelatae* of the Artemis temple at Ephesos (Fig. 171), constitute a very successful translation of Hittite orthostats into the Ionian idiom. Moreover, the frieze of the Ionian temple and the terracotta revetments (Pl. 68) are, as has long been recognized, decorated with rich figural scenes following the practice of Near Eastern building façades (Pl. 20).[897]

FIG. 171 – *Columna caelata from the archaic Artemis temple at Ephesos. After Durm, Baukunst der Griechen, p. 319, Fig. 301. About 550 B.C. See above.*

EPILOGUE

Our stylistic analysis has clearly demonstrated that at the beginning of their history, in the eighth and seventh centuries B.C., the Greeks were greatly influenced by the Near East and that Greek art came into existence as a result of impulses from this foreign source. From the Near East the Greeks took not only the Phoenician alphabet, the greatest intellectual achievement of mankind, but also a varied selection of elements in the fields of religion, mythology and literature. One need only recall the numerous Near Eastern influences on the Greek pantheon and the close links between Hesiod's *Theogony* and Hurrian-Hittite mythology. An altogether new mythological world with such fantastic figures as griffins, sphinxes, Centaurs, sirens, chimaeras, and images of Pegasos and the Gorgon fascinated Greece in this period. Moreover, the human figures of early Greek art betray unmistakable Near Eastern traits. Hair in the 'stepped-wig' style, the long and short chiton, the two types of belt, as well as garment folds in the early Archaic style are (as we have shown) direct imitations of Near Eastern fashions. Helmet shapes, various musical instruments, such vessel shapes as the aryballos, deinos (cf. footnote 803a), krater and foot krater represent versions or even imitations of Near Eastern works. Countless motifs, ornamental schemes and also guiding rules employed by Greeks artists were borrowed from their Near Eastern neighbours. The 'Archaic smile' was a Syrian discovery. Even the preceding short summary suffices to show that the Near Eastern peoples played a great part in the formation of Greek art and culture. This was a peaceful encounter of unique importance, with the Near East the donor and Greece the recipient. In this way the Greeks learned much from the Near East, but they were also able in a short time to take over the intellectual leadership of mankind. They created an entirely new world, which became the cradle of western civilization.

The small city-states of the Greeks, which naturally staked no claims to universal dominion, prepared a favourable soil for the development of freedom of action in all fields of social and cultural life. Commercial and artistic competition was the main driving force behind the Greek miracle. Merchants, artists and men of every occupation were always on the look-out for the finest, best and newest things. This free competition facilitated the emergence of a spirit of inquiry. Thus from the mysterious wisdom of Near Eastern priests and from the millennial lore of the Orient, philosophy and the exact sciences developed in the sixth century B.C. in the Ionian territory of Anatolia. From the monologues of Near Eastern poets there grew the intricate Greek drama, in which events were not narrated but portrayed in living action.

As early as the seventh and sixth centuries writing was no longer the privileged possession of the priestly caste or of court scribes, but the common property of the whole people. Inscriptions on vases, statues and bronze objects clearly show that writing was widely diffused and that a great many citizens were literate. A comparable social structure may be observed in the Phoenician and Aramaean cities of the Near East in the eighth and seventh centuries B.C. In these cities, too, an intense artistic activity developed that involved a broad segment of the population. Monumental art, however, remained the monopoly of the king. The decisive factor was not the competition of citizens and communities, but the absolute will of the ruler. Yet in Greece, where in addition to the king or tyrant leading citizens could also commission large and important works, the artist had unrestricted access to all that was best and newest. Thus, after three centuries of experiment and development, toward the middle of the fifth century Greek artists discovered the third dimension, light and shade, and perspective. These achievements laid the foundations for western art.

NOTES TO TEXT

1. On 'conceptual' art see Schaefer, *Leistung*, pp. 35–54; Schaefer and Andrae, *Propyl. Kunstgesch.*, pp. 12–18.

2. On the main principles of conceptual art see Unger, *Sumer. und akkad. Kunst*, pp. 20–5; ibid., *Assyr. und babyl. Kunst*, pp. 42ff.; ibid., *Obelisk*, pp. 31ff.

3. Schaefer, *Leistung*, p. 36.

4. *Ibid.*, pp. 35–7.

5. Unger, *Sumer. und akkad. Kunst*, p. 21.

6. Strommenger, *Mesopotamien*, Pls. 212–14, 232–44.

7. *Ibid.*, Pls. 224, 241, 253–4, 258.

8. *Ibid.*, Pl. 243 (below).

9. Schaefer and Andrae, *Propyl. Kunstgesch.*, p. 164; Unger, *Assyr. und babyl. Kunst*, p. 43.

10. H. Gressmann, *Altorientalische Texte zum Alten Testament*, Berlin–Leipzig, 1926, p. 339.

11. Unger, *Assyr. und babyl. Kunst*, Fig. 64; Frankfort, *Art and Architecture*, Pls. 103, 106.

12. Unger, *Obelisk*, p. 55.

13. Unger, *Sumer. und akkad. Kunst*, p. 21.

14. Frankfort, *Art and Architecture*, Fig. 107.

15. *Ibid.*, Figs. 103, 106.

16. Strommenger, *Mesopotamien*, Pl. 233.

17. *Ibid.*, Pl. 246.

18. Unger, *Assyr. und babyl. Kunst*, Fig. 65 (After A. Paterson, *Assyrian Sculpture*, The Hague, 1915).

19. It should be noted that Assyrian artists, despite their attempts to create a sense of depth in orthostat reliefs, overlooked the simplest details. For example, the forelegs of a lion on a relief of Assurnasirpal II are on the same plane in the relief as the chariot wheel behind which they are depicted (cf. our Fig. 1 or Strommenger, *op. cit.*, Pl. 203). On such questions see Frankfort, *Art and Architecture*, p. 91.

20. Unger, *Assyr. und babyl. Kunst*, Fig. 64.

21. *Ibid.*, p. 42.

22. Schaefer, *Leistung*, p. 35.

23. *Ibid.*, p. 34.

24. *Ibid.*, pp. 34, 51 and note 46.

25. Unger, *Sumer. und akkad. Kunst*, p. 16.

26. *Ibid.*, p. 19.

27. *Ibid.*, pp. 12, 23.

28. Schaefer, *Leistung*, pp. 34, 51 and note 46.

29. Cf. also B. Meissner, *Babylonien und Assyrien*, vol. I, Heidelberg, 1920, p. 315; W. von Soden, *Herrscher im Altertum*, Berlin–Göttingen–Heidelberg, 1954, p. 86.

30. Moortgat uses the expression 'pictorial prose' (cf. Strommenger, *Mesopotamien*, p. 37). His study 'Die Bildgliederung der jungassyrischen Wandreliefs', *Jahrbuch der Preussischen Kunstsammlungen*, 1930, was unfortunately unavailable to me. B. Hrouda's article 'Die Grundlagen der bildenden Kunst in Assyrien', *ZA*, vol. 23, 1965, pp. 274–97, came to my attention while this book was in the press.

31. Frankfort, *Art and Architecture*, p. 73, calls it 'pictorial epic'.

32. On the 'art of narration' see Kantor, Perkins, Güterbock, Hanfmann, von Blanckenhagen, Witzmann, *AJA*, vol. 61, 1957, pp. 44–91.

33. H. J. Kantor, 'Narration in Egyptian Art', *AJA*, vol. 61, 1957, pp. 44–54.

34. Strommenger, *Mesopotamien*, Pls. 66–9.

35. *Ibid.*, Pls. 122–3.

33. On the 'art of narration' in Babylonian art see Ann Perkins, *AJA*, vol. 61, 1957, pp. 54–62.

37. See H. G. Güterbock, 'Narration in Anatolian, Syrian and Assyrian Art', *AJA*, vol. 61, 1957, pp. 62–71.

33. Frankfort, *Art and Architecture*, p. 99, Pl. 108b.

33. H. G. Güterbock, *op. cit.*, pp. 62f., Pl. 21h; Parrot, *Assur*, p. 5, Fig. 8; Strommenger, *Mesopotamien*, Pl. 188; T. B. L. Webster, *Hellenistic Art* (ART OF THE WORLD), London, 1967, p. 105.

40. P. H. von Blanckenhagen, 'Narration in Hellenistic and Roman Art', *AJA*, vol. 61, 1957, pp. 79ff. On the 'art of narration' in Greek art before the Hellenistic age see G. M. A. Hanfmann, *AJA*, vol. 61, 1957, pp. 71–8.

41. E. Bielefeld, 'Zum Problem der kontinuierenden Darstellungsweise', *AA*, vol. 71, 1956, pp. 31–4; H. Kähler, *Rome and her Empire* (ART OF THE WORLD), London, 1963, p. 129.

42. L. Schnitzler, 'Die Trajansäule und die mesopotamischen Bildannalen', *JdI*, vol. 67, 1952, pp. 43–77.

43. *Ibid.*, pp. 44ff., 76ff.

44 Unger, *Obelisk*; A. Moortgat, *Die bildende Kunst des alten Orients und die Bergvölker*, Berlin, 1932, pp. 52ff., Pls. 28, 29; A. Jeremias, *Handbuch der altorientalischen Geisteskultur*, 2nd ed., Berlin–Leipzig, 1929, p. 404, Fig. 227.

45 B. Landsberger, *Sam'al*, Ankara, 1948, p. 57, n. 144; p. 24, n. 48 (end of note).

46 Unger, *Obelisk*, p. 30.

47 *Ibid.*, p. 51.

48 On Middle Assyrian sculpture see A. Moortgat, 'Assyrische Glyptik des 13. Jhd.', *ZA*, vol. 13 (47), 1941, pp. 50ff.; ibid., 'Assyrische Glyptik des 12. Jhd.', *ZA*, vol. 14 (48), 1944, pp. 23–44; T. Beran, 'Assyrische Glyptik des 14. Jhd.', *ZA*, vol. 18 (52), 1957, pp. 141–215; U. Moortgat-Correns, in K. Bittel (ed.), *Beiträge zur mittelassyrischen Glyptik in vorderasiat. Archäologie: Studien und Aufsätze A. Moortgat zum 65. Geburtstag gewidmet*, Berlin, 1964, pp. 165–77; Frankfort, *Art and Architecture*, pp. 65–72; Strommenger, *Mesopotamien*, p. 36.

49 Strommenger, *op. cit.*, Pls. 191–9.

50 *Ibid.*, Pls. 200–1.

51 *Ibid.*, Pls. 196–7.

52 *Ibid.*, Pl. 208.

53 *Ibid.*, Pl. 207.

54 For literature on reliefs at Balawat see Strommenger, *Mesopotamien*, p. 107.

55 *Ibid.*, Pls. 209–14.

56 Unger, *Assyr. und babyl. Kunst*, p. 29, Fig. 41.

57 On the hair tuft see Thureau-Dangin, *Arslan-Tash*, p. 85; ibid., *Til-Barsib*, p. 45.

58 Schaefer and Andrae, *Propyl. Kunstgesch.*, p. 688, Fig. 533.

59 Strommenger, *Mesopotamien*, Pls. 206 (above), 210 (above), 204 (below), 213 (below) and in second row from bottom.

60 On stylistic questions relating to the depiction of lions see Akurgal, *Spätheth. Bildkunst*, pp. 39–79.

61 On W-shaped stylization of thighs see Akurgal, *Kunst Anatoliens*, pp. 31–2.

62 Strommenger, *Mesopotamien*, Fig. 202 (above and middle, for the bull and the recumbent lion), Fig. 208 (above right, for the camels); Barnett, *Palace Reliefs*, Pl. 14.

63 Tine-shaped stylization may be noted in the rendering of several horses on the bronze gate at Balawat. Barnett, *op. cit.*, Pls. 155 (above and middle), 140 (above right), 142 (above left). See also Yadin, *Art of Warfare*, vol. II, p. 403 and Fig. on same page.

64 Strommenger, *Mesopotamien*, Fig. 207.

65 Schaefer and Andrae, *Propyl. Kunstgesch.*, Fig. 544; Strommenger, *op. cit.*, Fig. 208; Unger, *Assyr. und babyl. Kunst*, Fig. 82; Frankfort, *Art and Architecture*, Fig. 93.

66 Strommenger, *op. cit.*, Figs. 209–14. Strommenger correctly states that on this door one may distinguish a large number of masters (p. 107). See also W. Nagel, 'Meister- und Gesellenarbeit an neuassyrischen Reliefs', *JdI*, vol. 73, 1958, pp. 1–8, Pl. 1.

67 Unger, *Assyr. und babyl. Kunst*, Fig. 43.

68 *Ibid.*, Figs. 42, 53.

69 A. Scharff and A. Moortgat, *Ägypten und Vorderasien im Altertum*, Munich, 1950.

70 Frankfort, *Art and Architecture*, Fig. 94b; Strommenger, *Mesopotamien*, Fig. 218; Barnett and Falkner, *Sculptures*, Pl. 6.

71 Strommenger, *op. cit.*, Fig. 217.

72 Barnett and Falkner, *op. cit.*, Pls. 85, 98.

73 *Ibid.*, Pl. 71.

74 *Ibid.*, Pls. 71, 85, 99.

75 *Ibid.*, Pl. 2; Thureau-Dangin, *Arslan-Tash*, Pl. 3.

76 See especially the lion hunt relief of Assurbanipal II in Berlin (Unger, *Assyr. und babyl. Kunst*, Fig. 85).

77 Barnett and Falkner, *Sculptures*, Pl. 2. See also the portal lions at Arslan-Tash: Thureau-Dangin, *Arslan-Tash*, Pl. 3.

78 Thureau-Dangin, *op. cit.*, Pl. 3.

79 Barnett and Falkner, *Sculptures*, Pls. 6, 36; Strommenger, *Mesopotamien*, Fig. 218. See also the horses in the wall-paintings at Til Barsib (Parrot, *Assur*, Fig. 347).

80 Barnett and Falkner, *op. cit.*, Pl. 71.

81 *Ibid.*, Pls. 16, 44, 81–3.

82 On the rope between the chariot box and the shaft-end see E. F. Weidner, *Die Reliefs der assyrischen Könige*, (*Archiv für Orientforschung*, 1939-, Suppl. 4), Pt. 1, p. 4.

83 Unger, *Die Reliefs Tiglatpilesers III aus Arslan-Tash*, Istanbul, 1925, p. 15.

84 The ninth-century war chariot also sometimes has a three-man complement (cf. for example the bronze gate at Balawat: Strommenger, *Mesopotamien*, Fig. 214). The actual number of occupants, however, seems to have been two during the ninth century. The small chariot box also looks too small for a heavier load.

85 Unger, *op. cit.*, pp. 15, 18.

86 *Ibid.*, p. 16.

87 Thureau-Dangin, *Til-Barsib*, p. 45. The

same motif recurs on orthostat reliefs in the South-west Palace at Kalkhu (Strommenger, *op. cit.*, Fig. on p. 218 (above); Barnett and Falkner, *op. cit.*, Pl. 6).

88 Unger, *op. cit.*; Thureau-Dangin, *Arslan-Tash*.

89 Thureau-Dangin, *Til-Barsib*, pp. 45ff. The frescoes in Rooms XXII and XXVII were restored in the reign of Assurbanipal (p. 45).

90 Unger, *op. cit.*, pp. 15ff.; Thureau-Dangin, *Arslan-Tash*, pp. 85ff.

91 Thureau-Dangin, *Til-Barsib*, p. 46. Cf., for example, the great hunting scene with the chariot: Parrot, *Assur*, p. 345, Fig. 268.

92 Frankfort, *Art and Architecture*, p. 78.

93 Strommenger, *Mesopotamien*, Pls. 220–1.

94 *Ibid.*, Pls. 198–9.

95 *Ibid.*, Pl. 192.

96 E. A. Wallis Budge, *Assyrian Sculptures in the British Museum: Reign of Ashur-nasir-pal, 885–860 B.C.*, London, 1914, Pls. 29, 49; Akurgal, *Spätheth. Bildkunst*, p. 27, n. 67.

97 The spiral lock also occurs in sculptures of the reign of Tiglath-Pileser III: Barnett and Falkner, *Sculptures*, Pls. 36, 55.

98 Cf. also W. Nagel, 'Meister- und Gesellenarbeit an neuassyrischen Reliefs', *JdI*, vol. 73, 1958, pp. 1–8, Fig. 1.

99 Strommenger, *Mesopotamien*, Pls. 225–8.

100 *Ibid.*, Pl. 193.

101 *Ibid.*, Pls. 226–7.

102 *Ibid.*, Pl. 224; Parrot, *Assur*, p. 13, Fig. 15.

103 An exception are the Lamassu figures, which have almost the same long diagonal tufts that are found in the Classical style (Strommenger, *op. cit.*, Pl. 220). They are, however, quite different in form from the ninth-century examples.

104 Yadin, *Art of Warfare*, p. 300, Fig. 2; p. 420, Fig. 1; P. E. Botta and E. Flandin, *Monuments de Ninive*, 2 vols., Paris, 1849.

105 Parrot, *Assur*, p. 32, Figs. 36, 38; Strommenger, *Mesopotamien*, Pl. 225.

106 Parrot, *op. cit.*, p. 266, Fig. 341; p. 37, Fig. 43.

107 Strommenger, *op. cit.*, Pl. 220.

108 Parrot, *Assur*, p. 32, Figs. 36, 38.

109 A. Scharff and A. Moortgat, *Ägypten und Vorderasien im Altertum*, Munich, 1950, pp. 414–26.

110 Schaefer and Andrae, *Propyl. Kunstgesch.*, Fig. 556; Frankfort, *Art and Architecture*, Pls. 102, 106, 110; Strommenger, *Mesopotamien*, Pl. 248.

111 Unger, *Assyr. und babyl. Kunst*, Fig. 64.

112 Schaefer and Andrae, *Propyl. Kunstgesch.*, Fig. 564; Frankfort, *Art and Architecture*, Pl. 110; Strommenger, *Mesopotamien*, Pl. 248.

113 Strommenger, *op. cit.*, Pls. 252, 258.

114 *Ibid.*, Pl. 244.

115 *Ibid.*, Pls. 233–60.

116 *Ibid.*, Pls. 220–7.

117 *Ibid.*, Pls. 247, 251, 254, 258.

118 Barnett, *Palace Reliefs*, Figs. 61–2; Schaefer and Andrae, *Propyl. Kunstgesch.*, Figs. 564, 566; Frankfort, *Art and Architecture*, Pls. 108–11; Strommenger, *Mesopotamien*, Pls. 248–50, 257, 260–1.

119 Barnett, *Palace Reliefs*, Figs. 58, 78; Strommenger, *op. cit.*, Pl. 249; Parrot, *Assur*, Fig. 55.

120 Barnett, *op. cit.*, Fig. 121; Schaefer and Andrae, *Propyl. Kunstgesch.*, Fig. 562; Strommenger, *op. cit.*, Pl. 234; Parrot, *op. cit.*, p. 44, Fig. 53.

121 Strommenger, *op. cit.*, Pls. 255–6; Parrot, *op. cit.*, pp. 58–61, Fig. 65; Barnett, *op. cit.*, Figs. 67–8, 70, 72.

122 G. Rodenwaldt, *Die Bildwerke des Artemistempels von Korkyra*, Berlin, 1939, pp. 188–90; Akurgal, *Griechische Reliefs aus Lykien*, p. 9.

123 See also Unger, *Assyr. und babyl. Kunst*, p. 43.

124 Schaefer and Andrae, *Propyl. Kunstgesch.*, Fig. 559; Strommenger, *Mesopotamien*, Pl. 260; Barnett, *Palace Reliefs*, Fig. 90.

125 Frankfort, *Art and Architecture*, Pl. 112; Strommenger, *op. cit.*, Pl. 259.

126 Frankfort, *op. cit.*, p. 99.

127 *Loc. cit.*

128 See also a scene of lions in combat on an ivory plaque from Ziwiye, in which the lion-slayer places with his left hand a specially prepared object into the animal's mouth (A. Godard, *Le Trésor de Ziwiyè*, Haarlem, 1950, p. 93, Fig. 81).

129 O. Weber, *Assyrische Kunst*, Berlin, 1924, p. 13.

130 Strommenger, *Mesopotamien*, pp. 117–8, Pl. 261.

131 Schaefer and Andrae, *Propyl. Kunstgesch.*, Fig. 537 (see the lion beneath the horses); Frankfort, *Art and Architecture*, Pl. 84; Strommenger, *op. cit.*, Pl. 202.

132 Frankfort, *op. cit.*, p. 131.

133 See Unger, *Assyr. und babyl. Kunst*, p. 43.

134 Strommenger, *Mesopotamien*, Pl. 243.

135 Frankfort, *Art and Architecture*, Pls. 104–5; Strommenger, *op. cit.*, Pls. 238–40.

[136] The complete scene is reproduced in Frankfort, *op. cit.*, Pls. 104–5.

[137] Strommenger, *Mesopotamien*, p. 116.

[138] *Ibid.*, p. 116, Pl. 240.

[139] *Ibid.*, Pl. 239 (240).

[140] Frankfort, *Art and Architecture*, Pl. 104 (in middle of plate).

[141] Strommenger, *op. cit.*, p. 116.

[142] H. Weidhaas, 'Der Bit Hilani', *ZA*, 11 (45), 1939, p. 109.

[143] M. E. L. Mallowan, *Iraq*, vol. 12, 1950, and the following volumes.

[144] Strommenger, *Mesopotamien*, pp. 39, 103 ff.

[145] Thureau-Dangin, *Til-Barsib*.

[146] Thureau-Dangin, *Arslan-Tash*.

[147] Frankfort, *Art and Architecture*, pp. 73–81; Strommenger, *Mesopotamien*, pp. 39, 109–12; Parrot, *Assur*, p. 8.

[148] Parrot, *op. cit.*, pp. 30ff., Figs. 35–8; Strommenger, *op. cit.*, Pls. 220–7.

[149] Strommenger, *op. cit.*, p. 109, Figs. 51–3.

[150] *Ibid.*, pp. 39, 109–12.

[151] *Loc. cit.*

[152] *Loc. cit.*

[153] Parrot, *Assur*, p. 98, Figs. 107, 108.

[154] Strommenger, *op. cit.*, pp. 39, 113–15.

[155] Unger, *Assyr. und babyl. Kunst*, p. 38, Fig. 66.

[156] *Ibid.*, p. 38.

[157] O. Neugebauer, *The Exact Sciences in Antiquity*, 2nd ed., Providence (R.I.), 1957, pp. 29ff., 97ff.

[158] *Ibid.*, pp. 48, 101–2.

[159] L. W. King, *Babylonian Boundary Stones and Memorial Tablets*, London, 1912.

[160] Akurgal, *Spätheth. Bildkunst*, p. 134.

[161] Strommenger, *Mesopotamien*, Pls. 270–2.

[162] Akurgal, *Spätheth. Bildkunst*, Pl. 25a; *Tell Halaf*, vol. III, Pls. 92b, 94b, 95b.

[163] Schaefer and Andrae, *Propyl. Kunstgesch.*, Fig. 516; Strommenger, *Mesopotamien*, Pl. 272.

[164] Schaefer and Andrae, *op. cit.*, Pl. 517; Strommenger, *op. cit.*, Pl. 274.

[165] L. W. King, *op. cit.*, Pls. 72, 74, 103.

[166] Unger, *Assyr. und babyl. Kunst*, Fig. 31.

[167] Akurgal, *Spätheth. Bildkunst*, p. 32 and n. 20.

[168] At Zincirli on the reliefs from the North Hall and in Hilani III the male figures have only part of the bunched pleats visible at the rear under the cloak. *AiS*, p. 243, Fig. 150, Pls. 58–61.

[169] Akurgal, *Spätheth. Bildkunst*, p. 37, Figs. 19, 20, Pls. 43a, b.

[170] C. J. Gadd, *Stones of Assyria*, London, 1936.

[171] *AiS*, Pl. 3 (on the narrow side of Asarhaddon's stele).

[172] F. Krischen, *Weltwunder der Baukunst in Babylonien und Ionien*, Tübingen, 1956, p. 9.

[173] Unger, *Assyr. und babyl. Kunst*, p. 60.

[174] *Ibid.*, p. 31.

[175] *Ibid.*, p. 31 and Fig. 42.

[176] F. Krischen, *op. cit.*, Fig. 5; Strommenger, *Mesopotamien*, p. 122, Fig. 62.

[177] F. Krischen, *op. cit.*, pp. 30ff., Pls. 6–9.

[178] *Ibid.*, pp. 39ff.

[179] *Ibid.*, p. 49.

[180] *Ibid.*, p. 40; Strommenger, *Mesopotamien*, p. 121, Fig. 61.

[181] Parrot, *Assur*, p. 173, Fig. 220.

[182] Strommenger, *Mesopotamien*, p. 121, Fig. 61.

[183] Schaefer and Andrae, *Propyl. Kunstgesch.*, Pl. 29; Barnett, *Palace Reliefs*, col. Pls. 6, 7; Strommenger, *op. cit.*, col. Pl. 43; Parrot, *Assur*, p. 176, Pl. 224.

[184] Schaefer and Andrae, *op. cit.*, Fig. 521; Barnett, *op. cit.*, col. Pl. 4; Strommenger, *op. cit.*, Pl. 277; Parrot, *op. cit.*, p. 174, Fig. 221.

[185] The modelling of the thigh muscle is very faint. A W-shaped scheme can be discerned with difficulty: see the bull in Parrot, *Assur*, p. 221 (below).

[186] Strommenger, *Mesopotamien*, p. 40, 121, Fig. 61.

[187] A lucid survey of Aramaean history will be found in A. Moortgat, *Geschichte Vorderasiens bis zum Hellenismus in Ägypten und Vorderasien im Altertum*, Munich, 1959, pp. 329, 386ff., 400, 432, 454.

[188] *Ibid.*, p. 387.

[189] A. Dupont-Sommer, *Les Araméens* (Coll. L'Orient ancien illustré, 2), Paris, 1949.

[190] My first studies of Aramaean art were published several years ago: *Spätheth. Bildkunst* (see index on p. 163). See also my study *Kunst der Hethiter*, pp. 100–5.

[191] The article by the Italian scholar G. Garbini, 'Il problema dell'arte aramaica', *RSO*, vol. 34, 1959, pp. 141–7, has unfortunately been unavailable to me.

[192] See also the relief at Karadag: Bossert, *Altanatolien*, Pl. 761. In Assyrian reliefs too the Anatolian peoples are shown wearing a similar kind of head-dress (Barnett and Falkner, *Tiglathpileser*, Pls. 18, 47, 121).

[193] Barnett, *Nimrud Ivories*, Pl. 14 (M 1), Pl. 19.

[194] Frankfort, *Art and Architecture*, p. 198, Fig. 96.

[195] Akurgal, *Spätheth. Bildkunst*, pp. 27ff.

[196] *Ibid.*, pp. 23, 25, 27–8 (N 75), 32, 36, 38, 120–1 (N 206), 130 (N 278), 134, 136; Akurgal, *Kunst der Hethiter*, pp. 100–4.

[197] W. Andrae, in *MDOG*, vol. 80, 1943, p. 30; Akurgal, *Spätheth. Bildkunst*, p. 27, n. 74; B. Landsberger, *Sam'al*, Ankara, 1948, pp. 53 ff.

[198] Akurgal, *Kunst der Hethiter*, pp. 100–2.

[199] *Ibid.*, Pl. 129.

[200] *AiS*, p. 375, Fig. 273.

[201] *AiS*, Pl. 6; Bossert, *Altanatolien*, Pl. 955.

[202] *AiS*, pp. 175, 325, Pl. 54; Schaefer and Andrae, *Propyl. Kunstgesch.*, Pl. 36 (between Figs. 596 and 597), p. 707.

[203] Schaefer and Andrae, *Propyl. Kunstgesch.*, p. 707; Naumann, *Architektur Kleinasiens*.

[204] *AiS*, pp. 161, 346, Pl. 60; Schaefer and Andrae, *Propyl. Kunstgesch.*, Fig. 593.

[205] Akurgal, *Spätheth. Bildkunst*, pp. 121ff.

[206] J. Garstang, in *LAAA*, vol. I, 1908, vol. V, 1913; Bossert, *Altanatolien*, Pls. 875–83.

[207] L. Delaporte, *Malatya I: la Porte des Lions*, Paris, 1940; Bossert, *op. cit.*, pp. 791–5; Akurgal, *Kunst der Hethiter*, Figs. 106–7.

[208] R. D. Barnett, in *Annual of Department of Antiquities of Jordan*, 1951, Pl. 31.

[209] *AiS*, Pl. 62.

[210] Akurgal, *Kunst der Hethiter*, Pls. 106–7.

[211] Akurgal, *Kunst Anatoliens*, p. 46, Figs. 25–6.

[212] W. L. Brown, *The Etruscan Lion*, Oxford, 1960, Pl. 5a.

[213] *Ibid.*, Pl. 5b.

[214] *Ibid.*, p. 9.

[215] Akurgal, *Kunst Anatoliens*, pp. 58–9, Figs. 36–7.

[216] Akurgal, *Spätheth. Bildkunst*, pp. 80–6.

[217] *Carchemish III*, Pl. 38A.

[218] Akurgal, *Spätheth. Bildkunst*, pp. 84ff., Pl. 49a.

[219] *AiS*, Pls. 60B, 67.

[220] O. Nuoffer, *Der Wagen im Altertum*, Leipzig, 1904, p. 82.

[221] Barnett, *Nimrud Ivories*, Pls. 33–4.

[222] B. Landsberger, *Sam'al*, Ankara, 1948, pp. 37ff.

[223] *Ibid.*, p. 38.

[224] Akurgal, *Spätheth. Bildkunst*; ibid., *Kunst der Hethiter*, pp. 90–105; ibid., *In Historia* (*Zeitschrift für alte Geschichte*, fasc. 7, Wiesbaden, 1964), pp. 117ff.

[225] On the peoples of the Neo-Hittite principalities see B. Landsberger, *op. cit.*, pp. 83ff., 98ff.; H. G. Güterbock, 'Toward a Definition of the Term Hittite', *Oriens*, vol. 10,

1957, pp. 233–9; ibid., 'Carchemish', *JNES*, vol. 13, 1954, p. 114.

[226] P. Matthiae, *Ars Syra*, Rome, 1962, pp. 1–156 with Plates.

[227] Landsberger, *op. cit.*, pp. 107ff.

[228] Naumann, *Architektur Kleinasiens*, p. 360.

[229] On the *bit hilani* see R. Koldewey in *AiS*, pp. 183–95; F. Oelmann, 'Zur Baugeschichte von Sendschirli', *JdI*, vol. 36, 1921, pp. 85–98; F. Wachtsmuth, 'Die Baugeschichte von Sendschirli', *JdI*, vol. 38–9, 1923–4, pp. 158–69; ibid., *Der Raum*, vol. I, p. 77; H. Weidhaas, 'Der Bit Hilani', *ZA*, vol. 11 (45), 1939, pp. 108–68; R. Naumann, '*Hilani*, Hilammar und Torbau', *Veröffentlichungen der Deutschen Orientgesellschaft*, no. 61, pp. 44–9; ibid., *Architektur Kleinasiens*; Frankfort, *Art and Architecture*, pp. 162ff., 167ff., 170–1; ibid., 'The Origin of the Bit Hilani', *Iraq*, vol. 14, 1952, pp. 120–31; B. Hrouda, 'Die Churriter als Problem archäologischer Forschung', *Archaeologia Geographica* (Hamburg), vol. 7, 1958, p. 14.

[230] Naumann, *Architektur Kleinasiens*, pp. 354–8.

[231] Frankfort, *Art and Architecture*, pp. 139–40.

[232] Naumann, *op. cit.*, pp. 354ff.

[233] *Ibid.*, p. 356. Sir L. Woolley has also pointed to the links with Minoan-Mycenaean culture. *Antiquaries' Journal*, vol. 17, 1937, pp. 1 ff.; vol. 18, 1938, pp. 1 ff.; vol. 19, 1939, pp. 1 ff.

[234] Akurgal, *Kunst der Hethiter*, pp. 58ff., 76.

[235] *Ugaritica I*, p. 33; II, p. 21. See also Woolley, *op. cit.* and R. Naumann, 'Hausmodell von Tell Halaf', *Jahrbuch für kleinasiatische Forschung* (Heidelberg), vol. 2, 1953, p. 255.

[236] *AiS*, pp. 243–53; Naumann, *Architektur Kleinasiens*, p. 365.

[237] *AiS*, pp. 255–9, 290–300; Naumann, *op. cit.*, p. 365.

[238] Naumann, *op. cit.*, pp. 365–6.

[239] *AiS*, Pl. 67, pp. 255ff., 377ff.

[240] *AiS*, pp. 255, 377ff.

[241] Landsberger, *op. cit.*, p. 71; see also *AiS*, pp. 168ff., 380f.; F. Oelmann, 'Zur Baugeschichte von Sendschirli', *JdI*, vol. 36, 1921, p. 94.

[242] F. Wachtsmuth, in *JdI*, vol. 38–9, 1923–4, p. 161.

[243] The term Hilani IV was coined by F. Oelmann in his article quoted above, p. 92. In the publication of the excavations it is called 'Eastern Hall': *AiS*, pp. 159ff.

[244] *AiS*, p. 163, Pls. 73, 74; p. 165, Pl. 77.

[245] *Ibid.*, Pl. 60b, pp. 346ff.; Akurgal, *Kunst der Hethiter*, Pl. 131.

[246] *AiS*, pp. 350ff.

[247] *Ibid.*, Pl. 60b, p. 347; Akurgal, *op. cit.*, Pl. 131.

[248] *Ibid.*, pp. 151ff., 154ff.; Naumann, *Architektur Kleinasiens*, pp. 368, 374.

[249] *Ibid.*, Pls. 56, 57b, 58, 59 and Figs. 250–4 (pp. 338–45).

[250] *Ibid.*, Pl. 55, pp. 330–3.

[251] *Ibid.*, pp. 308–17.

[252] *Ibid.*, pp. 141ff., Pls. 20–1.

[253] Naumann, *op. cit.*, p. 374.

[254] *Loc. cit.*

[255] *AiS*, pp. 141ff.; Naumann, *op. cit.*, p. 374, Fig. 460.

[256] *AJA*, vol. 41, 1937, p. 9, Fig. 4.

[257] J. Garstang, in *LAAA*, vol. 5, 1913, Pl. 3.

[258] *Tell Halaf II*, pp. 376ff., Plan 1–3, 5, 10.

[259] Naumann, *op. cit.*, p. 365.

[260] *AJA*, vol. 41, 1937, p. 13.

[261] *Ibid.*, pp. 9ff., Fig. 7.

[262] J. Garstang, in *LAAA*, vol. 1, 1908, Pl. 42.

[263] *Ibid.*, Pl. 40 ff.

[264] Bossert, *Altanatolien*, pp. 877, 900.

[265] R. Naumann in *Tell Halaf II*, p. 381; ibid., *Architektur Kleinasiens*, pp. 260ff; A. Moortgat in *Tell Halaf III*, pp. 22ff.; B. Hrouda in *Tell Halaf IV*, p. 115.

[266] W. F. Albright, 'The Date of the Kapara Period at Gazan (Tell Halaf)', *Anatolian Studies*, vol. 6, 1956, p. 81.

[267] *Tell Halaf II*, Pl. 11.

[268] D. Opitz in *Tell Halaf III*, p. 117.

[269] H. Weidhaas, 'Der Bit Hilani', *ZA*, vol. 11 (45), 1939, p. 108; cf. also *AiS*, p. 189.

[270] *AiS*, p. 188, Fig. 84; Parrot, *Assur*, Fig. 10, p. 8.

[271] Weidhaas, *op. cit.*, pp. 110–11; *AiS*, p. 190.

[272] *AiS*, p. 190, Figs. 85–6.

[273] Frankfort, *Art and Architecture*, p. 139.

[274] *Ibid.*, p. 145.

[275] Akurgal, *Kunst der Hethiter*, Pls. 90–7.

[276] *AiS*, Pl. 46.

[277] L. Delaporte, *Malatya I: la Porte des Lions*, Paris, 1940, pp. 88–97; Akurgal, *Remarques stylistiques*, pp. 1–114.

[278] A. Scharff and A. Moortgat, *Ägypten und Vorderasien im Altertum*, Munich, 1959, pp. 386f.

[279] Bossert, *Altanatolien*, p. 572.

[280] Naumann, *Architektur Kleinasiens*, p. 130, Figs. 124–6.

[281] Thureau-Dangin, *Arslan-Tash*, Pl. 5 (2).

[282] G. Loud, 'Khorsabad II', *OIP*, vol. 40, 1938, Pl. 38, 41B, C and p. 30, Fig. 2.

[283] *AiS*, Pls. 53a, b; p. 237, Figs. 146; p. 244, Fig. 152; p. 255, Fig. 163; p. 291, Fig. 198; p. 293, Fig. 201; pp. 358 ff.

[284] *AJA*, vol. 41, 1937, p. 15, Fig. 8 (two bases in the Oriental Institute, Chicago and one base in the museum at Hatay, Antakya).

[285] *AiS*, p. 359.

[286] *AiS*, p. 360.

[287] G. Loud, 'The Megiddo Ivories', *OIP*, vol. 52, 1939, Pls. 34–5; Barnett, *Nimrud Ivories*, Pls. 3, 4, 21, 25 etc.

[288] Akurgal, *Kunst der Hethiter*, Pl. 134.

[289] E. Fugmann, *L'Architecture des périodes pré-hellénistiques* (vol. II (i) of *Hama: Fouilles et recherches de la Fondation Carlsberg, 1931–8*), Copenhagen, 1958, p. 205, Fig. 258.

[290] *AiS*, Pl. 33a; p. 197, Fig. 88; pp. 358ff.

[291] *AiS*, p. 361, Fig. 260; p. 320, Fig. 226; pp. 321 ff.

[292] *Carchemish II*, p. 155, Fig. 61.

[293] *Ibid.*, Fig. 60.

[294] Naumann, *Architektur Kleinasiens*, p. 130, Figs. 123–6.

[295] G. Loud, 'Khorsabad II', *OIP*, vol. 40, 1938, Pl. 32 (B 48), nos. 15–17, p. 31, p. 96, nos. 15–17.

[296] The base published by Frankfort (*Art and Architecture*, p. 88, Fig. 35) does not originate from Khorsabad, as stated, but from Niniveh (Kuyunjuk). The figure represented in Perrot and Chipiez, *Histoire de l'art*, vol. II, p. 223, Fig. 82; in Frankfort, *Art and Architecture*, p. 82, Fig. 35; and in O. Puchstein, 'Die ionische Säule als klassisches Bauglied orientalischer Herkunft' (*Sendschriften der Deutschen Orientgesellschaft*, no. 4), Leipzig, 1907, are each one of the four bases that originate from the Palace of Sennacherib. The figure given by Frankfort is redrawn from the one given by Puchstein, and has been confused with the bases from Khorsabad. The drawing in Perrot and Chipiez, *op. cit.*, is not faithful to the original. All four bases are in London.

[297] Schaefer and Andrae, *Propyl. Kunstgesch.*, Fig. 575.

[298] Barnett, *Palace Reliefs*, p. 136; Strommenger, *Mesopotamien*, p. 236 (above).

[299] G. Loud, 'Khorsabad I', *OIP*, vol. 38, p. 76, Fig. 88; p. 72, Fig. 83. Barnett, *Palace Reliefs*, pp. 133–4; Frankfort, *Art and Architecture*, Pl. 106 (above).

300 A fine photograph is in Parrot, *Assur*, p. 52, Fig. 60. On shapes of bases and capitals in this relief see O. Puchstein, *op. cit.*, p. 36, Figs. 44–5.

301 Perrot and Chipiez, *op. cit.*, vol. II, p. 225, Fig. 85; Barnett and Falkner, *Sculptures*, Pls. 110–11.

302 *AiS*, 'Kleinfunde', Pl. 63, pp. 82f.; see also Pl. 33 (above, right).

303 *Ibid.*, p. 303.

304 Barnett, *Nimrud Ivories*, Pl. 78, p. 210.

305 *AiS*, pp. 301–5.

306 Akurgal, *Kunst der Hethiter*, Pls. 66–9.

307 *Ibid.*, Pls. 90–1.

308 *Ibid.*, col. Pls. 16–17.

309 *Ibid.*, Pl. 88.

310 Front parts of lions were also featured on the pillars of Temples II and V at Bogazköy (Naumann, *Architektur Kleinasiens*, p. 395).

311 Frankfort, *Art and Architecture*, p. 160, Pl. 151c.

312 Akurgal, *Kunst der Hethiter*, Pl. 103.

313 *Carchemish II*, B 32.

314 *AJA*, vol. 41, 1937, p. 14, Figs. 6, 7.

315 *Tell Halaf II*, p. 68, Fig. 31.

316 W. Andrae, *Die Stelenreihen in Assur* (*Wissenschaftliche Veröffentlichungen der Deutschen Orientgesellschaft*, no. 24), Leipzig, 1913, pp. 30–5, Pl. 17, Figs. 33–4.

317 Perrot and Chipiez, *Histoire de l'art*, vol. II, p. 216, Fig. 74.

318 *AiS*, 'Kleinfunde', p. 32, Fig. 27, Pl. 12g.

319 F. Matz, *Geschichte der griechischen Kunst*, Frankfurt, 1950, Pl. 249a.

320 *OLZ*, 1920, p. 208.

321 Andrae, *op. cit.*, p. 34.

322 *Ibid.*, p. 34.

323 Bossert, *Altanatolien*, Fig. 823; R. Naumann, 'Hausmodell von Tell Halaf', *Jahrbuch für kleinasiatische Forschung*, vol. 2, 1953, p. 251, Fig. 6.

324 Naumann, *Architektur Kleinasiens*, p. 142.

325 Naumann, 'Hausmodell . . .', p. 253, Fig. 10; ibid., *Architektur Kleinasiens*, p. 140, Fig. 154.

326 Naumann, 'Hausmodell . . .', p. 247, Fig. 1b; *Tell Halaf III*, p. 15, Fig. 14.

327 *Tell Halaf III*, Pls. 138–9, pp. 117–18.

328 Barnett, *Nimrud Ivories*, Pl. 78 (S 254) (above, left).

329 *Ibid.*, Pl. 78 (S 258) (above, 2nd row).

330 Perrot and Chipiez, *Histoire de l'art*, vol. II, p. 726, Fig. 386.

331 G. Loud, 'Khorsabad I', *OIP*, vol. 38, p. 72, Fig. 83; p. 77, Fig. 89.

332 Barnett, *Palace Reliefs*, pp. 133–4; Frankfort, *Art and Architecture*, Pl. 106 (above).

333 Barnett, *loc. cit.*

334 Y. Yadin, in *Biblical Archaeologist*, vol. 22, 1959, p. 11, Fig. 8 (from Hazor); Bossert, *Altsyrien*, Pls. 1012–3 (from Megiddo).

335 *Carchemish III*, Pl. B 64 b.

336 Akurgal, *Remarques stylistiques*, pp. 1–114.

337 Akurgal, *Spätheth. Bildkunst*, pp. 6 ff., Figs. 1–9.

338 Akurgal, *Remarques stylistiques*, p. 46, Figs. 23–4.

339 *Ibid.*, pp. 98–114.

340 H. G. Güterbock, 'Narration in Anatolian, Syrian and Assyrian Art', *AJA*, vol. 61, 1957, p. 65.

341 Akurgal, *Spätheth. Bildkunst*, pp. 142 ff.

342 Akurgal, *Kunst der Hethiter*, Figs. 51, 65. For the same belt in Syria, see Bossert, *Altsyrien*, Pls. 608–9.

343 On the motif of the two-headed sphinx, the chimaera, see Akurgal, *Spätheth. Bildkunst*, pp. 125f. In addition to the five examples given here, see also the chimaera on the ivory plaque from Megiddo with strong Hittite features (G. Loud, 'The Megiddo Ivories', *OIP*, vol. 52, 1939, Pl. 11 (44g). Two further examples from the second millennium are in A. Dessenne, *Le sphinx: étude iconographique*, Paris, 1957, Pl. 18 (224, 226), pp. 94 ff.

344 Akurgal, *Spätheth. Bildkunst*, pp. 111–18.

345 On this position of the arm see Akurgal, *Kunst der Hethiter*, p. 77; K. Bittel, *In Historia* (*Zeitschrift für alte Geschichte*, fasc. 7, Wiesbaden, 1964), p. 125.

346 Akurgal, *Spätheth. Bildkunst*, pp. 125ff.

347 On this pictorial theme see H. J. Kantor, in *JNES*, vol. 21, 1962, pp. 114ff.

348 Akurgal, *Remarques stylistiques*, pp. 86ff.

349 *Ibid.*, pp. 46ff.

350 Schaefer and Andrae, *Propyl. Kunstgesch.*, Fig. 540; Barnett, *Palace Reliefs*, Pl. 9.

351 Schaefer and Andrae, *op. cit.*, Fig. 545.

352 H. Seyrig, 'Statuettes trouvées dans les montagnes du Liban', *Syria*, vol. 30, 1953, p. 25, Pl. 12.

353 E. Kunze, *Kretische Bronzereliefs*, Stuttgart, 1931, Pl. 49; P. Demargne, *La naissance de l'art grec*, Paris, 1964, pp. 356–7, Figs. 465–6, 469 (tr. by S. Gilbert and J. Emmons, London, 1964).

354 Barnett, *Nimrud Ivories*, Pl. 16 (S 3), (above, left); Pl. 23 (S8a–f, S 26), Pl. 27 (S 12), (above, left).

355 Akurgal, *Remarques stylistiques*, pp. 63–94.
356 *Ibid.*, pp. 108ff.
357 *AiS*, pp. 202–8, Figs. 94–101, Pl. 34.
358 *Ibid.*, pp. 208–29, Figs. 102–34, Pls. 35–45.
359 *Ibid.*, pp. 230–6, Figs. 137–8, 140, Pl. 46.
360 *Ibid.*, p. 244, Figs. 151–2; p. 271, Fig. 177; p. 369, Fig. 269; Pl. 65.
361 *Ibid.*, pp. 362–9, Figs. 262–8; Akurgal, *Kunst der Hethiter*, Pls. 126–7.
362 Akurgal, *op. cit.*, Fig. 108.
363 *AiS*, p. 211, Fig. 102, Pl. 39.
364 Strommenger, *Mesopotamien*, Pls. 204(below), 213 (below).
365 G. R. Meyer, *Durch vier Jahrtausende altvorderasiatischer Kultur*, Berlin, 1962, p. 136, Fig. 57 (p. 139); Unger, *Assyr. und babyl. Kunst*, Fig. 85.
366 *AiS*, p. 375, Fig. 273.
367 B. Landsberger, *Sam'al*, Ankara, 1948, p. 53.
368 *Ibid.*, pp. 53, 55 and notes 138–9.
369 Cf. *AiS*, p. 215, Figs. 106–7 with Pl. 34f (p. 207, Fig. 98).
370 *AiS*, p. 244, Figs. 151–2; p. 262, Fig. 168.
371 *Loc. cit.*
372 W. Orthmann, 'Hethitische Götterbilder', *Vorderasiatische Archäologie: Studien und Aufsätze A. Moortgat zum 65. Geburtstag gewidmet* (ed. K. Bittel, E. Heinrich, B. Hrouda, W. Nagel), Berlin, 1964, pp. 222ff.
373 Akurgal, *Kunst der Hethiter*, p. 86, Pl. 79 (below).
374 E. Fugmann, *L'Architecture des périodes prébelléniques* (vol. II(i) of *Hama: Fouilles et recherches de la Fondation Carlsberg, 1931–8*), Copenhagen, 1958, p. 156, Fig. 188 (5 E 978–9); p. 157, Fig. 189 (5 E 980–1); p. 175, Fig. 215 (6 B 597–8, 602); p. 193, Fig. 245; p. 203, Fig. 256; pp. 207–8, Figs. 261–4.
375 P. J. Riis, in *Hama II* (iii), 1948, pp. 19, 198; ibid., in *Gnomon*, vol. 35, 1963, fasc. 2, p. 206.
376 Fugmann, *op. cit.*, pp. 236, 268.
377 F. Seirafi and A. Kirichian, *Les annales archéologiques de Syrie*, xv, 1965, vol. II, pp. 3–20, Figs. 1–2, Pls. 4–10; W. Orthmann, in *AA*, 1964, pp. 138–46.
378 Fugmann, *op. cit.*, p. 207, Fig. 261.
379 Akurgal, *Kunst der Hethiter*, Pl. 103.
380 *Carchemish II*, B 28b; *Carchemish III*, B 48a, B 54b.
381 *Carchemish III*, B 58a.
382 *AiS*, p. 222, Fig. 121, Pl. 38c (Pl. 43b).
383 *Tell Halaf III*, Pls. 89, 116.
384 *Carchemish I*, B 9 – B 16.
385 *Carchemish II*, B 18 – B 26.
386 *Carchemish I*, B 2 – B 3.
387 *Carchemish II*, B 17b – B 18b.
388 *Carchemish III*, B 37 – B 47.
389 *Ibid.*, B 53 – B 60.
390 *Ibid.*, B 33.
391 *Carchemish II*, A 13d.
392 *Ibid.*, B 25, B 26a.
393 *Carchemish III*, B 53, B 54a.
394 *Carchemish II*, B 32.
395 *Carchemish III*, B 47.
396 Akurgal, *Kunst der Hethiter*, Pl. 109.
397 Bossert, *Altanatolien*, Pl. 828 (head of royal statue); Akurgal, *Spätheth. Bildkunst*, Pl. 10a (lion base of royal statue).
398 *Carchemish I*, B 10b.
399 Thureau-Dangin, *Til-Barsib*, Pls. 1–10.
400 *Ibid.*, Pls. 9–10.
401 *Carchemish II*, B 25, B 26a.
402 *Carchemish III*, B 54a; Bossert, *Altanatolien*, Pl. 828.
403 Akurgal, *Spätheth. Bildkunst*, Pl. 23a.
404 H. G. Güterbock, in *JNES*, vol. 13, 1954, p. 106.
405 *Carchemish III*, B 43b; Akurgal, *op. cit.*, Pl. 23; ibid., *Kunst der Hethiter*, Pl. 117.
406 *Carchemish III*, B 45a, B 46a.
407 H. G. Güterbock, *N. Özgüç: eti Müzesi Kilavuzu*, p. 26.
408 *Carchemish III*, B 54a; Bossert, *Altanatolien*, Pl. 828.
409 W. Orthmann, 'Hethitische Götterbilder', *Vorderasiatische Archäologie: Studien und Aufsätze A. Moortgat zum 65. Geburtstag*, Berlin, 1964, p. 223.
410 *Carchemish II*, B 25.
411 The splendid comprehensive study by the Italian archaeologist Maria Giulia Amadasi, *L'iconografia del carro da guerra in Siria e Palestina*, Rome, 1965, only became available to me while this book was in the press. A study of this subject has long been overdue. I should like to congratulate Professor Sabatino Moscati on the useful studies which his Institute has produced. See also no. 9 (P. Matthiae, *Studi sui rilievi di Karatepe*, 1963) and no. 13 (M. Bisi, *Il grifone: storia di un motivo iconografico nell'antico Oriente mediterrano*, 1965) in the series *Studi semitici*: both these treat important themes in Near Eastern art.
412 Akurgal, *Spätheth. Bildkunst*, pp. 87–8.
413 I. J. Gelb, 'The Double Names of the

Hittite Kings', *Rocznik orientalistyczny*, vol. 17, 1953, pp. 146–54.

414 H. G. Güterbock, 'The Deeds of Suppiluliuma as told by his son Mursili II', *JCS*, vol. 10, 1956, pp. 121f.

415 *Tell Halaf III*, pp. 37–99, Pls. 10–100; pp. 15–22.

416 *Ibid.*, pp. 99–110, Pls. 103–9; pp. 22–30.

417 *Ibid.*, pp. 35–7, Pls. 1–9; pp. 110–9, Pls. 110–49, 156–60.

418 *Ibid.*, Pl. 88 (A 3 152, A 3 153).

419 *Ibid.*, Pl. 102 (A 3 176).

420 *Ibid.*, Pl. 87 (A 3 150), Pl. 104 (Ba, 2).

421 *Ibid.*, Pl. 10a (107b, 108), Pl. 13b, Pl. 149.

422 *Ibid.*, Pls. 19b, 20b, 21, 22a.

423 *Tell Halaf III*, Pl. 146.

424 *Ibid.*, Pl. 93a.

425 *Ibid.*, Pl. 104.

426 G. Loud, *The Megiddo Ivories*, OIP, vol. 42, 1939, pp. 10f., Pl. 11f.

427 *Tell Halaf II*, Pl. 11; Parrot, *Assur*, p. 86, Fig. 95.

428 *Tell Halaf III*, Pls. 10, 108.

429 *Ibid.*, Pls. 87, 104, 107–8.

430 *Ibid.*, Pl. 41.

431 *Ibid.*, Pls. 89, 116.

432 *Ibid.*, Pls. 136–7.

433 *Ibid.*, Pls. 41–2.

434 See also *ibid.*, pp. 21f.

435 *Ibid.*, Pls. 70–8.

436 *Ibid.*, Pls. 83–5, 125.

437 *Ibid.*, Pl. 33a.

438 *Ibid.*, Pl. 43a.

439 *Ibid.*, Pl. 114.

440 Frankfort, *Art and Architecture*, Pl. 149b.

441 E. Gjerstad, in *Opuscula Archaeologica*, vol. IV, 1946, Pls. 7, 9, 10; Frankfort, *op. cit.*, p. 198, Fig. 96.

442 *Tell Halaf III*, Pls. 130–1, 133.

443 E. Fugmann, *L'architecture des périodes préhelléniques* (vol. II(i) of *Hama: Fouilles et recherches de la Fondation Carlsberg, 1931–8*), Copenhagen, 1958, p. 204, Fig. 257 (above, left).

444 *Tell Halaf III*, Pls. 18–20.

445 *Ibid.*, Pls. 27–8, 30, 35–6, 88, 102.

446 Barnett, *Nimrud Ivories*.

447 *Ibid.*, Pls. 19, 20.

448 *Tell Halaf III*, pp. 15ff.

449 *Ibid.*, pp. 23ff.

450 Strommenger, *Mesopotamien*, Pls. 191, 193. A relief from the reign of Assurnasirpal II, now in Berlin (Barnett and Falkner, *Sculptures*, Pl. 127; G. R. Meyer, *Durch vier Jahrtausende altvorderasiatischer Kultur*, Berlin, 1962, p. 157, Fig. 71), has a similar form to those of the reigns of Tiglath-Pileser and Sargon. The front edge of the cloak does not have the same fine curve, however, that we find with the examples of the latter half of the eighth century, but falls almost vertically.

451 Barnett and Falkner, *Sculptures*, Pl. 105.

452 *Tell Halaf III*, Pls. 94b, 95a, 96a.

453 *Ibid.*, Pls. 120, 128.

454 *Ibid.*, p. 342, Fig. 253.

455 *Ibid.*, Pl. 133; Parrot, *Assur*, p. 93, Fig. 102.

456 Barnett, *Nimrud Ivories*, Pl. 89; Parrot, *op. cit.*, p. 155, Fig. 189.

457 *Tell Halaf III*, Pl. 147.

458 Akurgal, *Spätheth. Bildkunst*, p. 65, note 156; pp. 67, 143.

459 M. E. L. Mallowan, in *Iraq*, vol. 2, 1935, pp. 197–8; *ibid.*, vol. 14, 1952, p. 48; *ibid.*, vol. 15, 1953, pp. 16, 22.

460 Barnett, *Nimrud Ivories*, pp. 133–5.

461 M. E. L. Mallowan, in *Iraq*, vol. 19, 1957, p. 17, note 1.

462 *Tell Halaf II*, p. 394; *Tell Halaf III*, p. 5.

463 *Tell Halaf IV*, p. 3, Pl. 1, Fig. 1.

464 *Ibid.*, pp. 65ff., Pl. 48, Figs. 7, 8; Pl. 30, Fig. 17.

465 *Ibid.*, p. 42, Pl. 33, nos. 61–3.

466 *Tell Halaf III*, p. 6.

467 *Ibid.*, Pls. 49, 50a, 51b, 55a, 64b, 65.

468 On the knuckle-bone handle see: Akurgal, *Kunst Anatoliens*, Pl. 3a, p. 108; *ibid.*, *Phrygische Kunst*, Pls. 57–9, pp. 81ff.

469 A. and J. Körte, *Gordion*, Berlin, 1904, pp. 67ff., Figs. 43–8.

470 Akurgal, *Kunst Anatoliens*, p. 81, Fig. 48; *ibid.*, *Phrygische Kunst*, Pls. 10–12, 17, 20, 23–5.

471 Akurgal, *Kunst Anatoliens*, p. 82, Fig. 49; *ibid.*, *Phrygische Kunst*, Pl. 13.

472 *Carchemish II*, B 30b.

473 Akurgal, *Kunst der Hethiter*, Pl. 142.

474 *Tell Halaf IV*, Pl. 62, no. 197.

475 Akurgal, *Kunst Anatoliens*, pp. 73ff., Fig. 43–4; *ibid.*, *Phrygische Kunst*, pp. 1–8, Figs. 1–9, Pls. 1–7; pp. 33–6.

476 *Tell Halaf IV*, pp. 66f.

477 A. and J. Körte, *op. cit.*, p. 72, Fig. 51.

478 Perrot and Chipiez, *Histoire de l'art*, vol. III, p. 797, Fig. 557.

479 R. Hampe, *Ein frühattischer Grabfund*, Mainz, 1960, Pls. 6–7, p. 40, Figs. 30–1.

480 *Tell Halaf III*, pp. 7f.

481 I mention here an Assyrian caryatid from the reign of Sargon, made of gypsum, which was found in Greece but has now been lost. F. Matz, *Geschichte der griechischen Kunst*, Frankfurt, 1950, Pl. 248a.

482 Akurgal, *Spätheth. Bildkunst*, pp. xiv, 74ff., 143ff.

483 *Carchemish I*, Pls. B 4 – B 8.

484 Strommenger, *Mesopotamien*, Pl. 231.

485 *Carchemish I*, Pl. B 8.

486 Barnett, *Nimrud Ivories*, Pls. 70–6.

487 Strommenger, *op. cit.*, Pl. 222.

488 Barnett, *op. cit.*, Pls. 8–12.

489 Akurgal, *Spätheth. Bildkunst*, Pls. 31, 32b, 34.

490 Akurgal, *Kunst der Hethiter*, p. 56.

491 *Ibid.*, Pl. 85, p. 40, Fig. 1.

492 *Carchemish I*, Pl. B 7b.

493 *Ibid.*, Pl. B 8.

494 Fr. W. von Bissing, in *AfO*, 6, 1930–1, p. 184.

495 *Carchemish I*, Pl. B 5b.

496 Parrot, *Assur*, p. 32, Fig. 36; Strommenger, *Mesopotamien*, p. 222. It must however be said that in the case of the hair-dress of the Gilgamesh figure this is not a matter of fashion but a characterization of the figure as a hero.

497 B. Landsberger and his pupils, *Sumeroloji Araştırmaları*, p. 1019; Forrer, *Provinzen*, p. 83.

498 B. Landsberger, *Sam'al*, Ankara, 1948, pp. 80ff.

499 *Ibid.*, p. 81.

500 For the literature about the reading of 'Assurdan', see E. Laroche, *Les hiéroglyphes hittites*, vol. I, Paris, 1960, p. 182, under Kargamis (p. 342).

501 J. Friedrich in *RHA*, vol. 56, 1955, pp. 27ff.

502 E. Laroche, *Les hiéroglyphes hittites*, Paris, 1960, vol. I, p. 182.

503 H. T. Bossert, 'Zur Geschichte von Karkamis', *Studi classici e orientali*, vol. I, 1951, p. 63.

504 *Ibid.*, p. 66.

505 On the funerary stele of the couple see Bossert, *Altanatolien*, Pl. 805; Akurgal, *Spätheth. Bildkunst*, Pl. 40; Catalogue of the Exhibition 'Kunst und Kultur der Hethiter'; Akurgal, *Kunst der Hethiter*, p. 102, Pl. 139.

506 D. B. Harden, *The Phoenicians*, London, 1962, Pl. 77.

507 Akurgal, *Spätheth. Bildkunst*, p. 28, Fig. 18, Pl. 41.

508 G. Contenau, *Manuel d'archéologie orientale*, vol. IV, 1947, pp. 2215–6, Fig. 1244.

509 M. Kalaç in the annual *Ex Oriente Lux*, vol. 18, 1964, pp. 280–3, Pl. 10.

510 E. Laroche, *Les hiéroglyphes hittites*, p. 287, w-pia, 66, 199; Contenau, *op. cit.*, vol. IV, p. 2216.

511 *Carchemish I*, Pl. B 8.

512 M. Kalaç, *op. cit.*, p. 283, Pl. 10.

513 Akurgal, *Spätheth. Bildkunst*, pp. 121–5.

514 Contenau, *op. cit.*, pp. 2215–6, Fig. 1244.

515 Akurgal, *op. cit.*, Pl. 42b.

516 M. Kalaç, *op. cit.*, p. 283, Pl. 7.

517 A. Moortgat, *Die bildende Kunst des alten Orients und die Bergvölker*, Berlin, 1932, p. 64.

518 See now the fine publication by N. Özgüç, *The Anatolian Group of Cylinder Seals: Impressions from Kültepe*, pp. 1–86, Pls. 1–35.

519 Akurgal, *Spätheth. Bildkunst*, pp. 7, 9(n. 57), 13, 23, 30 (n. 2), 106, 118 (n. 187), 137 (n. 281); ibid., *Kunst der Hethiter*, Pl. 140, col. Pl. 24.

520 *AiS*, Pl. 6; Bossert, *Altanatolien*, Pl. 955.

521 P. F. S. Poulsen, *Der Orient und die frühgriechische Kunst*, Berlin, 1912, p. 102; R. D. Barnett, in *JHS*, vol. 68, 1948, p. 20; E. Akurgal, in *AJA*, vol. 66, 1962, p. 376.

522 Akurgal, *Kunst der Hethiter*, Pl. 93 (below).

523 *Ibid.*, Pl. 102, col. Pl. 22.

524 The same illustration as in the previous note: a relief from Karabel near Izmir, which Franz Steinherr has recently identified with assurance as Tuthaliya IV (Steinherr, in *Istanbuler Mitteilungen*, vol. 15, 1965, pp. 17–23).

525 D. D. Luckenbill, *Ancient Records of Assyria and Babylonia*, Chicago, 1926, *s.v.* Urballai.

526 H. T. Bossert, 'Die phönizisch-hethitischen Bilinguen von Karatepe', *Oriens*, vol. 1, 1948, vol. 2, 1949; *Archiv orientalni*, vol. 18, 1950; *Jahrbuch für kleinasiatische Forschung*, vol. 1, 1950–1, vol. 2, 1952–3; H. T. Bossert and H. Çambel, *Karatepe: a Preliminary Report on a new Hittite Site*, Istanbul, 1946.

527 U. B. Alkim, in *Belleten*, vol. 12, 1948, pp. 533ff., Pls. 120–34; ibid., 'Les résultats archéologiques des fouilles de Karatepe', *RHA*, vol. 9, 1948–9, pp. 3 ff.; ibid., 'Explorations of Ancient Roads Passing Karatepe', *Anatolian Studies*, vol. 1, 1951, pp. 19–20.

528 H. Çambel, 'Karatepe: an Archaeological Introduction to a recently discovered Hittite Site in Southern Anatolia', *Oriens*, vol. 1, 1948, pp. 147–9; ibid., in *Belleten*, vol. 12, 1948, pp. 35–6.

529 P. Matthiae, *Studi sui relievi di Karatepe*, Rome, 1963, pp. 1–133, Pls. 1–32.

530 Akurgal, *Spätheth. Bildkunst*, p. 147 (postscript); ibid., *Kunst der Hethiter*, pp. 103–4, Pls. 141–50.

531 Akurgal, *Kunst der Hethiter*, Pls. 141–50.

532 *Ibid.*, Pls. 144–5.

533 *Ibid.*, Pls. 141, 144; P. Matthiae, *op. cit.*, Pl. 24; A. Dessenne, *Le sphinx: étude iconographique*, Paris, 1957, Pl. 38 (i).

534 Barnett, *Nimrud Ivories*, Pl. 1; Thureau-Dangin, *Arslan-Tash*, pp. 17–8, 30–1; Frankfort, *Art and Architecture*, Pl. 171.

535 E.g., the basalt stele of Kubaba from Carchemish: *Carchemish III*, Pl. B 62a; Bossert, *Altanatolien*, Pl. 858.

536 Frankfort, *Art and Architecture*, p. 198, Fig. 96; Barnett, *Nimrud Ivories*, Pls. 26 (above, left), Pl. 27 (above, left), 32 (middle), 44–5, 88–9.

537 H. Ranke, 'Ein ägyptisches Relief in Princeton', *JNES*, vol. 9, 1950, pp. 228–36, Pls. 9, 20a–c; cf. also similar examples in W. Wreszinski, *Atlas zur altägyptischen Kultur*, Leipzig, 1923–36, Pls. 198, 383.

538 E. Gjerstad, in *Opuscula Archaeologica*, vol. 4, 1946, Pl. 4 (middle); H. Mühlstein, *Die Kunst der Etrusker*, Figs. 7, 8; Frankfort, *Art and Architecture*, p. 200, Fig. 97.

539 *Syria*, vol. 31, 1954, Pl. 8; P. Matthiae, *Ars Syra. Contributi alla storia dell'arte figurativa sirana nelle età del Medio e Tardo Bronzo*, Rome, 1962, Pl. 25.

540 H. Çambel, in *Belleten*, vol. 12, 1948, pp. 35–6; ibid., in *Oriens*, vol. 1, 1948, pp. 147–9.

541 Akurgal, *Kunst der Hethiter*, Pls. 143–50; Çambel, *op. cit.*, Pl. 8, Fig. 2, Pls. 9–11, Fig. 7, Pl. 15; P. Matthiae, *Studi sui relievi di Karatepe*, Rome, 1963, Pls. 6, 7, 16–21, 22a, 23–4.

542 Schaefer and Andrae, *Propyl. Kunstgesch.*, pp. 569–71.

543 Barnett and Falkner, *Sculptures*, p. 22, Figs. 4, 10, 14, Pls. 25–6, 41–2, 50–1.

544 Akurgal, *Kunst der Hethiter*, Pl. 148.

545 *Ibid.*, Pls. 146–9.

546 *Carchemish II*, Pl. B 17b.

547 *AiS*, Pl. 62.

548 *Tell Halaf III*, Pl. 100.

549 A. Dessenne, *Le sphinx: étude iconographique*, Paris, 1957, p. 205 and notes 2, 3.

550 *AiS*, Pls. 34e, 38c, 43 (above).

551 H. Çambel, in *Belleten*, vol. 12, 1948, Pl. xi, Fig. 7, Pls. 12–14; Matthiae, *op. cit.*, Pls. 2–5, 8–15.

552 Matthiae, *op. cit.*, P. 2.

553 B. Landsberger, *Sam'al*, Ankara, 1948, pp. 39, 39–44.

554 On the Minoan-Mycenaean griffin and its survival, see Akurgal, *Spätheth. Bildkunst*, p. 81, no. 246.

555 On Phoenician art in general see D. B. Harden, *The Phoenicians*, London, 1962.

556 E. Gjerstad, in *Opuscula Archaeologica*, vol. 4, 1946, p. 2.

557 *Ibid.*, pp. 8ff.

558 Thureau-Dangin, *Arslan-Tash*, Pls. 19–26.

559 Barnett, *Nimrud Ivories*, Pls. 3, 14 (M 1).

560 *Ibid.*, Pls. 57–9, 88–9.

561 *Ibid.*, Pl. 8 (c 43); alternatively in *JHS*, vol. 68, 1949, Pl. 1 (below).

562 *JHS*, vol. 68, 1949, Pl. 1 (above).

563 Thureau-Dangin, *op. cit.*, Pls. 19ff.

564 G. Loud, 'Khorsabad II', *OIP*, vol. 40, 1938, Pls. 51–5.

565 Barnett, *Nimrud Ivories*, Pls. 59 (S 97, S 186), 88–9.

566 Parrot, *Assur*, p. 151, Fig. 185; Strommenger, *Mesopotamien*, Pl. 4 (between Pls. 268 and 269).

567 M. E. L. Mallowan, *Twenty-five Years of Mesopotamian Archaeology*, London, 1956, p. 56.

568 A fine photograph of the head will be found in the Catalogue of the Exhibition 'Schätze aus dem Irak', Berlin, March 1965, Pl. 51 (Cat. no. 128).

569 R. Herbig, in *OLZ*, 1927, pp. 917–22.

570 Barnett, *Nimrud Ivories*, pp. 145ff.

571 H. Carter, *The Histories of Herodotus of Halicarnassus*, Oxford, 1962, pp. 84–5.

572 Barnett, *op. cit.*, pp. 145ff.

573 Thureau-Dangin, *Arslan-Tash*, Pls. 34–5; G. Loud, 'Khorsabad II', *OIP*, vol. 40, 1938, Pls. 51–5.

574 Barnett, *op. cit.*, pp. 149ff.

575 Thureau-Dangin, *op. cit.*, pp. 136ff.

576 *Ibid.*, p. 136; Barnett, *op. cit.*, p. 126.

577 A. Dupont-Sommer, *Les Araméens* (Coll. L'Orient ancien illustré, 2), Paris, 1949, pp. 38ff.

578 *Ibid.*, p. 106.

579 Loud, *op. cit.*, Pls. 51–5.

580 M. E. L. Mallowan, 'Excavations at Nimrud', *Iraq*, vol. 13, 1951, pp. 1–20, Pls. 1–10; ibid., vol. 14, 1952, pp. 45–53, Pls. 12–17; ibid., vol. 15, 1953, p. 22; ibid., vol. 21, 1959, pp. 93–7.

581 Parrot, *Assur*, p. 154.

582 See the composition in Barnett, *Nimrud Ivories*, pp. 128–9.

583 Frankfort, *Art and Architecture*, Fig. 147.

584 Thureau-Dangin, *Arslan-Tash*, Pls. 30–1; H. J. Kantor, in *JNES*, vol. 19, 1960, p. 7.

585 Parrot, *Assur*, p. 156, Fig. 190; Barnett, *op. cit.*, Pls. 9, 22, 25 (S 11).

586 Akurgal, *Spätheth. Bildkunst*, p. 82, note 246.

587 W. Kraiker and K. Kübler, *Kerameikos V*, vol. 1, Berlin, 1954, pp. 201ff., Pl. 162.

588 E. Gjerstad, in *Opuscula Archaeologica*, vol. 4, 1946, Pl. 1; *KiB*, Pl. 104, 3 (1c7), 5.

589 W. Kraiker and K. Kübler, *op. cit.*, pp. 201ff.

590 E. Gjerstad, *op. cit.*, pp. 15, 17.

591 W. Kraiker and K. Kübler, *op. cit.*, p. 205.

592 Frankfort, *Art and Architecture*, Pls. 172 B, 173 B; *KiB*, p. 106 (4).

593 P. F. S. Poulsen, *Der Orient und die frühgriechische Kunst*, Berlin, 1912, p. 2, Figs. 12, 13; *KiB*, 106 (1, 2).

594 W. Andrae, in *ZA*, vol. 11 (45), 1939, pp. 88–98, Figs. 1–8, Pls. 10–14.

595 P. F. S. Poulsen, *op. cit.*, p. 68.

596 H. Walter and K. Vierneisel, *AM*, 74, 1959, pp. 40–1.

597 *AM*, vol. 74, 1959, Pl. 84, Fig. 2.

598 *Ibid.*, p. 40, Pl. 84, Figs. 3, 4.

599 *Ibid.*, Pl. 84, Fig. 3.

600 Akurgal, *Kunst Anatoliens*, p. 42, Fig. 20.

601 *Ibid.*, pp. 39ff., Figs. 17–19; see now Akurgal, *Urartäische und altiranische Kunstzentren*, Ankara, 1968, pp. 27–36.

602 P. F. S. Poulsen, *op. cit.*, p. 69, Fig. 71.

603 P. Amandry, in *Syria*, vol. 35, 1958, pp. 101–2.

604 F. Canciani and G. Pettinato, 'Salomos Thron', *Philologische und Archäologische Erwägungen (Zeitschrift des Deutschen Palästina-Vereins*, vol. 81, 1965, pp. 88–108).

605 Barnett, *Nimrud Ivories*; ibid., 'North Syrian and Related Harness Decoration', *Vorderasiatische Archäologie: Studien und Aufsätze A. Moortgat zum 65. Geburtstag gewidmet*, Berlin, 1964, pp. 21–7.

606 H. J. Kantor, in *JNES*, vol. 15, 1956, pp. 153–73; ibid., in *JNES*, vol. 21, 1962, pp. 93–117, Figs. 1–20, Pls. 11–15.

607 Barnett, *op. cit.*, p. 49.

608 P. J. Riis, in *Gnomon*, vol. 35, 1963, fasc. 2, p. 206.

609 Barnett, *op. cit.*, Pls. 16–17 (S 3).

610 *Ibid.*, p. 191.

611 M. E. L. Mallowan, in *Iraq*, vol. 15, 1953, pp. 1off.

612 Ibid., *Twenty-five Years of Mesopotamian Discovery*, London, 1956, p. 55.

613 Barnett, *op. cit.*, Pls. 18, 22 (above), 26–7.

614 R. Zahn, *Sammlung Baurat Schiller*, Auction sale catalogue 1929, pp. 12f., no. 106 A.B., Pls. 29, 40; Bossert, *Geschichte des Kunstgewerbes*, vol. 4, 1939, p. 149, Fig. 1; ibid., *Alt-Syrien*, p. 774; D. Ohly, *Athenische Goldbleche des 8. Jahrhunderts*, Berlin, 1953, p. 108 and n. 34 (p. 146).

615 C. Watzinger, *Handbuch der Archäologie*, vol. 1, p. 807.

616 R. Zahn, *op. cit.*, Pl. 40.

617 See the fine detail photograph in D. Ohly, *op. cit.*, Pl. 31.

618 See further similar examples of the hairdress mentioned in Barnett, *Nimrud Ivories*, Pls. 57, 59, 88–9.

619 Barnett, *op. cit.*, Pl. 70 (S 183); Strommenger, *Mesopotamien*, Pl. 264 (above).

620 R. S. Young, in *AJA*, vol. 66, 1962, Pls. 46–7.

621 *Ibid.*, p. 164.

622 See also R. S. Young, 'The Gordion Campaign of 1957', *AJA*, vol. 62, 1958, pp. 146ff.

623 *Ugaritica I–III*.

624 On the cultural remains of this period see V. R. d'A. Desborough, *The Last Mycenaeans*, Oxford, 1964; ibid., *Protogeometric Pottery*, Oxford, 1952.

625 Akurgal, *Phrygische Kunst*, pp. 112ff.; ibid., *Kunst Anatoliens*, pp. 1–7.

626 Akurgal, *Kunst der Hethiter*.

627 W. F. Albright, 'North-east Mediterranean – Dark Ages' in: *Studies presented to Hetty Goldman*, New York, 1956, pp. 144–64.

628 Akurgal, *Kunst Anatoliens*, pp. 9–20; ibid., 'The Early Period and the Golden Age of Ionia', *AJA*, vol. 66, 1962, pp. 369–79.

629 V. R. d'A. Desborough, *Protogeometric Pottery*, Oxford, 1952, pp. 181ff. and Appx. A. On this question see also the informative observations and remarks by J. Boardman, 'Early Euboean Pottery and History', *BSA*, vol. 52, 1957, pp. 1–29; ibid., 'Greek Potters in Al Mina', *Anatolian Studies*, vol. 9, 1959, pp. 163–9.

630 Desborough, *Protogeometric Pottery*, pp. 192–3.

631 Homer, *The Iliad*, Book XXIII, 744.

632 A. Goetze, *Kleinasien*, 2nd ed., Munich, 1957, pp. 139–40.

633 Apollodoros, 1, 41. Cf. T. J. Dunbabin,

The Greeks and their Eastern Neighbours, London, 1957, p. 56, n. 5; E. Kunze, Archäische Schildbänder: ein Beitrag zur frühgeschichtlichen Bildgeschichte und Sagenüberlieferung, Berlin, 1950, p. 83, n. 2.

634 H. G. Güterbock, Kumarbi, Zurich – N.Y., 1946, pp. 6–12.

635 Ibid., pp. 13–28.

636 Ibid., pp. 94ff.

637 W. F. Albright, in AJA, vol. 54, 1950, p. 164.

638 M. Robertson, in JHS, vol. 60, 1940, pp. 16, 21.

639 V. R. d'A. Desborough, Protogeometric Pottery, Oxford, 1952, pp. 181ff., 192–3.

640 See also the discussion by J. Boardman in JHS, vol. 52, 1957, pp. 24–5; ibid., in Anatolian Studies, vol. 9, 1959, pp. 163–9. The problem is also treated very well by T. J. Dunbabin, The Greeks and their Eastern Neighbours, London, 1957, pp. 25–31.

641 K. F. Johansen, 'Exochi', Acta Archaeologica, vol. 28, 1958, pp. 1–195.

642 Ibid., pp. 189, 191.

643 Ibid., p. 108, Fig. 207.

644 For a contrary view of the exceptional importance of Minoan art, as argued by Löwy, see E. Homann-Wedeking, Die Anfänge der griechischen Grossplastik, Berlin, 1950, pp. 98ff. On the problem of Minoan art see E. Kunze, Kretische Bronzereliefs, Stuttgart, 1931; P. Demargne, La Crète dédalique: études sur les origines d'un renaissance, Paris, 1947; ibid., La naissance de l'art grec, pp. 346 ff. See also D. Levi, 'Arkades', Annuario, vols. 10–12, 1927–9, pp. 15–710; ibid., 'I bronzi di Axos', Annuario, vols. 13–14, 1930–1, pp. 143–6; ibid., 'Scavi di Gortina', Annuario, vols. 17–18, 1955–6, pp. 1–82; J. K. Brock, Fortetsa: Early Greek Tombs, Cambridge, 1957.

645 F. Matz, Geschichte der griechischen Kunst, Frankfurt, 1950, Pl. 11.

646 H. Payne, Protokorinthische Vasenmalerei, Berlin, 1933, p. 10.

647 J. M. Davison, Attic Geometric Workshops, New Haven, 1961, Figs. 1, 5, 8 etc.

648 D. Ohly, Athenische Goldbleche des 8. Jahrhunderts, Berlin, 1953, Pls. 1 ff.

649 W. Schiering, Werkstätten orientalisierender Keramik auf Rhodos, Berlin, 1957, p. 107.

650 F. Matz, op. cit., pp. 83, 514 (n. 62), Pl. 27a.

651 E. Buschor, 'Kentauren', AJA, vol. 38,

1934, pp. 128ff. See also the comments by H. L. Lorimer in BSA, vol. 37, 1936–7, pp. 178 ff.

652 Hesiod, Theogony, 825ff.

653 E. Buschor, op. cit., p. 130.

654 L. W. King, Babylonian Boundary Stones and Memorial Tablets, London, 1912, Pl. 29A.

655 E. Kunze, in AM, vol. 55, 1930, p. 144.

656 F. Matz, op. cit., p. 485.

657 E. Homann-Wedeking, Anfänge der griechischen Grossplastik, Berlin, 1950, pp. 19, 116, 131.

658 D. Ohly, Athenische Goldbleche des 8. Jahrhunderts, Berlin, 1953, p. 108.

659 T. J. Dunbabin, The Greeks and their Eastern Neighbours, London, 1957, pp. 36ff.

660 Loc. cit.

661 Barnett, Nimrud Ivories, pp. 128ff.

662 Dunbabin, op. cit., pp. 37ff., Pl. 8, Figs. 4–7.

663 I am not quite sure whether this work (Dunbabin, op. cit., Pl. 8, Figs. 4, 5) is Syrian. With its Phoenicianizing Syrian hairdress and moulded eyes it constitutes a good parallel to the gold crown (our Pl. 39). The oval face with triangular chin, however, indicates that the statuette originates from an early Greek master. As I am not familiar with the original, and the photograph in Jenkins (R. J. H. Jenkins, Dedalica: a Study of Dorian Plastic Art in the Seventh Century, Cambridge, 1936, Pl. 11, 10) does in fact show non-Greek features, I should prefer to leave the question open. But the statuette does in both instances illustrate the great influence exerted by Syrian art upon Greece.

664 E. Kunze, in AM, vol. 55, 1930, pp. 147ff., Pls. 5–8; W. H. Schuchardt, Kunst der Griechen, p. 56f.; R. Hampe, Frühgriechische Sagenbilder in Böotien, Athens, 1936, pp. 36ff.

665 All told there were five statuettes; of one only the remains of a leg have been preserved. A. Brueckner and E. Pernice, 'Ein attischer Friedhof', in AM, vol. 18, 1893, pp. 127ff.; Perrot, in BCH, vol. 19, 1895, pp. 273ff.

666 Barnett, Nimrud Ivories, Pls. 70–4.

667 The helmet of the head of Amyklaion is also decorated with a meander. R. Hampe, Frühgriechische Sagenbilder in Böotien, Athens, 1936, p. 37; for a photograph in which the meander design can still be identified, see E. Homann-Wedeking, Anfänge der griechischen Grossplastik, Berlin, 1950, p. 23, Fig. 9.

668 Barnett, op. cit., Pl. 70, Fig. S 184.

669 D. Ohly, *Athenische Goldbleche des 8. Jahr-hunderts*, Berlin, 1953, p. 108 and n. 35 (p. 147).

670 R. Hampe, *Frühgriechische Sagenbilder in Böotien*, Athens, 1936, pp. 36ff.

671 *Ibid.*, pp. 37–8.

672 L. Alscher, *Griechische Plastik*, Berlin, 1954, pp. 29–31 and n. 46 (pp. 126–7).

673 Barnett, *op. cit.*, Pls. 57 (S 226), 88 (S 293), 96 (S 313).

674 *Ibid.*, Pls. 4, 88–9.

675 F. Matz, *Geschichte der griechischen Kunst*, Frankfurt, 1950, Pls. 65b, 89, 90a, 91a, 274a; R. J. H. Jenkins, *Dedalica . . .*, Cambridge, 1936, Pls. I 1, II 5, 10, VII 2, 4.

676 D. Levi, in *Annuario*, vols. 17–18, 1955–6, pp. 36ff., Figs. 39–44, 65, 69; J. Schäfer, *Reliefpithoi*, Pl. 6; P. F. S. Poulsen, *Der Orient und die frühgriechische Kunst*, Berlin, 1912, pp. 148ff., Figs. 173–4.

677 R. M. Dawkins (ed.), *The Sanctuary of Artemis Orthia at Sparta, Excavated and Described by Members of the British School at Athens, 1906–10*, Pls. 96a, 97(1), 119 (1–4), 121 (1–2).

678 See also an example from Athens (H. Payne, *Necro-Corinthia*, Oxford, 1931, Pl. 47, Fig. 11). A terracotta head in the National Museum at Athens has a diadem (F. Matz, *op. cit.*, Pl. 274a), which, as in the case of some Syrian prototypes, is decorated with rosettes. (Barnett, *op. cit.*, Pls. 70–1.)

679 R. J. H. Jenkins, *op. cit.*, Pls. VI (3–6).

680 Barnett, *op. cit.*, Pl. 73 (S 204 a, b).

681 Akurgal, *Spätheth. Bildkunst*, Pl. 37a.

682 F. Matz, *op. cit.*, Pls. 87–8.

683 *Ibid.*, Pl. 79.

684 *Ibid.*, Pl. 78.

685 *Ibid.*, Pls. 125–6.

686 *Ibid.*, Pls. 127–8.

687 K. Schefold, *Frühgriechische Sagenbilder*, Munich, 1962, 2nd ed., 1964, Pl. 38; L. Alscher, *Griechische Plastik*, Berlin, 1954, Figs. 70a–g.

688 R. A. Higgins, *Greek and Roman Jewellery*, London, 1961, Pl. 18E; P. F. S. Poulsen, *Der Orient und die frühgriechische Kunst*, Berlin, 1912, p. 142, Figs. 158, 160.

689 Barnett, *op. cit.*, Pls. 74–6.

690 F. Matz, *op. cit.*, Pl. 80. It is true that they are of hammered bronze plate; but the fact that the arms are pressed close to the body has nothing to do with insufficient strength in the bronze plate, as we can see from another figure from Dreros, which is also worked in embossed technique, but has arms that hang loosely (F. Matz, *op. cit.*, Pl. 80a (centre)).

691 F. Bilabel, *Die ionische Kolonisation* (*Philologus*, suppl. vol. 14, fasc. 1, Leipzig, 1920), p. 246.

692 G. Hafner, *Geschichte der griechischen Kunst*, p. 97.

693 P. Gilbert, 'Un trait d'expressionisme dans l'architecture de l'Egypte et de la Grèce', *Chronique d'Egypte*, vol. 36, 1961, pp. 255–68; ibid., *Passage en Grèce*, Brussels, 1959. E. Homann-Wedeking holds the view that there was only a slight degree of 'Egyptianization', which can be seen, for example, in the great *kouros* of Sunion (*Die Anfänge der griechischen Grossplastik*, Berlin, 1950, pp. 130–1). Knoblauch (*Studien*, p. 44, n. 115), on the other hand, holds that the influence of Egyptian sculpture is only felt later, after Greek monumental sculpture had already got under way. The great differences between early Greek monumental sculpture and Egyptian sculpture should not be used as arguments against Egyptian influence. These differences are undeniable, but so too is Egyptian influence. How otherwise could one explain the sudden transition from 'Daedalic' small-scale sculpture to monumental sculpture, in view of the fact the earliest Greek *kouroi* are represented in the same statuesque way? Knoblauch's position may be seen as a reaction against earlier statements which exaggerated the extent of Egyptian influence (see also N. Himmelmann-Wildschütz, *Bemerkungen zur geometrischen Plastik*, Berlin, 1964, p. 22).

694 L. Woolley, in *Antiquaries Journal*, vol. 17, 1935, pp. 1–15; ibid., in *JHS*, vol. 58, 1938, pp. 1–30, 133–70.

695 F. Salviat, in *BCH*, vol. 86, 1962, pp. 95–116, Figs. 1–11.

696 H. Payne, *Necro-Corinthia*, Oxford, 1931, pp. 67ff.

697 Akurgal, *Spätheth. Bildkunst*, pp. 76ff.; ibid., *Bayrakli*, pp. 93ff.

698 H. Payne, *Protokorinthische Vasenmalerei*, Berlin, 1933, Pl. 9, Fig. 7.

699 On this question see Akurgal, *Spätheth. Bildkunst*, p. 77.

700 H. Payne, *op. cit.*, Pls. 21–3.

701 L. Woolley, in *Antiquaries Journal*, vol. 17, 1937, pp. 1–15; ibid., in *JHS*, vol. 58, 1938, pp. 1–30, 133–170, especially p. 147.

702 Akurgal, *Kunst Anatoliens*, Figs. 41–2.

703 *Ibid.*, pp. 60, 66–70.

[704] E. Kunze, *Olympia Bericht II*, pp. 106ff., Pl. 45. Kunze was the first to identify the true character of these protomae and their 'homeland in the area immediately affected by Assyrian art' (p. 108).

[705] Akurgal, *Spätheth. Bildkunst*, p. 74 (for the discussion of the ivory lion from Zincirli, cf. also p. 48, Fig. 40).

[706] F. Salviat, *op. cit.*, pp. 95–116, Figs. 1–11.

[707] See above, n. 620.

[708] Salviat, *op. cit.*, p. 112.

[709] After this book had already gone to press there appeared the fine volume by H. Gabelmann, *Studien zum frühgriechischen Löwenbild*, Berlin, 1965, in which the most important of the questions dealt with here are discussed thoroughly and systematically. I was unfortunately not able to take note of this excellent study. However, I should like to express my delight that Gabelmann's work fulfils a long-felt need in exemplary fashion.

[710] Akurgal, *Spätheth. Bildkunst*, pp. 80–6.

[711] A. Conze, in *JHS*, vol. 46, 1926, p. 204, 8; F. Matz, *Geschichte der griechischen Kunst*, Frankfurt, 1950, Pl. 180.

[712] R. D. Barnett, in *JHS*, vol. 68, 1949, pp. 1–25, Pl. 11.

[713] On the problem of Greek griffin representations, see the fundamental works by U. Jantzen, *Griechische Greifenkessel*, Berlin, 1955 (Hanfmann, *Gnomon*, vol. 29, 1957, pp. 241–8); *Festschrift für H. Jantzen*, Berlin, 1951, pp. 26–9; *AM*, vol. 73, 1958, pp. 26–49, suppl. pp. 28–52. I should also like to mention the article by J. L. Benson, which contains informative comments (*Antike Kunst*, vol. 3, 1960, pp. 58–70, Figs. 3–4, Pls. 1–2). The fine and comprehensive study by Anna Maria Bisi, *Il grifone: storia di un motivo iconografico nell'antico Oriente mediterraneo*, Rome, 1965, only became available to me after this book had gone to the press.

[714] *Enciclopedia Universale dell'Arte*; Akurgal, *Kunst Anatoliens*, Figs. 39, 40.

[715] P. Amandry, in *Syria*, vol. 35, 1958, pp. 87ff.

[716] *Ibid.*, p. 95.

[717] U. Jantzen, *Griechische Greifenkessel*, Berlin, 1955, pp. 53ff., nos. 33–189.

[718] See similar heads from Olympia and Delphi in U. Jantzen, *op. cit.*, Pl. 26, pp. 65ff., 84.

[719] E. Kunze, *Archäische Schildbänder: ein Beitrag zur frühgeschichtlichen Bildgeschichte und Sagenüberlieferung*, Berlin, 1950, pp. 58ff.

[720] A. Dessenne, *Le sphinx: étude iconographique*, Paris, 1957.

[721] F. Matz, 'Kretische Sphingen', *JdI*, vol. 65–6, pp. 91–102.

[722] H. Walter, 'Der Sphinx', *Antike und Abendland*, vol. IX, pp. 63–72, Pls. 1 ff.

[723] On sphinxes see also the informative comments by J. Schäfer, *Studien zu den griechischen Reliefpithoi*, Kallmünz, 1957, pp. 31–3.

[724] H. Payne, *Protokorinthische Vasenmalerei*, Berlin, 1933, Pl. 17.

[725] K. Schefold, *Frühgriechische Sagenbilder*, Munich, 1962, 2nd ed., 1964; English translation by A. Hicks, *Myth and Legend in Early Greece*, London, 1966.

[726] E. Kunze, *Archäische Schildbänder . . .*, Berlin, 1950, pp. 64ff.

[727] *Ibid.*, pp. 61, 70–1, 134.

[728] *Ibid.*, pp. 83, 90, 93.

[729] *Ibid.*, pp. 71ff.

[730] H. J. Kantor, in *JNES*, vol. 21, 1962, pp. 93–117.

[731] E. Kunze, *op. cit.*, pp. 63ff.; K. Schefold, *op. cit.*, pp. 16, 35–5, 52, Pl. 22.

[732] H. Payne, *op. cit.*, Pl. 20(1).

[733] *Ibid.*, Pl. 20(2). For a fine example from Thasos, see F. Salviat and N. Weill, in *BCH*, vol. 84, 1960–1, pp. 347–86, Pls. 4–6.

[734] Hesiod, *Theogony*, 320–3.

[735] On the iconographic history of the chimaera in the Near East, see Akurgal, *Spätheth. Bildkunst*. See also the present volume, p. 187.

[736] Herodotus, I, 195.

[737] E. Kunze, *op. cit.*, pp. 74ff.

[738] N. Yalouris, *Athena als Herrin der Pferde*, Basle, 1950, pp. 1–102 with 16 Figures.

[739] *Ibid.*, p. 102.

[740] E. Bielefeld, 'Ein altanatolisches Motiv bei Kanachos', *Istanbuler Mitteilungen*, vol. 12, 1962, pp. 18–43, Pls. 4–9.

[741] E. Simon, 'Beobachtungen zum Apollon Philesios des Kanachos', *Charites: Festschrift für E. Langlotz*, 1957, pp. 38–46, Pls. 5–8.

[742] Herodotus, II, 44.

[743] F. Brommer, *Vasenlisten zur griechischen Heldensage: Herakles, Theseus, Aigeus . . .*, Marburg, 1956, pp. 7ff., 25ff., 54ff.

[744] On this see also T. J. Dunbabin, *The Greeks and their Eastern Neighbours*, London, 1957, p. 52.

[745] On Gilgamesh see H. Otten, in *Istanbuler Mitteilungen*, vol. 8, 1958, pp. 93–125.

746 H. Goldman, 'Sandon and Herakles', *Hesperia*, suppl. 8, 1949, pp. 164–74.

747 F. Dirlmeier, *Der Mythos von König Oedipus*, 2nd ed., Mainz, 1965.

748 H. J. Kantor, in *JNES*, vol. 21, 1962, pp. 93–116.

749 See also H. L. Lorimer, 'Über Zeus Dipaltos', *BSA*, vol. 37, 1936–7, p. 178, where it is correctly traced back to Assyrian prototypes.

750 K. Schefold, *Frühgriechische Sagenbilder*, Munich, 1962, 2nd ed., 1964, p. 17.

751 E. Kunze, *Olympia Bericht IV*, pp. 118–24, Pls. 38–46; F. Willemsen, in *AM*, vol. 69–70, 1954–5, pp. 12–32, Pls. 1–18.

752 E. Kunze, *op. cit.*, pp. 119f.

753 *Ibid.*, pp. 122–3.

754 *Ibid.*, Pls. 38–9; E. Kunze, *Neue Meisterwerke der griechischen Kunst aus Olympia*, Munich, 1948, Figs. 14–15; L. Alscher, *Griechische Plastik*, Berlin, 1954, Pl. 38a, b.

755 E. Kunze, *Olympia Bericht IV*, p. 123.

756 *Ibid.*, Pl. 42; L. Alscher, *op. cit.*, Pls. 39a–d.

757 H. Çambel, in *Belleten*, vol. 12, 1948, p. 49, Pl. xi, Fig. 7. P. Matthiae, *Studi sui rilievi di Karatepe*, Rome, 1963, Pl. 7.

758 Akurgal, *Kunst Anatoliens*, p. 46, Figs. 26, 28.

759 E. Kunze, *Neue Meisterwerke der griechischen Kunst aus Olympia*, Munich, 1948, Figs. 4–5; K. Schefold, *Frühgriechische Sagenbilder*, Munich, 1962, 2nd ed., 1964, Pl. 4b; D. Ohly, *Athenische Goldbleche des 8. Jahrhunderts*, Berlin, 1953, Pl. 28(2).

760 In Olympia bronze statuettes from the last quarter of the eighth century have also been found, with the same conical helmet with overhanging plume. *Olympia Bericht I*, p. 66, Fig. 69; pp. 66ff., Fig. 29.

761 On the question of the helmet types that originated in the Near East, see M. Pallottino, *Urartu, Greece and Etruria*, pp. 32ff.

762 *Olympia Bericht VII*, Pls. 62–7; P. Demargne, *La naissance de l'art grec*, p. 319, Figs. 405–6.

763 F. Matz, *Geschichte der griechischen Kunst*, Frankfurt, 1950, Pl. 63; cf. also Pls. 64, 66.

764 H.-V. Herrmann, *Olympia Bericht V*, pp. 81ff., Figs. 37–8. A fine photograph is in P. Demargne, *op. cit.*, p. 329, Fig. 422. Herrmann has pertinently compared the relief with the sculptures of Sakçegözü (p. 83), and correctly classified the piece.

765 A. Cuny, in *RHA*, vol. 7, 1945–6, p. 12; E. Dhorme, *Les premières civilisations*, pp. 303f.; T. J. Dunbabin, *The Greeks and their Eastern Neighbours*, London, 1957, p. 58.

766 F. Matz, *op. cit.*, Pls. 69–70.

767 P. Amandry, *Grèce et Orient*, Pl. 4, Figs. 4, 6.

768 Akurgal, *Kunst Anatoliens*, pp. 40ff., Figs. 25–6.

769 E. Kunze, *Kretische Bronzereliefs*, Stuttgart, 1963, pp. 267ff.; P. Amandry, *op. cit.*, pp. 1–20; Akurgal, *op. cit.*, pp. 35–51.

770 E. Kunze, *Neue Meisterwerke der griechischen Kunst aus Olympia*, Munich, 1948, p. 12, no. 20; nos. 21–2 (*Bericht I*, pp. 72ff., Pl. 21); *Antike*, vol. 15, 1939, pp. 36ff., Figs. 23, 25.

771 E. Kunze, *op. cit.*, pp. 12–13.

772 R. Hampe, *Frühgriechische Sagenbilder in Böotien*, Athens, 1936, p. 35.

773 H. Payne, *Protokorinthische Vasenmalerei*, Berlin, 1933, Pl. 9, Figs. 2, 7.

774 Ghirshman, *Perse*, p. 382, Fig. 585; p. 376, Fig. 512.

775 F. Matz, *op. cit.*, Pl. 188.

776 H. Payne, *op. cit.*, Pl. 13ff.

777 R. D. Barnett, 'Ancient Oriental Influences on Archaic Greece in the Aegean and the Near East', *Studies presented to H. Goldman*, New York, 1956, p. 232.

778 W. Nagel, *Altorientalisches Handkunstwerk*, Pl. 46; Parrot, *Assur*, p. 163, Fig. 212; Strommenger, *Mesopotamien*, Pl. 188.

779 R. Eilmann, in *CVA*, Berlin, 1, Pl. 20; K. Schefold, *Frühgriechische Sagenbilder*, 2nd ed., Munich, 1964, Pl. 36a.

780 E. Kunze, *Olympia Bericht IV*, p. 121, Pls. 40–1. For similar ornaments on the buttocks of figures in Greek vase-painting, see E. Kunze, *Olympia Bericht IV*, p. 121, and C. Karousos, in *JdI*, vol. 52, 1937, pp. 184f. See also an Attic vase fragment in Schefold, *op. cit.*, p. 65 (above). For the same decorative motif on vases, see Schefold, *op. cit.*, Pls. 9a, b, 10, 15–16, 18, 57a, 65a.

781 A. U. Pope, *A Survey of Persian Art*, vol. IV, 1958, Pl. 32 A, 33 B (on the thighs of two recumbent small animals). Ghirshman, *Perse*, p. 375, Fig. 498; p. 70, Fig. 91 (on the thighs of the two lions in the centre). A. Godard, *L'art de l'Iran*, Paris, 1962, (tr. by M. Heron, *The Art of Iran*, London, 1965), p. 44, Fig. 41.

782 This heart-shaped stylization of the shoulder and the hips of the body also occurs in Celtic art: P. Jacobsthal, *Early Celtic Art*, Oxford, 1944, Pl. 207; A. H. Springer, *Handbuch der Kunstgeschichte*, 6 vols., Leipzig, 1923, vol. I, p. 10, Fig. 28. The Celtic example probably derives from prototypes

in the frieze style. On a Luristan bronze, however, I later noticed that both the shoulder and the hips have the same heart-shaped stylization (Y. and A. Godard, *Bronzes du Luristan*: *Collections Graeffe*, The Hague, 1964, Pl. 35). Therefore the painters of the animal frieze must have derived their skill from Luristan prototypes.

783 R. M. Dawkins (ed.), *The Sanctuary of Artemis Orthia . . .*, Pl. 152, Fig. 2b.

784 H. Mühlstein, Fig. 65 (on the hips of the lion on the gold plaque from Praeneste). See also a horse with the same 'S'-shaped spiral: *Studi Etruschi*, vol. 30, 1962, p. 298, Pl. 24, Fig. 2. The source of this representation, which I encountered as the frontispiece to an Italian brochure, I owe to Mr. Massimo Pallottino.

785 C. Kardara, *Rodiaki Angeiografia*, p. 278, Fig. 270.

786 A. M. Tallgren, 'Caucasian Monuments', *ESA*, vol. 5, 1930, p. 129, Figs. 25a, b; Bossert (ed.), *Geschichte des Kunstgewerbes aller Zeiten und Völker*, vol. IV, p. 10, Figs. 1–2.

787 On Caucasian objects with 'S' spirals, see A. M. Tallgren, 'Archaeological Studies in Soviet Russia', *ESA*, vol. 10, 1936, p. 169, Figs. 25 (4); ibid., 'Caucasian Monuments', *ESA*, vol. 5, 1930, p. 39, Fig. 53, 54; F. Hančar, 'Einige Gürtelschliessen aus dem Kaukasus', *ESA*, vol. 6, 1931, p. 142, Fig. 2; p. 149, Fig. 3.

788 Akurgal, *Kunst Anatoliens*, p. 179.

789 *Loc. cit.*

790 *Loc. cit.* Cf. also the recent work by H. Gabelmann, who adds a few new comments (*Marburger Winckelmann-Programm*, 1964, pp. 6–12).

791 K. R. Maxwell-Hyslop, in *Iraq*, vol. 18, 1956, p. 152, and Figs. 1–5.

792 H. Payne, *Protokorinthische Vasenmalerei*, Berlin, 1933, Pl. 9, Figs. 3–4; Pl. 11, Figs. 1, 5 etc.; R. Hampe, *Ein frühattischer Grabfund*, Mainz, 1960, p. 56, Fig. 42.

793 Akurgal, *op. cit.*, pp. 56–8, Figs. 36–7.

794 R. Hampe, *op. cit.*, pp. 49ff., Figs. 30–3.

795 Apart from the examples collected by Hyslop (see note 791), cf. also a further representation on Assyrian reliefs, also reminiscent of Attic stemmed kraters (Barnett, *Palace Reliefs*, Pl. 107).

796 See also P. Jacobsthal, *Greek Pins and their Connexions with Europe and Asia*, Oxford, 1956, Figs. 209–18.

797 R. Hampe, *Ein frühattischer Grabfund*, Mainz, 1960, p. 48.

798 A. and G. Körte, *Gordion*: *Ergebnisse der Ausgrabungen im Jahre 1900*, Berlin, 1904, p. 72, Fig. 51.

799 *Ibid.*, Fig. 52.

800 The Phrygians exported splendid vessels to the Near East, as we have seen in our discussion of the Tell Halaf sculptures. On the other hand, they also imported Oriental works of art (*AJA*, vol. 66, 1962, Pls. 46–7; Akurgal, *Kunst Anatoliens*, Figs. 17, 20–1), and were under the influence of late Neo-Hittite art (Akurgal, *op. cit.*, p. 83). See also J. Boardman, in *Anatolia*, vol. 6, 1961, pp. 179–39. But the most important influences on Phrygian art were those from the Greek world (Akurgal, in *VIIIe Congrès International d'Archéologie Classique*, pp. 467–74, Pls. 114–17). Thus G. Wülker of Heidelberg has shown the influence of Greek bronzes on Phrygian works; she points in particular to the presence of bronze basins with Greek ring-handles at Gordion (our Fig. 149; oral communication).

801 Akurgal, *Phrygische Kunst*, p. 130 (table of mounds) see also pp. 39, 49, 103.

802 K. R. Maxwell-Hyslop, in *Iraq*, vol. 18, 1956, p. 152.

803 R. Hampe, *Ein frühattischer Grabfund*, Mainz, 1960, p. 48.

803a The Cycladic amphorae (E. Pfuhl, *Malerei und Zeichnung der Griechen*, 1923, vol. 3, Figs. 18–19, 99–100, 105) as well as the 'Lydion' have a shape such as we encounter among Urartian vessels (T. Özgüç, *Altintepe*, Pl. 3, Fig. 3; Pl. 13, p. 6, Fig. 7). The round Corinthian aryballoi occur already on Luristan bronzes (A. U. Pope, *A Survey of Persian Art*, O.U.P., 1958, vol. 4, Pl. 69A, C; 70 B) and on metalwork of northern Iran (Negahban, *Preliminary Report on Marlik Excavation*, Teheran, 1964, Pl. 12, Figs. 111, 140). The *deinos*, too, may probably be a Greek modification of Urartian and Phrygian bronze cauldrons (cf., e.g., Akurgal, *Kunst Anatoliens*, p. 50, Fig. 30; A. and G. Körte, *Gordion . . .*, Berlin, 1904, p. 68, Figs. 44–8; see also the present volume, Fig. 90).

804 R. M. Cook, *Greek Painted Pottery*, 2nd ed., p. 45.

805 See our note 711; P. E. Arias and M. Hirmer, *Le vase grec*, Pls. 22–3; F. Matz, *Geschichte der griechischen Kunst*, Frankfurt, 1950, Pl. 171.

806 E. Pfuhl, *Meisterwerke griechischer Zeichnung und Malerei*, p. 9 (tr. by J. D. Beazley, new ed., London, 1955).

807 The other deities, too, follow the same Hittite ceremonial scheme: see, e.g., Hermes and Kalypso (K. Schefold, *Frühgriechische Sagenbilder*, 2nd ed., Munich, 1964, Pls. 9a, b), Herakles and Deianeira (*ibid.*, Pl. 57e).

808 K. Schefold, *op. cit.*, Pls. 68–9.

809 *Ibid.*, Pls. 32, 57b, 70. In the last vase-painting four further couples in addition to Helen and Paris are represented in the same scheme.

810 On this ceremonial rule among the Hittites and other peoples, see above, p. 127, and Akurgal, *Spätheth. Bildkunst*, pp. 111–18; also below, p. 208.

811 Barnett, *Nimrud Ivories*, Pl. 26 (above, centre and left). On the early history of this motif, see pp. 82–3; compare the fine Syrian ivory 'Mistress of the Beasts', found at Gordion (*AJA*, vol. 66, 1962, Pl. 46).

812 A. U. Pope, *A Survey of Persian Art*, O.U.P., 1958, vol. 4, Pls. 28–34.

813 K. Schefold, *op. cit.*, Pl. 10, P. E. Arias and M. Hirmer, *Le vase grec*, Pls. 22–3.

814 On the griffin protome at the end of the chariot shaft see Akurgal, *Bayrakli*, p. 95.

815 Akurgal, *Kunst Anatoliens*, p. 238, Fig. 207; G. Mendel, *Catalogue du Musée de Brousse*, 1908, Pl. 1; M. Schede, *Meisterwerke*, Pls. 4a, b; see also Akurgal, *Bayrakli*, p. 95, n. 176.

816 T. L. Shear, *Sardis x*, Cambridge, 1926, Figs. 11, 17 and *Larisa II*, Pls. 8–10, 34–6; see also Akurgal, *Bayrakli*, p. 15, n. 175; A. Åkerström, *Architektorische Terrakotta-platten in Stockholm*, Lund, 1951, Pls. 1, 3.

817 Barnett, *Nimrud Ivories*, Pl. 27 (above, left).

818 K. Schefold, *Frühgriechische Sagenbilder*, 2nd ed., Munich, 1964, Pl. 10; Arias and Hirmer, *Le vase grec*, Pl. 22.

819 F. Matz, *Geschichte der griechischen Kunst*, Frankfurt, 1950, Pl. 12 (Late Geometric Attic pitcher in Tübingen, B 4; height 0.325 m.). See also M. Wegner, *Das Musikleben der Griechen*, Berlin, 1949, Pl. 1a.

820 Akurgal, *Kunst Anatoliens*, p. 15, Pl. 3.

821 L. Deubner, 'Die vielsaitige Leier', *AM*, vol. 54, 1929, pp. 194–200; M. Wegner, *op. cit.*, pp. 29ff.

822 M. Wegner, *op. cit.*, p. 48.

823 *Loc. cit.*

824 On other questions connected with seventh-century Cycladic vase-painting the reader may consult the informative study by the Danish archaeologist I. Strom, in *Acta Archaeologica*, vol. 33, pp. 221–78.

825 Akurgal, in *AJA*, vol. 66, 1962, pp. 372ff.

826 Akurgal, *Kunst Anatoliens*, pp. 175ff.

827 Ibid., pp. 178ff.; ibid., in *AJA*, vol. 66, 1962, pp. 373ff.

828 D. Ohly, 'Holz', *AM*, vol. 68, 1953, pp. 77–83, Pls. 13–15.

829 Barnett, *Nimrud Ivories*, p. 130, Fig. 48.

830 On this see F. H. A. Klinz, *Hieros Gamos*, Halle, 1933 (Dissertation); ibid., 'Hieros Gamos', *RE*, suppl. IV, col. 112.

831 Akurgal, *Kunst der Hethiter*, pp. 50–2.

832 In the text of *Anitta* it is stated: '. . . as soon as he enters the inner room, he will sit before me on my right hand'; see Akurgal, *Kunst der Hethiter*, p. 22.

833 Akurgal, *Spätheth. Bildkunst*, pp. 110–18; for the same motif on Roman cameos see ibid., p. 116, n. 173.

834 G. M. A. Richter, *The Archaic Grave Stones of Attica*, London, 1961, Figs. 31–3.

835 D. Ohly, in *AM*, vol. 68, 1953, p. 80.

836 *The Iliad of Homer*, tr. R. Lattimore, Chicago, 1962, pp. 487ff.

837 *Ibid.*, pp. 302–3.

838 D. Ohly, *op. cit.*, p. 78.

839 P. F. S. Poulsen, *Der Orient und die frühgriechische Kunst*, Berlin, 1912, p. 58, Fig. 58; W. L. Brown, *The Etruscan Lion*, Oxford, 1960, Pl. 1a.

840 D. Ohly, *op. cit.*, p. 78.

841 G. Daux, 'Chronique des fouilles et découvertes archéologiques en Grèce en 1961', *BCH*, vol. 86, 1962, p. 882, Pl. 30.

842 On ivory works from Ephesos see Akurgal, *Kunst Anatoliens*, pp. 192–218.

843 *Ibid.*, pp. 195–6.

844 Aristophanes, *The Clouds*, 599–600.

845 P. F. S. Poulsen, *op. cit.*, p. 102; R. D. Barnett, in *JHS*, vol. 68, 1948, p. 20; see also Akurgal, 'Early Period and Golden Age of Ionia', *AJA*, vol. 66, 1962, p. 376.

846 M. Mazzarino, in *Atenaeum*, vol. 21, 1943, pp. 57–8; C. Roebuck, *Ionian Trade and Colonisation*, p. 3.

847 *Sappho: a New Translation* by M. Barnard, Berkeley-Los Angeles, 1958.

848 E. Buschor, *Beiträge zur Geschichte der griechischen Textilkunst*, Munich, 1912, p. 36; see also E. von Lorentz, in *RM*, vol. 52, 1937, pp. 165ff.

849 Akurgal, *Kunst Anatoliens*, p. 198, Figs. 158–9.

850 H. Kenner, *Über das Weinen und das Lachen in der Kunst*, Vienna, 1960 (Österr. Akademie der Wissenschaften, Philos.-histor. Klasse, *Sitzungsberichte*, no. 234, vol. 2), pp. 63 ff.

851 E. Buschor, *Altsamische Standbilder*, vol. IV, Berlin, 1960, Figs. 238–48.

852 Akurgal, *Phrygische Kunst*, p. 85.

853 N. Firatli, 'Finds from the Phrygian Necropolis of Ankara', *Belleten*, vol. 23, 1959, pp. 206–8, Figs. 1–5.

854 R. S. Young, in *AJA*, vol. 62, 1958, p. 152 and n. 30, Pl. 26, Fig. 19.

855 J. Boardman, 'Ionian Bronze Belts', *Anatolia*, vol. 6, 1961, pp. 179–89.

856 Akurgal, *Phrygische Kunst*, pp. 81–93; ibid., *Kunst Anatoliens*, pp. 100–3, 206 and n. 170, 172. On the Phrygian fibulae found in Greece, see U. Jantzen, 'Phrygische Fibeln', *Festschrift für Friedrich Matz*, pp. 39–43, Pls. 8–11; Knudson, 'From a Sardis Tomb: a Lydian Pottery Imitation of a Phrygian Metal Bowl', *Berytus*, vol. 15, 1946, pp. 59–69.

857 Akurgal, *Kunst Anatoliens*, p. 83; see also below, n. 868.

858 I. Strom, in *Acta Archaeologica*, vol. 33, pp. 221–78.

859 G. M. A. Hanfmann, 'Ionia: Leader or Follower?', *Harvard Studies in Classical Philology*, vol. 61, 1953, p. 22.

860 Akurgal, 'Early Period and Golden Age of Ionia', *AJA*, vol. 66, 1962, pp. 374–5.

861 A. Greifenhagen, 'Schmuck und Gerät eines lydischen Mädchens', *Antike Kunst*, vol. 8, 1965, pp. 16ff., Pl. 5.

862 *Ibid.*, p. 17, Fig. 1.

863 R. D. Barnett, 'Median Art', *Iranica Antiqua*, vol. 2, 1962, p. 89, Fig. 6; ibid., in *British Museum Quarterly*, 26, Pl. 42; A. Greifenhagen, *op. cit.*, p. 17, Fig. 1.

864 R. D. Barnett, 'Median Art', p. 88, Fig. 5.

865 W. Schiering, *Werkstätten orientalisierender Keramik auf Rhodos*, Berlin, 1957, suppl. 7, 8.

866 *Ibid.*, Pl. 16, Figs. 1, 5, 6; C. Kardara, *Rodiaki Angeiografia*, p. 35, Fig. 6; p. 92, Fig. 58; p. 155, Figs. 122–3; p. 279, Fig. 271.

867 Akurgal, *Bayrakli*, p. 86.

868 Akurgal, *Phrygische Kunst*, pp. 46–7; ibid., *Kunst Anatoliens*, p. 83; cf. also note 857.

869 C. Kardara, *op. cit.*, pp. 35–88.

870 K. Schefold, 'Knidische Vasen und Verwandtes', *JdI*, vol. 57, 1942, pp. 131, 134–6, 138.

871 R. M. Cook, in *Gnomon*, vol. 37, 1965, pp. 502–7.

872 F. Villard, *Monuments et mémoires publiés par l'Académie des Inscriptions et Belles-Lettres (Fondation Eugène Piot)*, vol. 48, pp. 25–8, 36–47, Pls. 3–5, Figs. 1–2.

873 *Ibid.*, pp. 36ff.

874 *Ibid.*, p. 41.

875 A. Greifenhagen, 'Schmuck und Gerät eines lydischen Mädchens', *Antike Kunst*, vol. 8, 1965, p. 19.

876 E. Gjerstad, in *Opuscula Archaeologica*, vol. 4, 1946, Pl. 14.

877 Akurgal, *Kunst Anatoliens*, pp. 41, 46, Figs. 25–8.

878 H. Luschey, *Die Phiale*, Bleicherode, 1939, pp. 61ff.

879 *Ibid.*, pp. 61–2.

880 O. M. Dalton, *The Treasure of the Oxus*, London, 1926, Pl. 8 (no. 18).

881 Akurgal, in *Antike Kunst*, vol. 9, 1966.

882 B. B. Piotrovsky, *Vanskoye tsarstvo: Urartu*, Moscow, 1959, P.s. 54–5.

883 See also the Urartian examples in Akurgal, *Kunst Anatoliens*, p. 34, Figs. 9, 10.

884 Akurgal, in *Antike Kunst*, vol. 9, 1966.

885 A. Godard, *Le trésor de Ziwiyè*, Haarlem, 1950, p. 23, Fig. 13.

886 P. Calmeyer, in *Berliner Jahrbuch für Vor- und Frühgeschichte*, p. 31, Fig. G 1, p. 33, Fig. H 2, p. 37, Fig. I(1); E. L.-B. Terrace, *The Art of the Ancient Near East in Boston*, Fig. 42 (P. Calmeyer, *op. cit.*, p. 37, Fig. I(1)); E. Porada, *The Art of Ancient Iran*, ART OF THE WORLD, London, 1965, p. 122, Pl. 33.

887 E. Porada, *op. cit.*, p. 113, Pl. 28.

888 Akurgal, *Kunst Anatoliens*, pp. 219ff.

889 Arias and Hirmer, *Le vase grec*, Pl. 29. A woman on a cuirass from Olympia (F. Matz, *Geschichte der griechischen Kunst*, Frankfurt, 1950, Fig. 34) wears the same costume that we find on Phoenician tridacna shell renderings (our Fig. 105).

890 D. Levi, in *Annuario*, vols. 33–4, 1955–6, p. 260, Fig. 56; K. Schefold, *Frühgriechische Sagenbilder*, 2nd ed., Munich, 1964, Fig. 33.

891 *JHS*, vol. 22, 1902, Pl. VI (1).

892 F. Matz, *op. cit.*, Pl. 290.

893 Akurgal, *Kunst Anatoliens*, p. 282, Fig. 251.

894 R. D. Barnett, in *Iranica Antiqua*, vol. 2, 1962, Pl. 6; E. H. Minns, *Scythians and Greeks*, Cambridge, 1913, p. 172, Fig. 69.

895 K. Schefold, in *ESA*, vol. 12, 1938, pp. 9, 12, 36; ibid., *Handbuch der Archäologie*, vol. II, p. 454 (table).

896 Akurgal, *Kunst Anatoliens*, pp. 288–93; ibid.,

'Vom äolischen zum ionischen Kapitell', *Anatolia*, vol. 5, 1960, pp. 1–7.

[897] The revetment depicted here originates from Düver, near Burdur in south-western Anatolia. At this site grave robberies took place, the proceeds of which found their way to various museums all over the world. See A. Akeström, *Bulletin* of the Museum of Mediterranean and Near Eastern Antiquities (Medelhavsmuseet), Stockholm, vol. 4, 1964, pp. 49–53, Figs. 1–4.

NOTES

The following abbreviations are used for journals:

AA	Archäologischer Anzeiger: Beiblatt zum Jahrbuch des Deutschen Archäologischen Instituts, Berlin
AfO	Archiv für Orientforschung, Berlin
AJA	American Journal of Archaeology, Boston
AM	Mitteilungen des Deutschen Archäologischen Instituts, Athenische Abteilung, Berlin
Annuario	Annuario della Scuola archaeologica di Atena, Rome
BCH	Bulletin de Correspondence Hellénique, Paris
BSA	Annual of the British School at Athens, London
CVA	Corpus Vasorum Antiquorum, Paris
ESA	Eurasia Septentrionalis Antiqua, Helsinki
JCS	Journal of Cuneiform Studies, New Haven
JdI	Jahrbuch des Deutschen Archäologischen Instituts, Berlin
JHS	Journal of Hellenic Studies, London
JNES	Journal of Near Eastern Studies, Chicago
LAAA	Annals of Archaeology and Anthropology, Institute of Archaeology, Liverpool
MDOG	Mitteilungen der Deutschen Orientgesellschaft, Berlin
OIP	Oriental Institute Publications, University of Chicago
OLZ	Orientalische Literaturzeitung, Leipzig
RHA	Revue Hittite et Asianique, Paris
RSO	Revista degli Studi Orientali, Rome
VA	Vorderasiatische Abteilung der Staatlichen Museen, Berlin
ZA	Zeitschrift für Assyrologie, Leipzig

The following abbreviations are used for published works:

AiS	F. v. Luschan (ed.), *Ausgrabungen in Sendschirli*: *Mitteilungen aus den orientalischen Sammlungen der Berliner Museen.* I: Fasc. XI, 1893 III: Fasc. XIII, 1902 IV: Fasc. XIV, 1911 V: Fasc. XV, 1943
Akurgal, *Bayrakli*	E. Akurgal, *Bayrakli*: *Zeitschrift der Philosophischen Fakultät*, Ankara, vol. 8, 1950.
Akurgal, *Kunst Anatoliens*	E. Akurgal, *Die Kunst Anatoliens von Homer bis Alexander*, Berlin, 1961.
Akurgal, *Kunst der Hethiter*	E. Akurgal, *Die Kunst der Hethiter*, Munich, 1961; English translation by C. McNab: *The Art of the Hittites*, London, 1962.
Akurgal, *Phrygische Kunst*	E. Akurgal, *Die Phrygische Kunst*, Ankara, 1955.
Akurgal, *Remarques stylistiques*	E. Akurgal, *Remarques stylistiques sur les reliefs de Malatya*, Ankara, 1946.
Akurgal, *Spätheth. Bildkunst*	E. Akurgal, *Die späthethitische Bildkunst*, Ankara, 1949.
Barnett, *Nimrud Ivories*	R. D. Barnett, *A Catalogue of the Nimrud Ivories, with other Examples of Ancient Near Eastern Ivories in the British Museum*, London, 1957.
Barnett, *Palace Reliefs*	R. D. Barnett, *Assyrian Palace Reliefs and their Influence on the Sculptures of Babylonia and Persia*, London, 1960.

Barnett and Falkner, *Sculptures* R. D. Barnett and M. Falkner, *The Sculptures of Assur-Nasir-apali II (883–819 B.C.), Tiglath-Pileser III*, London, 1962.

Bossert, *Altanatolien* H. T. Bossert, *Altanatolien*, Berlin, 1942.
Bossert, *Altsyrien* H. T. Bossert, *Altsyrien*, Berlin, 1951.
Carchemish I *Report on the Excavations at Djerabis on behalf of the British Museum.* Part I. Introductory by D. G. Hogarth. London, 1914.

Carchemish II *Report on the Excavations at Jerablus on behalf of the British Museum.* Part II. *The Town Defences.* By C. L. Woolley. London, 1921.

Carchemish III *Report on the Excavations at Jerablus on behalf of the British Museum.* Part III. *The Excavations in the Inner Town.* By L. Woolley. *The Hittite Inscriptions.* By R. D. Barnett. London, 1952.

Frankfort, *Art and Architecture* H. Frankfort, *The Art and Architecture of the Ancient Orient*, Harmondsworth, 1954.

Ghirshman, *Perse* R. Ghirshman, *Perse: Proto-iraniens, Mèdes, Achéménides*, Paris, 1963. Translated by S. Gilbert and J. Emmons: *Persia from the Origins to Alexander the Great*, London, 1964.

Naumann, *Architektur Kleinasiens* R. Naumann, *Architektur Kleinasiens*, Tübingen, 1955.
KiB F. Winter, *Kunstgeschichte in Bildern,* Leipzig.
Olympia Bericht I–IV E. Kunze and H. Schleif, *Bericht über die Ausgrabungen in Olympia*, mit Beiträgen von R. Eilmann und U. Jantzen. Berlin, 1944.

Parrot, *Assur* A. Parrot, *Assur*, Paris, 1961. Translated by S. Gilbert and J. Emmons: *Niniveh and Babylon*, London, 1961.

Perrot and Chipiez, *Histoire de l'art* G. Perrot and C. Chipiez, *Histoire de l'art dans l'antiquité.* Vol. II: *Chaldée et Assyrie*, Paris, 1884. Vol. III: *Phénice-Cypre*, Paris, 1885.

Schaefer, *Leistung* H. Schaefer, *Die Leistung der ägyptischen Kunst*, Leipzig, 1929. Herausgegeben von der Vorderasiatischen-Ägyptischen Gesellschaft, Vol. 28.

Schaefer and Andrae, *Propyl. Kunstgesch.* A. Schaefer and W. Andrae, *Propyläen Kunstgeschichte*, II, 2nd ed., Berlin, 1925.

Strommenger, *Mesopotamien* E. Strommenger, *Fünf Jahrtausende Mesopotamien*, Munich, 1962. Translated by C. Haglund: *Mesopotamia*, London, 1964.
Tell Halaf I–IV Max Freiherr von Oppenheim, *Tell Halaf.*
I: *Die Prähistorischen Funde.* By H. Schmidt. Berlin, 1943.
II: *Die Bauwerke.* By F. Langenegger, K. Müller, R. Naumann. Berlin, 1950.
III: *Die Bildwerke.* By A. Moortgat . . . D. Opitz. Berlin, 1955.
IV. *Die Kleinfunde aus historischer Zeit.* By B. Hrouda. Berlin, 1962.

Thureau-Dangin, *Arslan-Tash* F. Thureau-Dangin, A. Barrois, G. Dossin, M. Dunand, *Arslan-Tash*, Paris, 1931.

Thureau-Dangin, *Til-Barsib* F. Thureau-Dangin and M. Dunand, *Til-Barsib*, Paris, 1936.
Ugaritica I–III C. F. A. Schaeffer, *Ugaritica: Etudes relatives aux découvertes de Ras Shamra.* Paris, 1939.
II: *Nouvelles études . . .* Paris, 1949.
III: *Sceaux et cylindres hittites . . . et autres découvertes de Ras Shamra.* Paris, 1956.

Unger, *Assyr. und babyl. Kunst* E. Unger, *Assyrische und babylonische Kunst*, Breslau, 1927.
Unger, *Obelisk* E. Unger, *Der Obelisk des Königs Assurnassirpal I aus Ninive*, Leipzig, 1932 (*Mitteilungen der altorientalischen Gesellschaft*, vol. 6, fasc. 1–2).

Unger, *Sumer. und akkad. Kunst* E. Unger, *Die sumerische und akkadische Kunst*, Breslau, 1926.
Yadin, *Art of Warfare* Y. Yadin, *The Art of Warfare in Biblical Lands in the Light of Archaeological Discovery*, London, 1963.

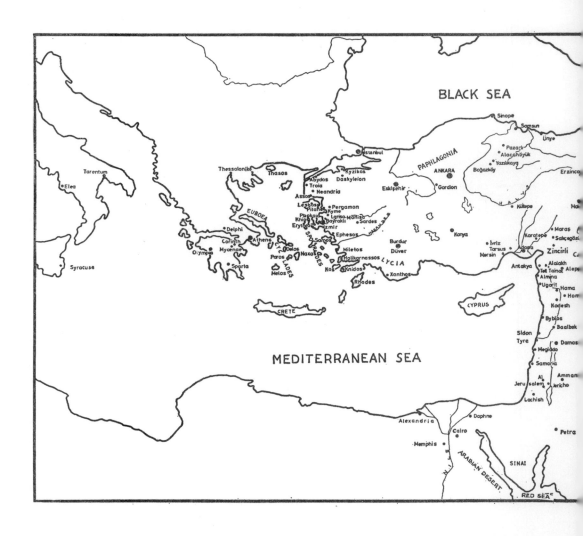

EASTERN MEDITERRANEAN AND NEAR EAST
ILLUSTRATING THE CONNECTIONS BETWEEN EASTERN AND GREEK ART

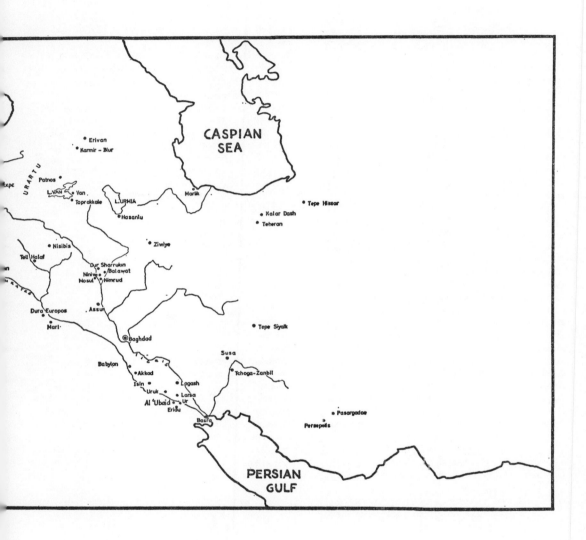

CASPIAN
SEA

URARTU

Erivan
Karmir – Blur
Patnos
L. VAN
Van
Toprakkale
L. URMIA
Hasanlu
Marlik
Tepe Hissar
Kalar Dash
Teheran
Ziwiye
Nisibis
Tell Halaf
Dur Sharrukin
Ninive
Balawat
Mosul
Nimrud
Assur
Dura Europos
Mari
Tepe Siyalk
Baghdad
Babylon
Susa
Akkad
Tchoga-Zanbil
Isin
Lagash
Uruk
Larsa
Al 'Ubaid
Ur
Eridu
Basra
Pasargadae
Persepolis

PERSIAN
GULF

247

INDEX

(The numerals in italics refer to the plates and figures.)